This book is dedicated to Melissa, Lili, and Aubrey.
—Brad

Credits

Executive Editor
Carol Long

Project Editor
Rosanne Koneval

Technical Editor
Mark Coffman

Production Editor
Tim Tate

Copy Editor
Jeri Freedman

Editorial Director
Robyn B. Siesky

Editorial Manager
Mary Beth Wakefield

Production Manager
Tim Tate

Vice President and Executive Group Publisher
Richard Swadley

Vice President and Executive Publisher
Barry Pruett

Associate Publisher
Jim Minatel

Project Coordinator, Cover
Lynsey Stanford

Compositor
Maureen Forys, Happenstance Type-O-Rama

Proofreader
Publication Services, Inc.

Indexer
Robert Swanson

Cover Image
© Jupiter Images / Image Source

Cover Designer
Michael E. Trent

About the Authors

Bradley L. Jones is an international bestselling author and speaker who currently works for `Internet.com`. Recognized as a Microsoft Most Valuable Professional (MVP), he is constantly working with technology and using it to help do more. While Bradley has written a number of books on techie languages, you can also find his books on using the Windows operating system, including *Windows XP in 10 Simple Steps or Less* as well as *The Windows Vista Bible: Desktop Edition*.

Bradley can also be found online at various sites including `Codeguru`, `Developer.com`, `HTMLGoodies`, `Flashkit`, and more. You can try to catch him on email or some of the Live Services as `LiveEssentials@Live.com`.

Marcus J. Schmidt is a senior marketing manager and community manager in the Windows Business Group at Microsoft Corporation. He's building a vibrant consumer community around some of the world's most widely used products—Windows & Windows Live. Every day, Marcus sees, hears, and learns how people use these products every day. He enjoys sharing and showcasing the contributions of the community to the world through Microsoft's websites and e-mail newsletters as well as on Facebook, Twitter and, of course, Windows Live. You can connect with Marcus at `marcusatmicrosoft.spaces.live.com`.

Acknowledgments

I would like to acknowledge the girls in my life for their support. This includes my wife, Melissa, and my two girls, Lili and Aubrey, whose pictures you'll see throughout this book. Time with my family is priceless and writing a book takes a good chunk of that time. Thus the value of this book is high!

I would also like to acknowledge the support provided by a number of people at Microsoft and throughout the community. This includes those in the Microsoft MVP program such as PJ, Brian, and others as well as several local Microsoft's people whose indirect support is also appreciated. This includes Bill, Dave, and Larry, who are always willing to do what they can to lend a hand when asked.

I would like to thank the folks at Wiley who spent countless hours taking the words I've written and turning them into cleaner prose for you to read. Carol, Rosanne, Jeri, and Mark were all pinnacle in making this book be the best it could be.

Finally, thank you. A book is only good if it gets read. As such, thank you for picking up this book and taking a few minutes to read it. Hopefully you'll find value in what is presented. If so, please drop me an email (`Essentials@Jones123.com`) and let me know, or post a review on your favorite book site!

—Brad Jones

Contents at a Glance

Contents

Introduction

Welcome to Windows Live Essentials Applications and Services. These are free applications and services available from Microsoft that anybody can download on their computer and use without any additional costs. The services are used on the Internet, so one requirement for using these is an Internet connection for your PC.

Although these services are offered for free, it doesn't mean they are trivial. In fact, if you are using a Home version of Windows Vista, then some of these applications were likely included with your system. This includes Windows Mail, Photo Gallery, and more. These were not included on Windows XP or Windows 7; however, as indicated, you can now download them online.

> **NOTE** *The requirements for using the applications or services are as follows:*
> - *Operating system: Windows XP with Service Pack 2 (32-bit edition only), Windows Vista (32-bit or 64-bit editions), Windows 7 (32-bit or 64-bit editions), or Windows Server 2008. (Windows Live Movie Maker is not supported on Windows XP.)*
> - *Processor: 1 GHz or higher for Windows Vista; 800 MHz or higher for Windows XP.*
> - *Memory: 128 MB of RAM (256 MB or more recommended) for Windows XP; 512 MB for Windows Vista.*
> - *Resolution: Minimum 1024 x 768.*
> - *Internet connection: Internet functionality requires dial-up or broadband Internet access (provided separately). Local or long-distance charges may apply.*
> - *Browser: Windows Live Toolbar requires Microsoft Internet Explorer 6 or later.*
> - *Graphics or video card: Windows Live Movie Maker requires ATI Radeon 9500 (or higher) or nVidia GeForce FX 5900 (or higher).*

Who This Book Is For

This book is intended for anyone running Windows XP or later that wants to get more out of their computer without spending any more money. If you are looking for free applications to work with the media on your machine, to send emails, to chat with your friends, to create blogs, to store your files and documents, to create movies, or to do a variety of other things, then this book is for you.

You will learn how to download and install a number of applications as well as how to access services on the Web. If you are comfortable using a browser to access the Internet, then you'll be able to easily take advantage of the free things that Microsoft has provided!

What This Book Covers

This book covers a number of applications and services. There is no requirement to read this book from beginning to end, so it is worth knowing what each chapter covers in advance so that you know which ones to jump to first.

In Chapter 1, "What Are Windows Live Essentials?" you'll learn about the Windows Live Essentials and Services. You'll learn where these are located, how to access them and what you need to do to begin using them.

In Chapter 2, "Instant Messaging with Windows Live Messenger," you'll learn how to use this service to send short messages (Instant Messages, called IMs) to your contacts. You'll not only be able to send short text messages, but also learn how to interact with others in different ways as well. This includes playing games, talking, or sharing items.

In Chapter 3, "Emailing with Windows Live Mail," you'll see how to use the Windows Live Mail program on your machine to work with email. If you don't have an email account, you'll be shown how to use the Windows Live Mail account to receive or send emails to others.

In Chapter 4, "Blogging and Writing with Windows Live Writer," you'll learn how to use the Windows Live Writer application to setup and create a blog so you can share your thoughts and insights with others, or to simply write your own prose for others to read. You'll learn to use Windows Live Writer to share pictures, videos, and more.

In Chapter 5, "Managing Pictures with Windows Live Photo Gallery," you'll learn how to use this application to manage, sort, and filter the photos and videos on your computer. You'll also learn how to use the Windows Live Photo Gallery to fix photos you've taken.

In Chapter 6, "Creating Movies with Movie Maker," you'll be able to take your photos and videos and knit them into your own movies that you can share with others. You'll see how to add a sound track, transitions, and other basic movie editing features.

In Chapter 7, "Organizing with Windows Live Calendar," you'll see how to use the calendar features in the Windows Live Applications to keep track of appointments, birthdates, and other key events. You'll even be able to share your calendar or access the calendars that have been shared by others.

In Chapter 8, "Socializing with Windows Live Spaces," you'll learn how to set up an area online where you can interact socially with others. Your personalized Windows Live Space will allow you to see what is going on with your friends as well as share what is going on with you.

In Chapter 9, "Interacting with Windows Live Groups," you'll learn how to join and interact with groups of people that have similar interests. You'll not only learn how to find different groups to chat with, but also how to create your own new group topics.

Finally, in Chapter 10, "Storing Things Online with SkyDrive," you'll learn how to take advantage of a Live service to store your files, photos, and documents on the Internet so that you can get them from anywhere at any time as long as you have an Internet connection. You'll also learn how to share items on SkyDrive with others.

Of course, these descriptions are brief. You can check out the Table of Contents to get a better idea of the details covered in each chapter. The focus of each chapter is to provide you with the key information you need to tap into and take advantage of each of these applications and services.

How This Book Is Structured

As mentioned, this book covers a number of different applications and services. You should read Chapter 1 to see how to install and begin using any or all of these applications. After reading Chapter 1, you should feel free to skip around the book to those applications or services that you are most interested in using. With a few applications in a couple of the chapters, you might be told to read part of another chapter; however, for the most part, each chapter can stand on its own once you've read Chapter 1.

What You Need to Use This Book

In order to use this book, you will need a computer with an Internet connection to download the Essential applications. In Chapter 1, you will learn the specific operating system and requirements necessary to run each of the different services. In general, you will need to be running Microsoft Windows XP, Windows Vista, or Windows 7.

Once you've downloaded the Essential Applications, you'll be able to run them without an Internet connection. There are a number of Live Services that are also covered in this book. While using these services, you will need to be connected to the Internet. These services included Live Messenger, Live Spaces, Live Groups, and SkyDrive.

Conventions

To help you get the most from the text and keep track of what's happening, we've used a number of conventions throughout the book.

NOTE *Notes provide additional information related to the current topic being presented.*

TIP *Tips are used to provide information that can make your work easier—special shortcuts or methods for accomplishing something easier than the norm.*

WARNING *Warnings provide information about things to watch out for, whether simply inconvenient or potentially hazardous to your data or systems.*

As for styles in the text, we show filenames and URLs within the text like so:

```
home.live.com
```

What Are Windows Live Essentials?

IN THIS CHAPTER, YOU WILL:

▸ Discover the applications you can add to Windows at no cost

▸ Set up your own Windows Live ID

▸ Walk through adding the Windows Live Essentials Applications to your computer

▸ Run the Windows Live Essentials Applications

▸ Install the Windows Live Toolbar

▸ Search the Internet with Bing

▸ Access Windows Live Applications from the Windows Live Toolbar

▸ Customize the Windows Live Toolbar

IF YOU are reading this book, then chances are you own a copy of Windows and want to get more from it. While Windows comes with a number of great applications, there are always more applications you can get. While you can lay out hundreds of dollars for software to do things such as produce videos, work with documents, manage your email, track your time, or do a variety of other things, you can also get applications that can do these things for free.

Windows Live Essentials is a set of applications that you can download from Microsoft at no cost. There are also Windows Live Services, which are services that you can access and use on the Internet. With these essential applications and services, you can extend what you can do with Windows in many different ways.

Introducing Windows Live Applications

When you install Windows Live Applications, which you'll do later in this chapter, you will be asked to select the applications you want to install. Each application might include some prerequisites; however, in almost all cases, everything you need will be installed at the same time that you install the application. In most cases, these applications will be downloaded to your computer so that you can use them whether you are connected to the Internet or not. The applications you will be able to install include those listed in Table 1.1.

TABLE 1.1 The Windows Live Essentials

LIVE ESSENTIAL	BRIEF DESCRIPTION
Messenger	This is a program that lets you interact with other people (contacts). You can send text messages, play games, share pictures, and much more.
Mail	This is an email program that is installed onto your computer. It allows you to access multiple email accounts as well as interact with your calendar, newsgroups, feeds, and more.
Photo Gallery	With this program, you'll be able to work with pictures and videos. You'll be able to organize them as well as fix and manipulate them. If you are using Windows Vista, then you already have a version of Photo Gallery.
Writer	This writing program will help you to create blog posts. You'll be able to post to a Windows Live account as well as to other blogging programs such as Blogger, Live Journal, TypePad, and WordPress.
Movie Maker	Movie Maker will allow you to work with video clips. You'll be able to create your own movies with transitions, effects, and a soundtrack using your video clips or images. You'll even be able to publish the result to the Web or elsewhere.
Family Safety	This is a program for helping to keep kids safe on the Internet. You'll be able to restrict web sites, contacts, time, and more. It provides the tools to monitor online usage.
Toolbar	This is an add-on for Internet Explorer to give you quick access to some of the Windows Live Essentials programs as well as to Windows Hotmail, searching, and more.
Silverlight*	This is a program that provides advanced support for a rich experience. It improves what you can do on Windows Live, the Microsoft sites, and more by supporting better graphics, high-definition video, and more.
Office Outlook Add-in & Office Live Add-in*	These add-in programs extend what you can do with Microsoft Outlook and Microsoft Office. They allow you to store and access information on the Web as well as allow you to pull information from the Web, such as email, to your local machine.

*These are secondary programs but are a part of the Windows Live Essentials.

In addition to the Windows Live Applications, there are also a few additional Windows Live Services that are worth your attention. A few are listed in Table 1.2. These services will also be covered in this book. In addition to the following services, there are several others that are can be found within Windows Live. All of these services are available online, so they require an Internet connection to use.

TABLE 1.2 Windows Live Services

SERVICE	BRIEF DESCRIPTION
Windows Live ID	A unique identifier that you can use to sign into various live services.
Spaces	This is a social networking platform that allows you to also create your own blog.
Groups	A part of the Windows Live Services that allow you to create or join social groups where you can interact or share.
SkyDrive	This service provides you storage on the Internet where you can place files and share them with others.
Calendar	Use an online calendar to manage your time and your appointments as well as to coordinate with others.

Requirements

Not everyone will be able to set up and use the Live Essentials Applications. You need to make sure you are running an acceptable version of Windows and that your computer is tough enough. In general, the requirements for running these applications are very similar to what you need to run Windows.

Of course, you should make sure you are running the correct version of Windows. You need to be running Windows Vista, Windows 7, or Windows Server 2008. All of the programs, except for Windows Live Movie Maker, will also work on the 32-bit version of Windows XP with Service Pack 2.

> **NOTE** *Windows Vista came with versions of some of the Live programs built in (such as Mail and Photo Gallery). These programs are not a part of the newer Windows 7.*

In addition to the operating system, there are system requirements your computer must meet. You should have a computer with a 1-GHz or better processor (800 MHz or higher for Windows XP). It is recommended that you have 512MB of RAM in your computer. If you are using Windows XP, you can get away with only having 128MB of RAM; however, 256MB is the recommended minimum if using Windows XP.

Because you are downloading these applications from the Internet, you'll need an Internet connection. If you are using Windows Live Mail, you'll need to have the connection to send and receive mail.

You should operate with a minimum resolution of 1024x768. Using Windows at a lower resolution doesn't give you much area to work with anyway. Additionally, if you plan to use Movie Maker, then you will also need a good video/graphics card. Microsoft recommends an ATI Radeon 9500 or higher as well as an nVidia GeForce FX 5900 or higher. Odds are, if you are using Windows Aero on Windows Vista or later, you will likely be able to use Movie Maker.

The last requirement I'll mention is a browser. If you are going to use the Windows Live Toolbar, you will need Microsoft Internet Explorer 6 or later.

NOTE *Some of the programs have additional requirements. In most cases, these will be installed when you install the program. For example, Windows Live Writer requires that you have the Microsoft .NET Framework 2.0 (or higher) installed. This will be installed automatically when you install Writer. Photo Gallery requires SQL Server 2005 Compact Edition. Again, this should be installed for you when the program installs. Finally, Photo Gallery and Movie Maker require DirectX 9 or later to be installed (at least some of the components). Again, in most cases, this will be done automatically for you.*

WARNING *You will need administrator rights to install the programs on your computer.*

Downloading and Installing the Windows Live Applications

The first steps to using the Windows Live Applications are to download and install them. You can download and install any or all of the applications that you want. If you choose to not install them all, you can always do the same process over to install any additional applications.

To start the process of installing the Windows Live Applications, you need to first download a file from `download.live.com`. When you go to this URL, you should find that it is somewhat similar to Figure 1.1.

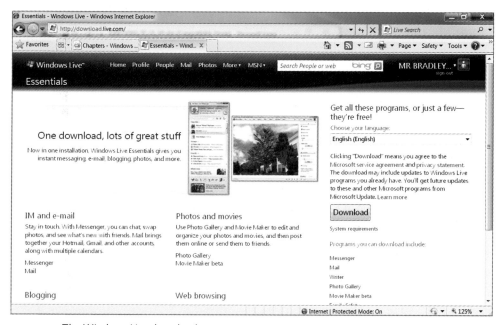

FIGURE 1.1 The Windows Live download page

Web pages evolve with time, so the page you see might be slightly different; however, you should find a link or button to allow you to download the Windows Live Applications. In Figure 1.1, you can see that there is a download button on the right. Clicking the download button on this page will begin the downloading process. It is most likely that Windows will ask if you want to Run or Save the file being downloaded. You'll need this file (called `wlsetup-web.exe`) in order to install the Windows Live Applications. Choose to either Run or Save the program. If you choose to Save the file, then once you download it, you will need to then run it.

> **NOTE** *The file* `wlsetup-web.exe` *is not all of the applications, but rather a file that will in turn download all the files. The* `wlsetup-web.exe` *file will be approximately a 1MB download.*

TIP *The actual applications will be downloaded when you run the setup program. If you plan to install the Live Applications on several machines, then you might want to download the entire installation package at once (a file that is approximately 133MB). You can do this by clicking the Download button shown in Figure 1.1. Once the download of the 1MB setup file starts, choose to cancel. You'll be presented with an option to Try again. Clicking this "Try Again" option for downloading will now download the complete 133MB file containing the applications.*

Once you've downloaded the `wlsetup-web.exe` file, run it by double-clicking on its icon. You could also have chosen to run this program as a part of the download. When you run this program, you may need to tell Windows to allow the program to run (you'll need to have administrator rights to your machine). The program will start by showing what is in Figure 1.2.

FIGURE 1.2 Starting the Windows Live Applications Installer

Once the installer starts loading, you will be presented with a selection of the various applications you can download and install, as shown in Figure 1.3.

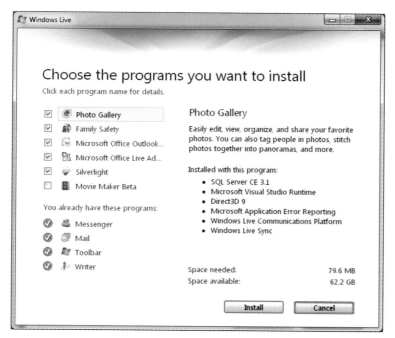

FIGURE 1.3 Choosing the applications to install

You can check the items you want to install. As you click on the names of each application, information about it will be displayed to the right. You can go ahead and install all the applications now, or you can install a few now and later run the installation program again to install others. You'll also see at the bottom of the page the amount of space needed to install the selected items. This amount will increase or decrease based on what you select.

Once you've selected the applications you want to install, click the Install button. This will start the installation process. If you have Internet Explorer open from having downloaded the setup files, you will be prompted to close it, as shown in Figure 1.4.

You might be prompted to close other programs as well. You can close the programs yourself, or you can choose one of the two options presented: either allow the installation to close the programs for you or choose to ignore the programs that are open. In general, you should close the programs or let the installation program close them.

You should press the Continue button to continue the installation process. You will see that the installation process will begin as shown in Figure 1.5. As the programs are downloaded and installed, you will see the status.

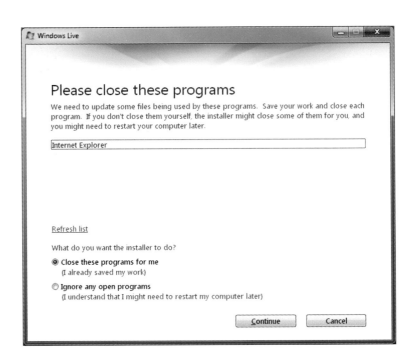

FIGURE 1.4 Please close these programs.

FIGURE 1.5 Installing the Windows Live Applications

As the programs install, information will be displayed about the applications. Note that if you followed the alternative suggestion earlier and downloaded the full applications, then when you start the install, it will progress more quickly because you've already done the downloading.

Once the downloading is completed from the setup program, you will be prompted to accept the Windows Live service agreement for the programs. The best way to understand the service agreement is to simply read it. Once you have, you'll need to click on the Accept button, shown in Figure 1.6, in order to continue. If you choose to cancel, you won't end up installing the programs.

FIGURE 1.6 Accepting the licensing agreement to use the Windows Live Applications

Once you've accepted the Live service agreement, you'll next be prompted to set a few options, as shown in Figure 1.7. These options will allow you to determine if you want to use Microsoft's search feature as your default instead of another search engine such as Google, Yahoo!, or others. You can also set MSN.com as your home page.

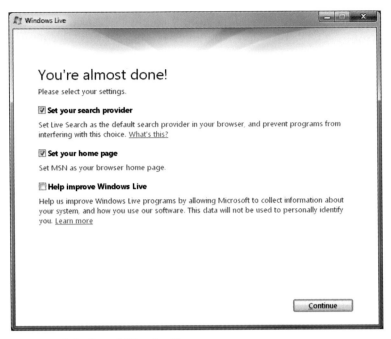

FIGURE 1.7 Selecting additional settings

In addition to the two options mentioned, you might also have one or two additional options for providing feedback to Microsoft. Figure 1.7 shows two options for providing feedback. The descriptions of these two options explain what they do. In either case, nothing specific about you will be returned to Microsoft, so selecting these options will not give Microsoft any personal insights on you.

Once you've selected the options you want to set, you can select the Continue button to continue with the installation of your Windows Live Essentials options. Pressing the Continue button will bring you to the Welcome window, as shown in Figure 1.8.

If you already have a Windows Live ID, you can click the Close button because you've installed the applications and are ready to start using them. Later in this chapter, you'll learn about the Windows Live Toolbar that can make accessing the applications a little easier. Alternatively, if there is a specific application you want to begin using, then now would be the time to jump to that chapter in this book!

If you don't have a Windows Live ID, you can click the Sign up link on the Welcome dialog to start the process of creating a Windows Live ID. The next section walks through this process.

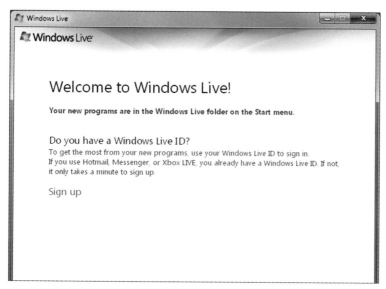

FIGURE 1.8 Do you want to set up a Windows Live ID?

Setting Up a Windows Live ID

In order to use the Windows Live Service mentioned earlier, you will need a Windows Live ID. As stated, if you already have one, you can close the dialog box and move on to the next section about using the Windows Live Essentials Applications. If not, you can click on the Sign up link. This will start the process of creating a Windows Live ID, as shown in Figure 1.9.

> **NOTE** *You can also create a new Windows Live ID by going to* www.1ive.com. *From there select Sign in to go to the Windows Live Sign in dialog, which contains a link for creating a new ID.*

Figure 1.9 contains a form for setting up your Windows Live ID as well as for entering information about yourself. Most of the information on this form is required and is fairly straightforward.

The first bit of information you need to enter is a Windows Live ID. This actual ID is an email address. This address can be one you create as a part of the setup process, or it can be an existing email address that you already have.

Library Resource Center
Renton Technical College
3000 N.E. 4ᵗʰ Street
Renton, WA 98056

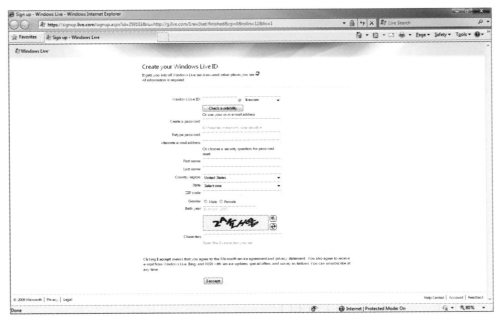

FIGURE 1.9 Creating a Windows Live ID as part of the installation

If you choose to use an existing email address, then you will need to click the link to use your own email address. This will allow you to then enter your own email address. The rest of the information on the form will remain the same. Don't bother trying to use a bogus email address because you will still have to validate that it is real. After you enter an email address, Windows Live ID automatically sends an email to that address, and you must respond to it in order to validate your account.

WARNING *If you use your own email address as your Windows Live ID, then you won't be able to use the Windows Live Hotmail service online. Of course, you can still use Windows Live Mail covered in Chapter 3.*

If you choose to set up an email address ID as a part of the sign-up process, then you will need to check to see if the ID you want is available. Do this by entering a value for Windows Live ID, by selecting an email extension (`live.com` or `hotmail.com`) and then clicking the Check availability button.

If the value you enter is available, a message will be posted to the form saying that it is available. If it is not available, then a list of alternatives will be presented that you can use to select an alternative. Figure 1.10 shows the alternatives that were selected when I tried to get `BradJones@live.com` as an ID. I have the option to select one of these alternatives or to enter a new value into the Windows Live ID box and try again.

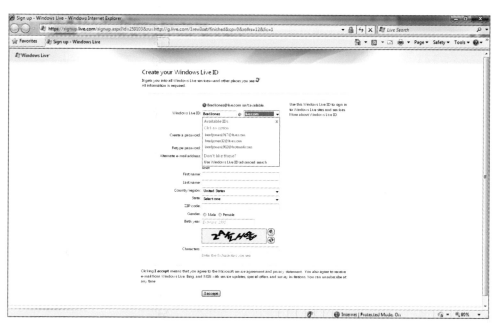

FIGURE 1.10 Checking for available IDs

As another option, if you don't like the suggestions for alternative IDs, you can use the Windows Live ID advanced search. A link to this search is included at the bottom of the alternative ID suggestions as shown in Figure 1.10. This will display a box similar to the one shown in Figure 1.11.

Using the advanced search dialog box, you can enter up to three words. A search will be done using these words. The resulting available IDs will be displayed for you to use to select your ID. You can enter words and then click the link to search for Windows Live ID options. If there is one you like, you can click on it. You'll then be returned to the form for setting up the rest of your ID. If you decide you don't want to use the advanced search, you can click the X in the upper-right corner to close the box and return to the Windows Live ID form.

FIGURE 1.11 Advanced Search for a new Windows Live ID

Once you've found an available ID, you can continue to enter the rest of the information. While the Windows Live ID is the most important piece of information, second to that will be your password. You'll need your ID and password to access Windows Live Services. You won't necessarily need these to use the Windows Live Essentials Applications. However, if you decide to do anything online—such as share images from the Windows Live Photo Gallery or post to a blog with Windows Live Writer— then you'll need both your ID and password.

While you need to enter a password you'll remember, you also should make sure it is a password that others won't easily guess. For that reason, the standard rules for creating a password apply. You shouldn't use your favorite pet's name, your children's names, your birth date, or other obvious items. In fact, when you click on the password box, you'll get a message stating that you should create a strong password that contains seven to sixteen characters that are both upper and lower case. To make it even stronger, you should also include a number or symbol along with the mixed-case letters. As you enter a password, the form will tell you how good it is. Figure 1.12 shows the various levels you might see. You are free to use any password you want, but you should work to get a strong status if you want to reduce the chance of someone gaining access to your Windows Live ID.

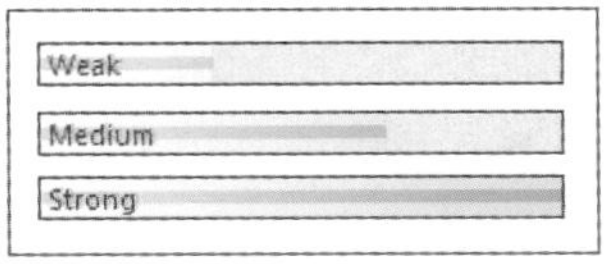

FIGURE 1.12 Password Status

After the password, most of the information on the form is straightforward. You should complete the form and then click the "I accept" button. This will process the form and create the Windows Live ID. If you have any errors on the form, messages will be displayed to help you correct then.

WARNING *The button for creating a Live ID is titled "I accept." This is because by creating a Live ID, you agree to the Microsoft service agreement and privacy statement. You can read those by clicking on the links in the form. If you don't agree with those, then you should not create a Live ID. If you are like most people, you'll probably click I accept without bothering to read either the agreement or the statement. . . .*

Once you've correctly completed the form, you'll be greeted with a page prompting you to get started with Windows Live, as shown in Figure 1.13. Note that the page you see will have your new Windows Live ID presented instead of bookauthor@live.com, which is the ID I created.

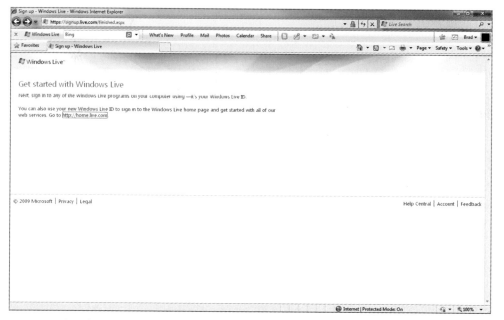

FIGURE 1.13 Windows Live ID created; time to get started

At this point, you have a Windows Live ID, and you are ready to do all of the things in this book—or at least the ones you've installed as shown earlier! On the getting started page shown in Figure 1.13, there is a link to home.live.com, which is the Windows Live home page. You can use that link to go to this page now, or you can go to the Windows Live home page at any time in the future by using that URL. The first time you go with a new ID, you will see something similar to Figure 1.14.

FIGURE 1.14 Windows Live Home Page

As you go through this book, you'll learn more about using the Windows Live home page as well as customizing some of the information on it. This will include linking images, setting up friends, getting to online mail, and much more. You can even access this home page from your mobile devices, as shown in Figure 1.15.

FIGURE 1.15 The mobile view of the Windows Live home page

Editing Your Windows Live Profile

Of course, if you find that something in your profile isn't right or changes, then you'll want to change that information. You can do this by logging into Live and going to your account settings.

The easiest way to get to your account information is to go to `account.live.com`. This will take you to the account settings page. If you are not already logged into Live, then you will be taken to the Windows Live login page, as shown in Figure 1.16.

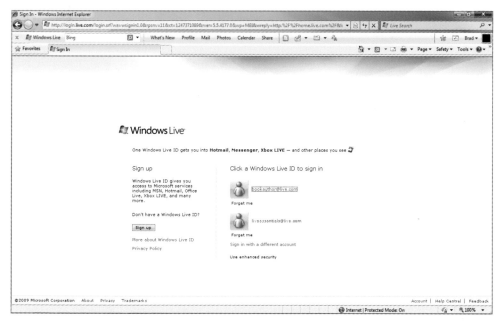

FIGURE 1.16 Logging in to Windows Live

You may or may not have accounts listed on the right side. If your account is listed, you can select it and use it to sign into Live. If your account is not listed, you can select the option to sign in with a different account. Either way, you will need to provide the Windows Live ID you created and your password. Once you provide these, you will be taken to the Windows Live Account page, as shown in Figure 1.17.

It is worth pointing out that there is a second path you can take to get to the account page. If you are logged in to Windows Live, then on the upper-right side of any of the Live pages, including `account.live.com` and `home.live.com`, you will see the name you entered into your account information along with a little down arrow. If you click on the down arrow, you will be given a few account options similar to those shown in Figure 1.17. Selecting View your account will also take you to your account page.

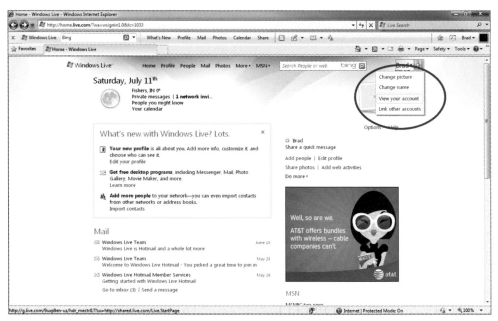

FIGURE 1.17 Account drop-down options

Whether you go directly to the account page or use the drop-down menu from one of the Windows Live pages, the end result will be a page similar to the one in Figure 1.18, only showing your information. From this page, you'll be able to access and change various information on your account.

The important parts of the Account page are on the left side. You have several options you can select as well as the ability to change the information that is being displayed. You can click on the Change or Add links to change the various items such as your password, alternate email address, and more. You can also choose to add a mobile number to your Windows Live account. If you want to change the information you originally entered to create your account, then you should click on the Registered information link. This will pull up a form as shown in Figure 1.19. This form is similar to the one you saw when you registered (as shown in Figure 1.12).

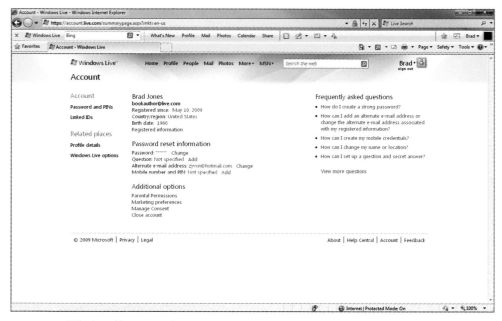

FIGURE 1.18 Windows Live account page

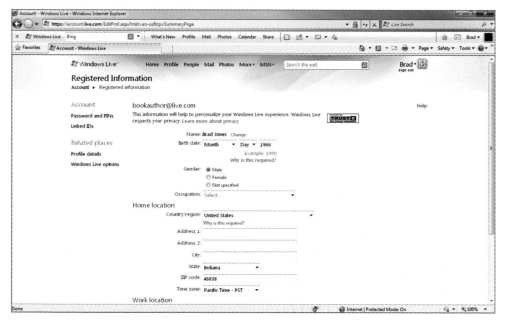

FIGURE 1.19 Updating account information

From the form shown in Figure 1.19, you can make changes. Once you've completed your changes, you can click Save to save them or Cancel to throw them out.

> **NOTE** *You can change nearly all of the information associated with your account. The one thing you can't change is the Live ID that you created. If you want to change the actual Live ID, then you will need to create a new account.*

Using the Windows Live Toolbar

At this point, you've learned how to create a Windows Live ID, you have learned how to log into your account, and you've seen how to update your information. Now it is time to start using the Windows Live Applications and services.

You learned how to install the Windows Live Applications earlier in this chapter. If you did so, then those applications will be on your Windows Start menu. You also had the option to install the Windows Live Toolbar. If you installed this toolbar, then it will be shown in Internet Explorer. In fact, if you look at Figure 1.19, you'll see that the Windows Live Toolbar is actually being shown in my browser windows. It is the toolbar across the top that contains the Windows Live search box and then a number of options to the right. I show it again in Figure 1.20 as a standalone toolbar.

FIGURE 1.20 The Windows Live Toolbar

The Windows Live Toolbar will allow you to have easy access to the Windows Live Search as well as access to many of the Windows Live Applications. There are a number of things you can do from the Toolbar any time you have your browser open. This includes:

- ▶ Keeping tabs on people in your network
- ▶ Using Bing (previously called Live Search)
- ▶ Viewing a snapshot of your email
- ▶ Viewing photos
- ▶ Using Windows Live Calendar
- ▶ Sharing your favorite links
- ▶ And much more

In addition to using the Windows Live Toolbar to do all of the preceding, you can also add custom buttons to allow you to do even more. In the following sections, you'll learn some of the highlights of what you can accomplish with the Windows Live Toolbar.

> **NOTE** *Some of the details of these functions will be left to other chapters in this book. For example, in the following sections you'll learn about accessing photos, email, and calendaring; however, the specific details of using these features will be covered in later chapters when Windows Live Photo Gallery, Windows Live Mail, and the other Windows Live Applications are covered.*

Keeping Tabs on People in Your Network

One of the first options you'll see on the Windows Live Toolbar is What's New. This is not an option to see what is new for Windows Live or even for the Windows Live Toolbar. Rather, it is an option to see what is new with people you are connected with on Windows Live. You'll learn more about connecting with people in Chapter 2, which covers using instant messaging with Windows Live Messenger, Chapter 7 on socializing with Live Spaces, and Chapter 9 on interacting with Groups. Once you start interacting with others, then you'll find that the What's New option on the toolbar will highlight recent happenings. Figure 1.21 shows what is new in my network today.

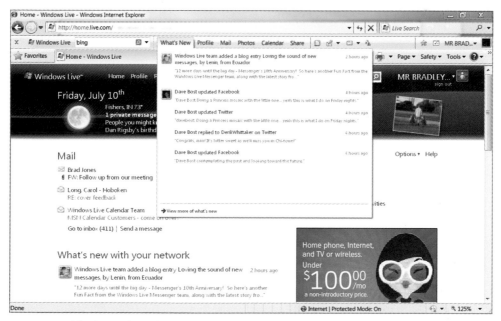

FIGURE 1.21 What's New from the Windows Live Toolbar

As you can see, the figure shows various types of information, including social networking interaction-related information. This includes information from my friends in my network as well as social feeds and groups I belong to. What will be displayed are new things that they have done, so you can keep tabs on them. You can see that there are even times, which reveal how old the information is.

> **NOTE** *What you see on the What's New page is similar to the information you'd see on your Windows Live Home Page (*home.live.com*).*

Using Bing: The Search Engine Previously Known as Live Search

Many people consider Google the gateway to everything on the Internet. Google is actually just one of many search engines that can be used to find things on the Web. Microsoft has also created a search engine that comes with the Windows Live Essentials called Bing (previously called Live Search).

You can get to Bing by going to either www.Live.com or www.Bing.com. Either way, you will arrive at the same relatively simple page, where you can enter search criteria for your search.

> **NOTE** *Microsoft regularly changes the background image on its search page. Therefore, you will likely see a different image than the one shown in Figure 1.22. If you move your mouse around on the image, you'll find that there will be information displayed about the image shown.*

The Windows Live Toolbar brings Windows Bing (Live Search) to your browser so that you have access to search at any time. Just as with the Windows Bing search page, you can simply enter a term into the search box, click the magnifying glass icon, and you'll be on your way to discovering matches on the Web.

FIGURE 1.22 Windows Bing (Live Search)

Even more than that, you can restrict your search to specific areas. As you can see in Figure 1.23, there is a drop-down list that can be used to refine your search. You can narrow your search to just news, maps, images, feeds, the current site, or the current computer. Simply enter your search term (or terms) and click the option you want to search. The results will then be displayed.

FIGURE 1.23 Focusing a Bing search

Access Windows Live Applications from the Windows Live Toolbar

The Windows Live Toolbar will also allow you to access a number of different applications. This includes applications such as Windows Live Mail, Windows Live Calendar, and more.

Viewing Email from the Toolbar

In Chapter 3, you will learn how to use email associated with Windows Live. This will include the Windows Live Mail program and Windows Live Hotmail. The Windows Live Toolbar is all about shortcuts and getting you to programs quicker.

 While you'll learn about email in Chapter 3, it is good to know now that the Windows Live Toolbar will give you access to your mail without having to go to the mail programs. Rather, you'll be able to click on the Mail option on the tool bar and get a list of your most recent emails. In Figure 1.24, you'll see my current email listed from the Windows Live Toolbar. Of course, if you didn't use a Microsoft Live.com or Hotmail. com email address to set up your Windows Live ID, then you will actually be presented with a message asking you to sign up for a Windows Live Hotmail account instead.

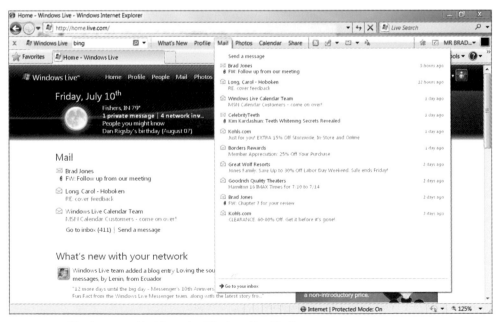

FIGURE 1.24 Windows Live Mail from the Windows Live Toolbar

As you can see in the figure, this is simply a list of the most recent mail messages in my Windows Live Hotmail account. I can also choose to go to my inbox by clicking on the link at the bottom of the list of messages.

> **NOTE** *This list of mail messages is not a replacement for the mail program. It is simply a quick shortcut for seeing your most recent messages.*

Viewing Shared Photos

Just as with mail, you can also get a quick view of photos by using the Photo option on the Toolbar. When you select Photos, you'll get a view of the most recent photos that have been shared in your Live network. As you can see in Figure 1.25, several of my Live network friends have shared images.

The Windows Live Toolbar gives you quick access to these photos. You'll learn more about viewing and manipulating them in Chapter 5. You'll learn more about interacting with others via Windows Live in a number of chapters within this book, including Chapter 8.

FIGURE 1.25 Shared Photos viewed from the Windows Live Toolbar

Checking Your Windows Live Calendar

Chapter 7 will talk about setting up and using calendar functionality. You'll be able to schedule appointments, events, and other activities that you can then use or share with others. As with the other features, the Calendar option on the Windows Live Toolbar allows you quick access to current items on your calendar, as shown in Figure 1.26. You'll be able to add events, go to your calendar, or simply figure out what day it is.

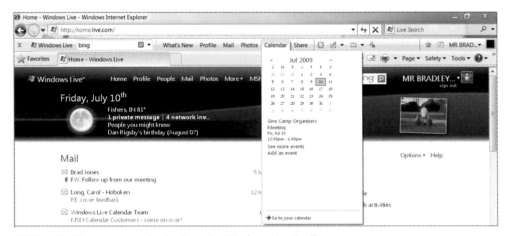

FIGURE 1.26 Viewing your calendar from the Windows Live Toolbar

Sharing Your Favorites

Another option on the Windows Live Toolbar is for saving and sharing favorites. Your favorites are sites that you like enough that you want to remember them. You can save your favorites in a browser like Internet Explorer; however, Windows Live will let you save a favorite that you can share.

 To save a favorite that you'll be able to share, you can click on the Share option on the Windows Live Toolbar when you are on the site you want to remember and share. This will pull up the dialog shown in Figure 1.27.

You can fill in the name and description of the Web page you want to save. Once you've entered the information, click the Share button. The page's address will be written to your Windows Live SkyDrive's public favorites. You'll be able to let others access the shared links from there. You can learn more about SkyDrive, sharing favorites, and more in Chapter 10.

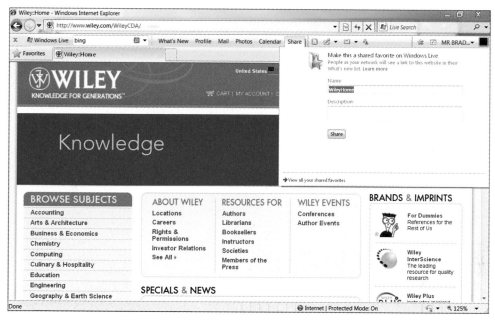

FIGURE 1.27 Sharing a favorite site

Translating to Other Languages

The Windows Live Toolbar has several other features that you can use in addition to those that have already been covered. If English isn't your first language, then you might want to try the Translation option. This option will allow you to translate the text on a web page to a different language. This option is accessible via the Translate icon on the Windows Live Toolbar.

When you click the Translate this page icon, the current web page will be displayed twice on the page, side by side, with a few additional options. In Figure 1.28, you can see my blog page shown after the Translate button has been clicked.

You can actually change the translation language using the drop-down list. In Figure 1.28, I've selected the option to translate from English to Russian. In the drop-down list, you'll see there are a number of options to translate to or from English.

You'll also see that there are options to change the view. The default view is to have the original page to the left and the translation to the right. You can choose to put one above the other, or you can choose to have one hover over the other. Regardless of the display, this is a chance for you to get a quick view of a page in a different language—all from the one-click convenience of the Windows Live Toolbar.

FIGURE 1.28 A translated page

Customizing Your Windows Live Toolbar

There are a number of buttons and options on the Windows Live Toolbar that I've not covered. Additionally, there are a number of buttons not on the toolbar that you can add. You can add additional buttons and customize your Windows Live Toolbar by clicking on the "Get new buttons" icon. As shown in Figure 1.29, this will display a list of some of the buttons that are available as well as a link to a location where you can get others.

FIGURE 1.29 Adding additional buttons to your Windows Live Toolbar

The buttons you can add to your Windows Live Toolbar are not limited to those from Microsoft. If you click the Find more buttons link shown in Figure 1.29, you'll be taken to a web page that will allow you to select from hundreds of options that you can add to your Toolbar. There are options for adding links sites and functions such as eBay, LinkedIn, maps, events, movies, music, Webkinz, news, games, and much more.

WARNING *When you choose to add a button, most likely a file will be downloaded and installed. Therefore, you should only install buttons from sites or companies you trust.*

In addition to adding buttons, you can remove and customize the buttons that are already on the Windows Live Toolbar. Within the dialog shown in Figure 1.29, you'll also see a link for Toolbar options. Clicking this link will pull up a dialog similar to Figure 1.30.

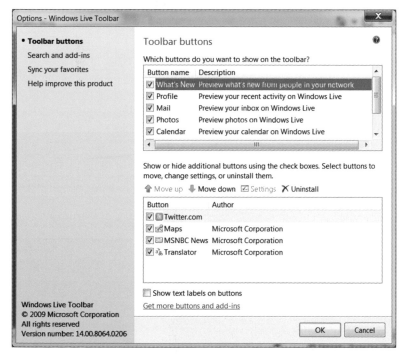

FIGURE 1.30 Setting Windows Live Toolbar options

As you can see, from the Windows Live Toolbar options dialog, you can check or uncheck items being displayed on your toolbar. You can also change the order by clicking on an item to highlight it and then clicking the Move up or Move down option. You can uninstall a button you've added or that is on the page by clicking the Uninstall option. If a button or add-in has settings, you'll also be able to adjust them here as well.

Once you've made your changes, you can click the OK button to save them. You can select Cancel if you change your mind and want to leave your settings as they were before pulling up the dialog.

In Conclusion

This chapter covered a lot of information to get you started with Windows Live Essentials. You learned how to install the Windows Live Applications on your computer and how to install additional add-ons such as the Windows Live Toolbar, which gives you quick access to many of the Live Essentials features as well as the ability to create button links to many other features.

This chapter was core for getting the applications onto your machine. From here, you can actually jump to any chapter in this book. Pick the chapter that has the Live Application or Service you are most interested in using now.

Instant Messaging with Windows Live Messenger

IN THIS CHAPTER, YOU WILL:

- ▶ Sign into Windows Live Messenger
- ▶ Adjust your sign-in options
- ▶ Set up contacts and groups
- ▶ Send instant messages
- ▶ Invite others into conversations
- ▶ Respond when you're contacted
- ▶ Block people from sending you instant messages
- ▶ Personalize and customize Windows Live Messenger
- ▶ Move beyond text instant messages

WHEN YOU think of Windows Live Messenger, you probably imagine people sending short bursts of text to each other. The latest version of Messenger takes online chatting to a whole new level of sophistication. Sure, you can still send those little text blurbs back and forth with a friend, but now you can also share photos, do audio/video calling, play games together, and even host chats for entire groups of people.

Windows Live Messenger has become such a key part of people's lives online that it has been used for things like marriage propos- als and long-distance holiday celebrations. When you can't be somewhere in person, and a telephone conversation just won't do, being able to connect with friends and family over Windows Live Messenger becomes the ideal way to stay in touch.

NOTE *Windows Live Messenger marked its 10th anniversary in 2009. More than 300 million people all around the world use it to keep in touch by exchanging quick text messages and even audio and video conversations. In fact, at any given time, there are about 40 million active Windows Live Messenger conversations underway.*

Earlier in its lifetime, this product was known as MSN Messenger, but the past several versions have carried the Windows Live name, and now it represents a key component of Windows Live Essentials. The most recent release introduced many significant changes to the product and included even closer integration with the rest of Windows Live.

Signing into Windows Live Messenger

To begin using Windows Live Messenger, you must first sign in with your Windows Live ID. Enter your ID and password into Windows Live Messenger as shown in Figure 2.1

If you don't already have a Windows Live ID, you can sign up for one by clicking on the Sign up link. As you sign in, there are a few options to consider:

▶ Check Remember me if you want Windows Live Messenger to remember your ID the next time you run the application. If you check this box, you won't have to enter your ID again.

▶ Check Remember my password if you also would like Windows Live Messenger to store and enter your password for you. If you're using a public computer, you should keep this check box turned off.

▶ Check Sign me in automatically if you would like Windows Live Messenger to use your stored ID and password to sign you in every time you are connected to the Internet. If you check this box, the two boxes above are also checked.

WARNING *If you are using a public or shared computer or if you are worried about anyone accessing your account on your PC, you should not check any of these options. That way your ID, password, and access to your account are protected.*

FIGURE 2.1 Initial sign-in experience for Windows Live Messenger

By default, Windows Live Messenger signs you in as Available, and the border around your display picture will be shown in green. An available status tells your Messenger contacts that you are there and ready to have a conversation. If you would like to sign in as something other than available, click the Sign in as: drop-down list, illustrated in Figure 2.2, and select Busy (informing people not to contact you right now), Away (you're not at your computer), Appear offline (useful for seeing who else is online but appearing to be offline yourself). You can also jump directly into other options (more on these later in the chapter).

FIGURE 2.2 Sign-in as menu options

Adjusting Sign-In Options

If you chose to have Windows Live Messenger remember your ID and password, when you sign in in the future, you can click the down arrow near the Sign in as: area (see Figure 2.3) to adjust your sign-in options, including asking Windows Live Messenger to remove your account from the remembered list by clicking on the (Forget me) link.

FIGURE 2.3 Click the down arrow button to show the sign-in options.

Setting Up Contacts and Groups

After signing in, the main Windows Live Messenger window will be displayed (see Figure 2.4), as well as a small at-a-glance Today window. The Today window shows you top news and sports headlines, a quick view into your Hotmail inbox, and other information and links.

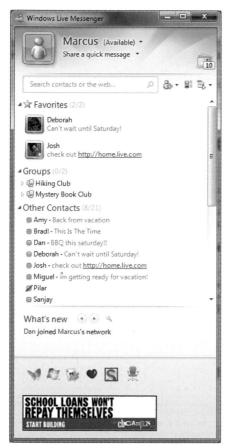

FIGURE 2.4 Main Windows
Live Messenger Window

If you have already been using other parts of Windows Live to add people to your network, you may already have contacts displayed within Messenger, similar to what you see in Figure 2.4. If you don't have any contacts, Windows Live Messenger will prompt you to add them, which is easy to do. Click on the Add a contact link or the Add a contact or group button, which will pop up a menu as shown in Figure 2.5.

FIGURE 2.5 Add menu

To begin, select Add a contact and you will see a window like the one in Figure 2.6. Enter your contact's email address to have an invitation sent. Optionally, you can also enter a mobile device (phone) number to send messages as text messages and assign this new contact to a category of contacts. Messenger creates a default category of "Favorites" in which you can place your top, most frequently used Messenger friends.

> **NOTE** *If you add a mobile device (phone) number, you can send messages to your contact's phone as text messages. They may be charged by their carrier for these messages, however.*

FIGURE 2.6 Add a contact

> **TIP** *If you have contacts using Yahoo! Messenger, you can add them as contacts and communicate with them by using Windows Live Messenger. Just type in their Yahoo! Instant messaging address (e.g.,* name@yahoo.com*).*

If you would rather instant message simultaneously with a group of people, select Create a group from the Add menu shown in Figure 2.5. Before you begin Creating your group, Windows Live will display a small reminder about the differences between groups and categories, as shown in Figure 2.7.

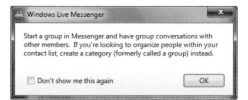

FIGURE 2.7 Reminder about the differences between groups and categories

This distinction is important, especially if you have used previous versions of Windows Live Messenger. In these earlier versions, categories were actually known as groups. In this current version, groups refer specifically to Windows Live Groups, which are covered in greater detail in Chapter 9. Categories, on the other hand, are simply ways of organizing people inside your contact list and are discussed further below.

After clicking the OK button in Figure 2.7, you will start creating your group by giving it a name in the window shown in Figure 2.8.

FIGURE 2.8 First step in creating a group, providing a name

After naming your group, you can enter email addresses for the members of your group as well as a brief introductory message about the group. The invitation for an example group (a Mystery Book Club) is illustrated in Figure 2.9.

Groups can be larger than 20 people, but only groups of up to 20 can carry on group instant messaging sessions using Windows Live Messenger. You will see these groups inside the main Messenger window (see Figure 2.4), under the Groups heading.

FIGURE 2.9 Inviting members to a group

As mentioned previously, Windows Live Messenger creates a "Favorites" category for you initially. You can add other categories by selecting Create a category from the Add menu shown in Figure 2.5. Messenger again provides a brief explanatory window about what a category is. Click the OK button, and then you'll see a window similar to Figure 2.10.

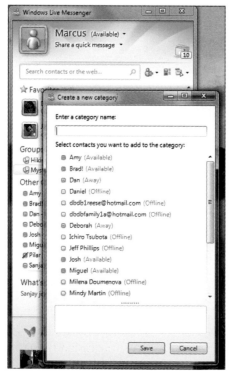

FIGURE 2.10 Creating a category and adding members

Type in your new category name (e.g., "Family" or "Coworkers") and then select the contacts to add to that category. As you click on the contact names, they will appear in the larger box near the bottom of the window. Click the Save button when you're finished assigning members to this new category.

Sending Instant Messages

Now that you have your contacts created, as well as any groups and categories in place, it's time to start communicating. To initiate an instant messaging conversation with one of your contacts, just double-click on their name in the main Messenger window (see Figure 2.4), and you will see a conversation window, depicted in Figure 2.11.

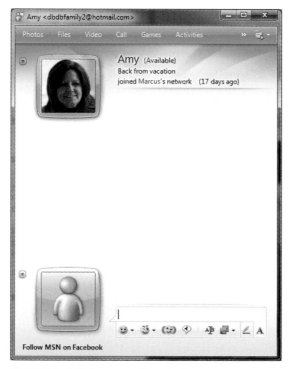

FIGURE 2.11 Initial conversation window

To send a message, just start typing in the small white balloon area near the bottom of the window. After you type in your message, press Enter. Your message will then appear in the top of the conversation window. As the other person you're chatting with enters his or her message, you'll see it appear immediately after yours (Figure 2.12 shows a conversation in progress).

FIGURE 2.12 Conversation in progress

NOTE *If you initiate a conversation with someone who isn't online, Windows Live Messenger will go into Offline Instant Messaging mode and store your message to be delivered the next time your contact signs into Messenger.*

You don't need to wait for the other person's message to appear before you begin typing another message. You'll see a typing indicator on the right above the white balloon area to let you know when your counterpart is typing something to send to you.

NOTE *The text at the bottom of the conversation window is an advertisement.*

> **TIP** *The conversation window can be resized just like any other window. You can make it wider to show more text or smaller to take up less space. You can even resize the regions inside the window (e.g., stretch your conversation balloon out to be larger).*

In addition to typing plain text, you can send other things as part of the conversation, all depicted by icons below the text balloon. Each of these icons and what they do are reviewed in the sections that follow.

Emoticons

Emoticons enable you to express your emotions (and more) in the form of small icons. Click on the icon to see all the different options available. Each emoticon has a text shortcut that, when typed, will change to the emoticon. For example typing :-) will display the smile emoticon.

When you click on the emoticon button, you'll see some of the emoticons that are built into Messenger (shown in Figure 2.13).

FIGURE 2.13 Some of the built-in emoticons

Click on any of them to add them to your conversation, or hover over each type to see a brief description of the emoticon and the text shortcut. As you start to use emoticons, those recently used will appear in the middle of the list. Featured emoticons, downloaded as part of Messenger theme packs or from third parties, are shown at the top. Click on the Featured emoticons or More link to see other available featured emoticons.

Clicking on the Show all link in Figure 2.13 will pop up a new window with all of the Emoticons currently available in Messenger. This Emoticons window lists emoticons divided into two groups. The groups on the top are the ones that are pinned to the list shown in Figure 2.13. The group on the bottom is the entire list of available emoticons. If you want to pin an emoticon to the list on the top, you first need to select one and click Unpin to free up space (you can only have 40 pinned emoticons). Then select an emoticon from the bottom list, click Pin, and it will be on your pinned list.

You can even create your own emoticons. Click the Create button to select an image from your PC. It will be automatically resized and then you can provide a text shortcut and a name for your emoticon.

Winks

A wink is like an emoticon but with animation and sound. Figure 2.14 shows some of the winks built into Messenger. Clicking on Featured winks or See more offerings will take you to a web site where you can download additional winks from a third party, many of which have a small cost associated with them.

FIGURE 2.14 List of winks

Clicking on any of these will add them to your conversation window, complete with animation and sound. When the wink is finished playing, a small icon will remain with a Play link to view it again. An example of a wink in action is shown in Figure 2.15.

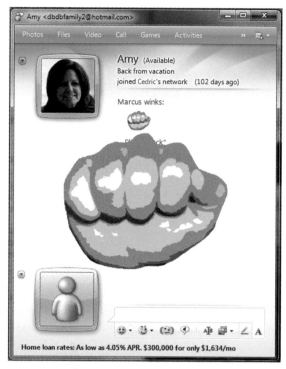

FIGURE 2.15 A wink in a conversation window

Other Icons: Nudge, Voice Clip, Formatting

If you think your conversation partner might need a little prompting to respond, clicking the Nudge icon will shake the conversation window and play a chime to draw attention. You probably don't want to nudge too often as it can be considered annoying.

Click on the Voice Clip icon (or press and hold F2) to record and send a brief voice comment. If you haven't already configured Messenger to work with your PC's audio configuration, you may be prompted to set this up prior to recording.

You can also adjust the font or the background image of your conversation by clicking on either of those two icons.

After clicking the Font icon, the window displayed in Figure 2.16 is displayed. From here, select your font, style (regular, italic, etc.), size, and effects, including color.

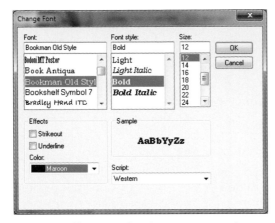

FIGURE 2.16 Choosing a font for your conversation

 When clicking on the Background button, you'll get a pop-up of featured and recently used backgrounds (similar to emoticons and winks). Click on any that you would like to use, or click on Featured backgrounds or More to visit a third-party web site to download backgrounds (possibly for a fee). Clicking on Show all will display a list of current backgrounds (see Figure 2.17). On this window, click Browse to select an image from your PC to use as your own custom background.

FIGURE 2.17 Choosing a background image for your conversation

WARNING *Depending on your choices of fonts and backgrounds, you might create a display environment that can be difficult to read. Consider more simple fonts, standard sizes and colors, and unintrusive backgrounds.*

When you're ready to end a conversation, simply close the conversation window. If this is your first conversation, Messenger will ask you if you want to save your conversations on your PC. If you're using a public or shared computer, it's recommended not to save your conversations. You can change this option later if you want.

NOTE *After you end a conversation by closing the window, if the other person continues the conversation, the window will appear again.*

Inviting Others to Join a Conversation

Sometimes you want to bring more than one person into a conversation without setting up a complete Windows Live Group (as discussed earlier in this chapter and in Chapter 9). For example, you may have a conversation going with one friend about plans for the weekend and want to confirm those plans with another friend.

To add someone else, just click Invite on the top of any conversation window, as shown in Figure 2.18. If you don't see the Invite option, make the window slightly wider or click the >> button to show any menu options that are hidden from view.

After clicking Invite, choose who to add into the conversation by clicking on their names in the next window that appears. Then click the OK button to return to the conversation window but with your new participant added (Figure 2.19).

FIGURE 2.18 Getting ready to invite someone

Responding When Contacted

When any of your contacts in Messenger want to begin a conversation with you, they will go through the same steps you would go through, outlined earlier in this chapter in the "Sending Instant Messages" section. If you are signed into Messenger, you will receive a pop-up notification in the lower-right corner of your screen to let you know that someone is contacting you. An example of this is shown in Figure 2.20.

FIGURE 2.19 The conversation window after adding a second person

FIGURE 2.20 One of your contacts initiating a conversion

You can configure how these notifications are displayed by clicking on the Options link inside the notification, or by selecting Options from the Tools menu inside Messenger. More details on this and other options can be found later in this chapter.

If you have Windows Live Messenger minimized or pinned to your task bar, you will also see the icon flash and then stay highlighted to inform you of the incoming conversation. To respond, click either on the pop-up notification or on the icon in the task bar to show the conversation window and begin to respond. All of the same options shown in Figure 2.11 and discussed previously in this chapter apply when you respond to a conversation started by someone else.

Blocking People in Messenger

You may find it necessary to block some people from contacting you for whatever reason. Messenger makes blocking unwanted contacts simple. To block someone, right-click on any contact within Messenger, and then select Block contact from the menu (see Figure 2.21). A small dialog box will inform you of the implications of blocking a contact. Click the OK button to confirm that you want to block a contact, or click the Cancel button to abort the process.

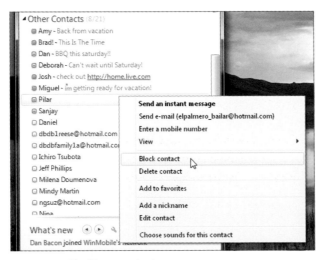

FIGURE 2.21 Blocking a contact

After you block a contact, you will still see them in your contact list, but their status icon will show a red slash mark through the status indicator, as shown in Figure 2.22.

FIGURE 2.22 Indication of a blocked contact

If you want to do more than just block a contact, click on Delete contact from the menu shown in Figure 2.21. Before deleting the contact, Messenger will ask if you also want to block the person and delete them from your Hotmail contacts as well, if the contact is shared between the two.

When people want to add you as a Messenger contact, you will be asked to confirm that you'll allow them to do so. You'll either receive a pop-up window asking for confirmation while in Messenger or the next time you start and sign in to Messenger.

> **TIP** *If you receive contact invitations from people you don't know, you should decline those invitations and block the sender from sending any others. This will help keep unwanted messages from being sent to you.*

Personalizing and Customizing

Messenger provides quite a few different ways to customize the program to fit your personal style and day-to-day use. The three most common optional changes—display picture, status, and scene—are covered in the following subsections.

Display Picture

The first thing most people do when using Messenger is to customize the picture displayed in the conversation window. After all, it's you having the conversation with your friends and family, so you should be more than the default gray Messenger person. To change your display picture, click on the picture in the upper-left corner of the main Messenger window (see Figure 2.4) to bring up the Display Picture window illustrated in Figure 2.23.

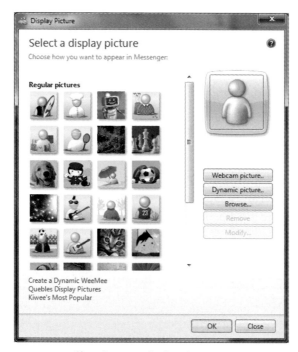

FIGURE 2.23 Changing your display picture

Messenger includes many built-in display pictures for you to choose from in the Regular pictures area. But you have a whole lot of other fun options, too, including:

▶ Click on the Webcam picture button to take a still picture or a short movie from your PC's webcam.

▶ Click on Dynamic picture to create display pictures that change based on selected emoticons like smile, wink, or many more, all on the window shown in Figure 2.24.

▶ Click on Browse to select a picture stored on your PC.

▶ Or click on any of the links below the Regular pictures area to go to a third-party web site and configure a display picture (fees may apply)

NOTE *The links on the lower-left corner of Figure 2.23 (Create a Dynamic WeeMee, Quebles Display Pictures, and Kiwee's Most Popular) are links to third-party websites with offers to download and/or purchase items.*

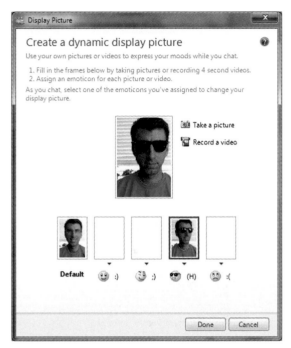

FIGURE 2.24 Creating dynamic pictures for emoticons

Status

The next option most frequently changed within Messenger is your status. As you recall from earlier in this chapter, when Messenger first starts, you are signed in as Available unless you specify another status when signing in (see Figure 2.1). It's easy to change your status at any time. Click on the area displaying your name (near the top of the window shown in Figure 2.4 and next to your display picture) and select a new status from the menu shown in Figure 2.25. You may also completely sign out of Messenger from this menu as well as access the other options displayed.

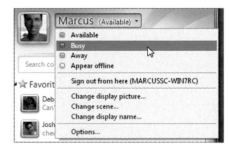

FIGURE 2.25 Set a new status, sign out, or select other options from this menu.

Scene

Another popular option for most people who are using Messenger is to change the Messenger's scene or display theme. Select Change scene from the Tools menu to show the Scene window illustrated in Figure 2.26.

FIGURE 2.26 Selecting a new scene and color scheme

Many of the scenes are similar to other themes used within Windows Live. Each scene also recommends a corresponding color scheme (shown near the bottom of the window). You can chose any color scheme you wish, however, independent of any scene selected.

Take a look at Figure 2.27 for an example of how Messenger might look after a few customizations. It's definitely more personalized than the default options you saw previously in Figure 2.4.

 Messenger includes a large number of additional personalization and customization options, which you can access from the menu button in the main Messenger window. From this menu, select Tools to see the various options shown in Figure 2.28.

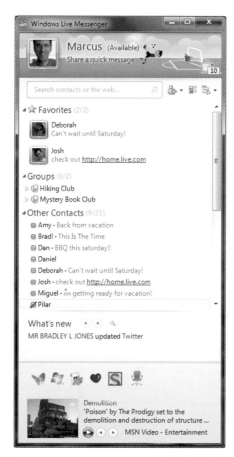

FIGURE 2.27 A more customized version of Messenger

FIGURE 2.28 Tools available inside Messenger

TIP *If you don't want to receive notifications of Messenger activities (like your contacts signing in), you can turn those off by clicking Options from the Tools menu. Then select Alerts from the list of option settings and uncheck the boxes for notifications you no longer wish to receive.*

Moving Beyond Text

While text might still be the predominant way most people communicate over Messenger, you certainly aren't limited to just typing back and forth with your friends. After you start a Messenger conversation, a whole range of options are available across the top of the conversation window (see Figure 2.11). The most popular options are discussed further in the subsections that follow.

Photos

You know how fun it can be to sit down with a friend or family member and flip through a stack of pictures? With Messenger, you can do just that, albeit virtually. Just click on Photos at the top of any conversation window to select some pictures from your PC, and then share them. The result will be similar to what you see in Figure 2.29. You and the person you're talking with can click on any of the photos in your "stack" and talk about them as you view them.

FIGURE 2.29 Sharing photos

NOTE *Photo sharing doesn't work when chatting with more than one person.*

Files

If you want to actually transmit a file (possibly a photo), Messenger provides two options when you click on Files at the top of a conversation window. You can select Publish files online and will be taken to a Windows Live SkyDrive page, where you can configure a new folder to share files (for more information on SkyDrive, see Chapter 10).

More often, however, people select Send a file or photo, choose something from their PC, and then send it to the other person. Your contact receiving the file will be prompted to accept it, and then to store it on their PC. Figure 2.30 shows an example of a file (in this case a Microsoft Word document) being transmitted inside a Messenger conversation window.

FIGURE 2.30 Transferring a file

Video Calls

The most sophisticated communication option inside Messenger is video calling. Clicking Video will enable a two-way audio/video session between you and your contact. If you haven't already configured the audio and video options inside Messenger, you'll be prompted to do so.

Just like a telephone, your Messenger will "ring" the other person's Messenger, the video call must be accepted, and then it will begin. The quality of the transmission will depend on many factors, including the equipment, bandwidth, and Internet conditions. But generally most people find Messenger video calls to work quite well.

Call

Not to be confused with a video call, clicking Call will initiate a voice-over-IP (VOIP) audio-only session. You can choose to call your contact's computer, or to call a phone number. This technology is called Windows Live Call and is only available in certain parts of the world. Additional fees apply for PC-to-phone calls and are charged by a third party.

TIP *A headset with a microphone is recommended for the best results when doing audio calling.*

Games & Activities

Messenger has even more ways to have fun—built-in games and sharable activities! You can play games online with anyone in your contact list. While you have a conversation window open, click Games on the top bar, and the window will expand to show you the game options, similar to what's shown in Figure 2.31.

Choose from the list of games (either the Top Games or All Free Games), and then click the Start Game button to begin playing.

If you're not in the mood for games, try clicking on Activities to find some other things you can do together, all right inside the conversation you're having.

FIGURE 2.31 Some of the games you can play

In Conclusion

In this chapter, you found out about one of the key applications in the Windows Live Essentials suite—Windows Live Messenger. You learned how to sign in to Messenger, adjust your sign-in options, as well as set up contacts and groups. You discovered how to start communicating with people as well as how to respond to someone contacting you. You explored the customization and personalization options within Messenger. And finally, you found out about how to move beyond text to use Messenger for things like photo/file sharing, voice/video calling, and even playing games.

Emailing with Windows Live Mail

IN THIS CHAPTER, YOU WILL:

▶ Learn about Windows Live Mail

▶ Discover how to add email accounts to Windows Live Mail

▶ Create and send email messages to friends, family, or anyone else you know

▶ Save draft messages to send or edit later

▶ Personalize your email messages with formatting, color, and styles

▶ Customize your email messages with stationery

▶ Identify yourself in your email messages with your own personalized signature

▶ Learn how to forward and reply to email messages

▶ Discover how to embed attachments or photos into your messages

▶ Manage the people you know via Windows Live Contacts

▶ Manage junk mail and prevent it from entering your Inbox

▶ Learn how to add and read RSS feeds from Windows Live Mail

IN THE past, people would write letters, stick them in an envelope, add a stamp, and mail them off to another person. That was the way one sent mail. In the world of the Internet, people now tend to send messages via the Internet and email. Instead of taking days, electronic messages can travel almost instantly.

Emails can contain text, images, and more. You can send plain, simple text, or you can format it with special fonts, bolding, and much more. You can even use stationery for your messages!

Of course, to send email you need an email account and a program for creating emails. If you followed the instructions in Chapter 1, you most likely have a Windows Live ID. In fact, the Windows Live ID you created in Chapter 1 can be used as an email ID. If you don't have an email program, then you can use the Windows Live Mail application as well as the Windows Live Hotmail service.

> **NOTE** *With Windows Live Mail, you can use multiple email accounts.*

Understanding Email Accounts

In this chapter, you will learn about Windows Live Mail (see Figure 3.1). This is one of the Windows Live Essential Applications that you learned how to download in Chapter 1. Once it is downloaded and installed, you will find it on your Start menu under the Windows Live folder.

FIGURE 3.1 The Windows Live Mail program in use

The Windows Live Mail program will operate on your computer. You will be able to use this program to set up or access email accounts. You'll also be able to use the program to track events and to manage a calendar and access web news feeds.

In order to get email, you need to have a company provide you with email service. This is a service that routes emails to you and takes your emails and sends them off to other people. Think of a service provider as the postal service for emails! While Windows Live Mail will allow to you read, compose, and otherwise work with emails, it is not an email service provider. If you are already reading emails on your machine, then you already have an email service. Most Internet service providers provide you with email services as well. If you are unsure if you have an email service, don't fret. Microsoft provides email processing through its online Windows Live Hotmail service.

While you will use Windows Live Mail on your local machine, you can also use Windows Live Hotmail to create, read, and otherwise work with email online. You access Windows Live Hotmail online at `mail.live.com`. With Hotmail, you can use your Windows Live ID as your email address. Additionally, at the time this book was written, Microsoft was providing 5GB of storage online for your email messages. They even stated that this amount of storage could be expected to increase with time.

Windows Live Mail can use the Windows Live Hotmail email address and can pull your Hotmail email down to your local computer. You can then use the Windows Live Mail program to read and respond to those email addresses.

NOTE *For the most part, this chapter will focus on Windows Live Mail and will not focus on Windows Live Hotmail.*

NOTE *In Chapter 7, you will learn how to use the Calendar feature of Windows Live. The calendar is located within Windows Live Mail.*

Creating a Mail Account

The first time you run Windows Live Mail, you will likely be prompted to set up or create an email account, as shown in Figure 3.2.

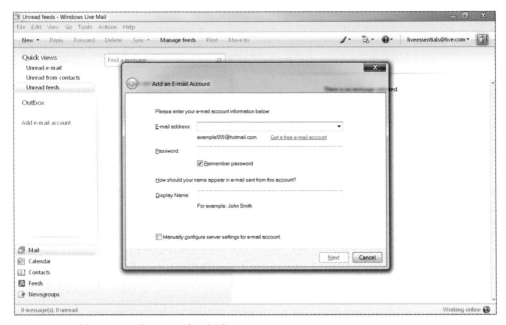

FIGURE 3.2 Adding an email account for the first time

If you don't already have an email account or service, then you can click the Get a free email account link to initiate both of these. When you do this, you will be prompted to log in with your Windows Live ID. If you don't already have a Windows Live ID, then you should return to Chapter 1 of this book to see how to create one. Your Windows Live ID will be used as your email address. You should go ahead and log in to Windows Live using your ID. Once you do, a Windows Live Hotmail account will be created, and Windows Live Hotmail will open, as shown in Figure 3.3.

Of course, if you already have a Windows Live ID, then you can simply enter it into the dialog box in Figure 3.2. Enter your Windows Live ID, your password, and the name you'd like to be displayed when sending emails. You can keep this formal, such as "Bradley Jones," or you can make it whimsical such as "Brad!" The thing to remember is that this will be on all of the emails you send. You can change the value later if you wish.

NOTE *If you have an email address from your Internet service provider (ISP), then you can set it up as well. This is covered later in the section, "Tapping into Existing Mail Accounts."*

Once you've entered the values, click the Next button to continue setting up your account with Windows Live Mail. If you entered a valid address and password, then you should see a confirmation message similar to the one shown in Figure 3.4.

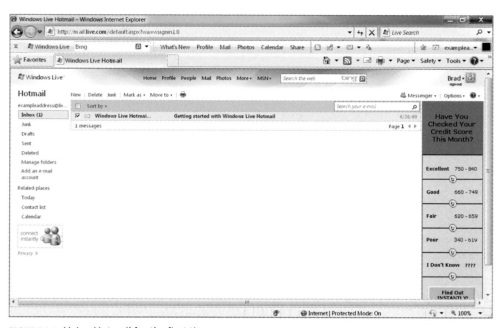

FIGURE 3.3 Using Hotmail for the first time

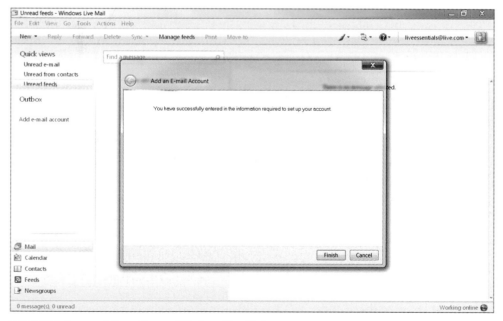

FIGURE 3.4 Successfully setting up Windows Live Mail

Clicking the Finish button will take you to Windows Live Mail. Of course, the first thing you need to do to get into Windows Live Mail is to sign in with your Windows Live ID. If you are not already signed into Windows Live, you will be prompted to sign in. Figure 3.5 shows one of the possible sign-in boxes you might receive. You'll need to enter your Windows Live ID and password if you want to send or receive email using the Windows Live Hotmail service.

FIGURE 3.5 Signing into Windows Live Mail

If you don't sign into Windows Live, you can still get into Windows Live Mail. You will simply get errors if you try to send or receive email unless you have a different email service provider set up.

TIP *Using your Windows Live ID with Windows Live Mail gives you a number of added benefits. In addition to also being able to access Windows Live Hotmail, you can also interact from Windows Live Mail with Windows Live Messenger, Windows Live Groups, Windows Live Calendar, and more. Additionally, you'll be able to pull your contacts from Windows Live Spaces and Windows Live Groups and use them when emailing.*

If this is the first time you are entering Windows Live Mail and if you are using your Windows Live ID, then you will be prompted to download folders, as shown in Figure 3.6. You should click the Download button to begin this process.

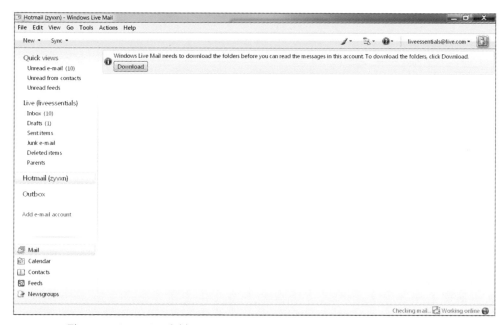

FIGURE 3.6 The prompt to set up folders

Folders are used for organizing email messages. The download process will check your Windows Live Hotmail account and synchronize any custom folders you might have there. If you've never used Windows Live Hotmail or don't have any custom folders, then this will simply finish the setup process.

The Windows Live Mail Layout

At this point, you have set up Windows Live Mail with your Windows Live ID. Figure 3.7 shows the layout that you should see if you are using a new account. In this case, the Windows Live ID that was used was ExampleAddress@Live.com.

There are a number of things to note in Figure 3.7. On the left, you can see the default folders. These are the default folders set up in the previous section. Table 3.1 gives a brief description of each of these. Later in this chapter, you'll learn how to set up additional folders. To see the emails in each folder, simply click on the folder's name. You can simply click on Inbox to go back to seeing your new email messages.

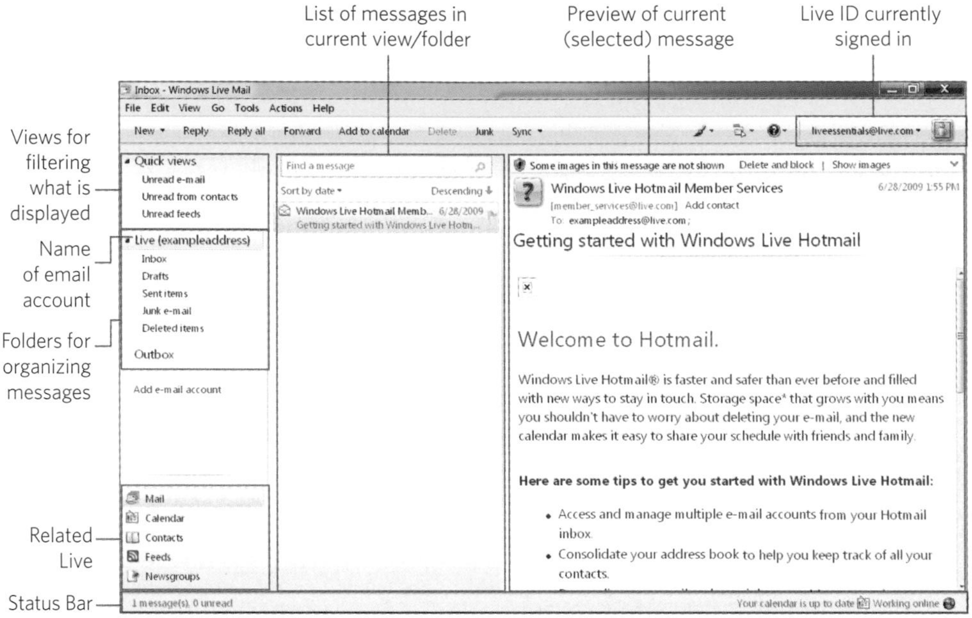

List of messages in
current view/folder

Preview of current
(selected) message

Live ID currently
signed in

Views for
filtering
what is
displayed

Name
of email
account

Folders for
organizing
messages

Related
Live

Status Bar

FIGURE 3.7 Windows Live Mail's layout

TABLE 3.1 The Standard Folders for Windows Live Mail

FOLDER	DESCRIPTION
Inbox	Every email message you receive will initially be placed in the Inbox folder.
Drafts	This folder contains written, saved emails that have not yet been sent.
Sent Items	This folder maintains a copy of all the emails you have sent.
Junk e-mail	Messages that are flagged as spam are placed in this folder.
Deleted Items	Messages you've deleted go into this folder. These messages are still accessible to you until they are removed from this folder.
Outbox	When you create a message and send it, the message will be placed in the Outbox and then sent. Frequently, the message goes into the Outbox and is immediately sent so quickly that you might not even notice it was there. If you are not connected to the Internet, then when you send a message, it will be placed in the Outbox until you are connected and it can be sent on its way.

Above the folders, you see Quick Views. These are additional options that you can click on to see different groupings of your emails. In Figure 3.7, there is only one email, so these groups are not critical. In Figure 3.1, however, you can see that there are a lot more emails that have been received. Therefore, being able to see the unread

emails or just the ones from your contacts becomes more helpful. If you click on these views, then the displayed list of emails will be filtered to show just those you indicated.

In addition to the Quick Views options, there are several other ways to sort your displayed email lists. You can see in Figure 3.7 that the default sort of your messages is by date. However, if you click on the Sort by option, you will see that you can change the order to one of a variety of options such as subject, size, priority, etc. (see Figure 3.8).

Most of the other features highlighted in Figure 3.7 should be straightforward. Several will be covered throughout the rest of this chapter.

FIGURE 3.8 Options for sorting messages

In addition to sorting by the various options, you can make the list ascending or descending. You do this by clicking on the Ascending or Descending option shown next to the sort option. This value will switch back and forth each time you click on it.

Tapping into Existing Mail Accounts

You can add additional email accounts to Windows Live Mail. This is great if you have more than one email address but don't want to have to log-in to separate accounts to read all of your email. The previous section showed you how to pull Windows Live Hotmail into Windows Live Mail. You can also pull in Gmail, email from your ISP, or email from a number of other places. Of course, to do this, you will need to know a few things, including:

▶ Your email address for that account

▶ Your email user name (usually the left half of your email address)

▶ Your email password

▶ Your email account type (usually POP3 or HTTP)

▶ Your outgoing (SMTP) mail server (usually something like smtp.*something*.com)

▶ Your incoming (POP3) mail server (usually something like mail.*something*.com or pop3.*something*.com)

If you want to associate another Windows Live Hotmail account with your Windows Live Mail, all you need is the Windows Live ID and the password. For other accounts, you'll need the preceding information. If you are unsure of something—such as the outgoing and incoming mail servers—then simply ask your ISP. They usually post this information on their support site or will provide it if you ask.

Once you have the preceding information in hand, you are ready to add a new account. Click on the Add e-mail account link on the left side of Windows Live Mail to begin the process. This will give you the exact same dialog you saw in Figure 3.2 at the beginning of this chapter. If you are setting up another Windows Live ID, then simply enter the information as you did before. If you want to use a different email account, then in addition to entering your email address, password, and display name, also check the Manually configure option at the bottom. This will allow you to enter the additional information needed to set up the email account, as shown in Figure 3.9.

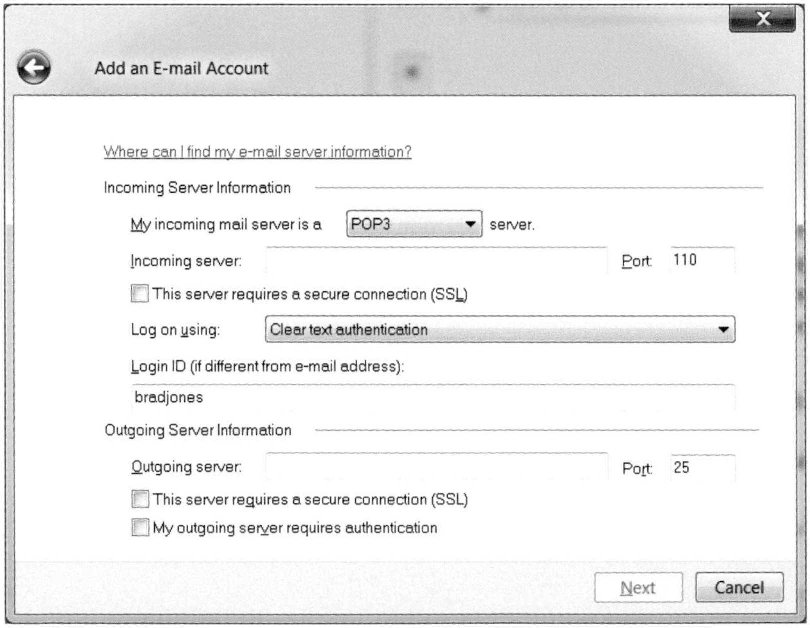

FIGURE 3.9 Setting up an external email account

There is a lot of information needed in Figure 3.9. If you are unsure of a value, the best thing to do is check the help information from your ISP or from the mail provider. Most ISPs can provide this information if you contact their technical support. Once you've entered the information and clicked Next, you should get a success message similar to the one in Figure 3.10. You'll also see the account added to the left side of Windows Live Mail.

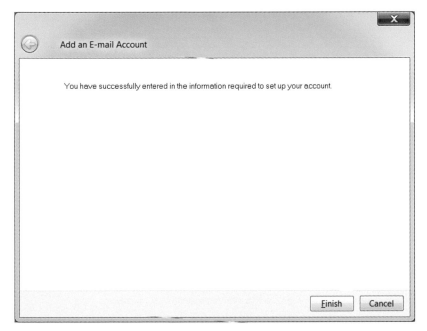

FIGURE 3.10 The success message after adding an account

In the success dialog, there is one additional check box. You can set the new account as the default mail account. The default account is the one used when you create an outgoing message. You can always change this later, but it's best to set the default account to the account you send the most messages from.

> **WARNING** *If more than one person uses your computer, then you should set up Windows Live Mail in each person's Windows account. This will keep the mail accounts separate*

USING WINDOWS LIVE MAIL WITH OTHER MAIL SERVICES: GOOGLE GMAIL

On some services, you need to enable the ability to use offline mail programs such as Windows Live Mail. For example, you can configure Google's Gmail to be read in Windows Live Mail, but you first must enable email forwarding on Google. To do this, sign into Gmail and click Settings at the top of the Gmail page. Once on the Settings screen, select the Forwarding and POP/IMAP tab.

On that tab, select the option to Enable IMAP for all mail. You can fill out other settings as well. You can then click Save Changes. Of course, if you are not sure of the Gmail settings to use in Windows Live Mail, click the Configuration Instructions on the Forwarding tab to get the values you need for the dialog that was shown in Figure 3.9. The values that you needed at the time this book was written were:

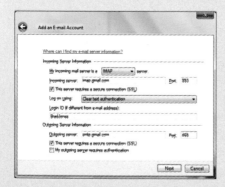

Reading a Message

When you first install Windows Live Mail, you should already have a message in your inbox welcoming you to Windows Live Hotmail. This will appear in the middle pane of Windows Live Mail. If you don't see this message, then make sure that the Inbox on the left side is selected.

You can read this message in the same way that you will read other messages you will receive. Click on the message to select it. By default, you should see the preview pane shown on the right, where you will see a preview of the message. In Figure 3.11, you can see that a message has been selected and is previewed in the area on the right.

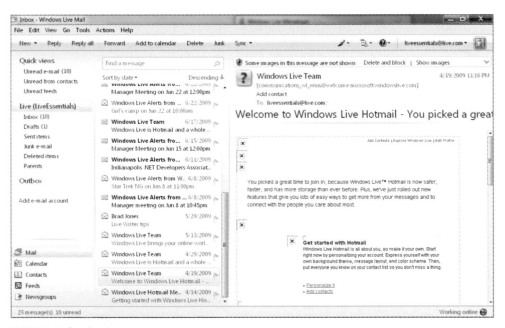

FIGURE 3.11 Previewing a message

Your first thought when looking at the preview might be that the message is really messed up. It seems to have broken images and the message isn't formatted well. It also has a big warning at the top stating that not everything has been shown. This is just a preview. If the message is from someone you don't know, then the message could contain harmful things such as images, documents, videos, and other downloadable items that may contain viruses or other bad things. As such, you don't want to open these on your computer unless you know they are safe. Because of this, Windows Live Mail lets you decide if you want to show the images in your received emails. If you know that the email is safe, you can click on the Show images link at the top of the preview pane, and the images will be added. This will often improve the layout of the message as well.

If you don't know who the message is from, you should avoid showing the images as well as avoid clicking the links, no matter how interesting they may sound. Clicking on a link in a message can also load a virus or malware on your computer.

If the message is junk mail, then you can click the Delete and block link. This will remove the message from your Inbox and future messages from that person or email address will automatically go into your junk folder instead of your Inbox.

WARNING If you don't know whom an email is from, don't click on its links and don't display its images. That can install bad things onto your computer. Additionally, if you get an email from someone you know and it seems to be something very odd, like a simple message saying "Look at this" with a link, then you should also use caution. Many virus programs can mimic the name and address of other people so that the email seems real to trick you into clicking a bad link. Of course, antivirus software can help prevent problems.

WARNING If you get an email saying that you just won the lottery, that a person needs help transferring money, or anything else that seems too good to be true, then it probably isn't true. These types of scams are very common. Also, if you get emails saying you need to change your password due to a security breach, there is a good chance that this too is a scam to get you to enter your ID and password on a fake site.

TIP If a message looks like it is junk, then click the Junk button on the toolbar to move it to your junk folder.

If a preview looks good and you want to look closer at the message, then you can open it. To open an email message you double-click on it within the center column shown in Figure 3.11. Alternatively, you can right-click on the message to display a pop-up menu. From that menu, select Open. This will then display the message in a new window.

After you open a message, it will be marked as read. In fact, if you preview a message, it will also be marked as read. In the list of messages, unread messages are in bold.

A read message will be unbolded. If you decide you want to indicate that a message hasn't been read, you can right-click on it and select Mark as unread.

Creating a New Mail Message

Once you have an email account set up on Windows Live Mail, you are ready to start composing and sending messages. Windows Live Mail provides you with the ability to easily create messages.

USING THE EMAIL EDITOR

To create a new message in Windows Live Mail, select New → E-mail message from the toolbar. Alternatively, you can press Ctrl+N or File → New → E-mail message from the menu. Regardless of how you begin, you will be greeted with the New Message dialog, as shown in Figure 3.12.

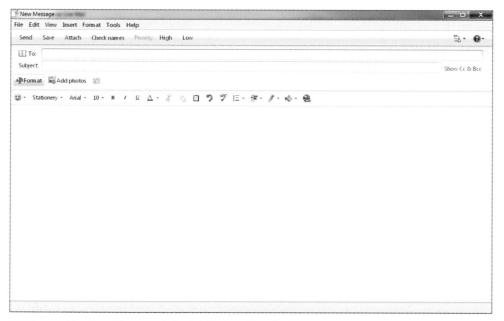

FIGURE 3.12 The New Message dialog in Windows Live Mail

In the New Message dialog, you will need to enter the email address of the person you are sending a message to. You will also want to enter a subject and a message.

You can send an email message to one or more people. You enter the recipients' email addresses into the To field in the New Message editor. If you are sending the message to more than one person, you can enter each of their email addresses into the To field, separated by a semicolon.

SELECTING AN EXISTING CONTACT

If you have set up contacts for Instant Messageing (IM), groups, or from previous email messages, then you can select from your contacts by clicking on the icon next to the To field. This will display your list of contacts. In Figure 3.13, you can see my list of contacts (slightly edited to hide email addresses).

NOTE *If you have not set up any contacts in any of your Windows Live Essentials Applications or Services, then this dialog will initially be empty.*

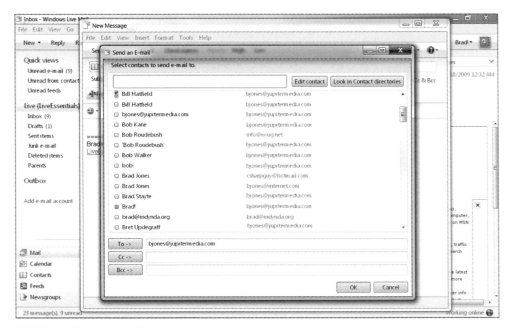

FIGURE 3.13 The contacts list

As you can see in this dialog, you can search your contacts or simply enter their addresses into the To field. To add a contact from the list, you can either double-click on their name or you can select their name and then click the To button near the bottom. You can also simply type email addresses into the To box at the bottom of this dialog.

In addition to having a To box, you also can see in Figure 3.13 that there are Cc and Bcc boxes. Just as with regular mail, Cc allows you to copy someone on the email message.

Any email addresses entered into the To and Cc boxes will be seen by everyone receiving your email message. If you want to send the message to someone else, but don't want everyone to see their name or email address, then you can use the Bcc field, which is for a blind carbon copy. The people who are listed in the To and Cc boxes will not see any of the names or email addresses of the people listed in the Bcc box.

Once you've entered the addresses from your contacts list, you can click OK. This will return you to the New Message dialog. Once there, you will notice that the Cc and Bcc boxes have been added to the message box.

FORMATTING YOUR MESSAGE

Once the email address is entered, you are ready to create the message. You can enter a Subject line to describe your message and then enter the text you want to send in the main area of the New Message window. When you enter text, you have the ability to add formatting, highlighting, and more. In Figure 3.12, you can see a toolbar with a number of defaulted controls. Table 3.2 briefly states what each formatting item does.

TABLE 3.2 Formatting a Message

TOOLBAR ITEM	PURPOSE	DESCRIPTION
☺ ▾	Emoticons	Insert an emoticon (small picture) into the message.
Stationery ▾	Stationery	Insert stationery into the message. Stationery is a background picture on the message.
Arial ▾	Font	Pick a font to use in the message. This will change any text highlighted in the message to the selected font, or it will use the selected font when typing at the current location in the message.
10 ▾	Font size	This sets the font size.
B	Bold	This bolds the text.
I	Italic	This italicizes the text.
U	Underline	This underlines the text.

continues

TABLE 3.2 Formatting a Message *(continued)*

TOOLBAR ITEM	PURPOSE	DESCRIPTION
	Font Color	This sets the color of the text.
	Cut	This cuts the currently highlighted text.
	Copy	This copies the currently highlighted text.
	Paste	This pastes the information that was previously cut or copied.
	Undo	This undoes your last action.
	Spell Check	This checks the spelling in your message.
	Format as List	This changes the currently selected text to a numbered list, or it starts a numbered list. ⦙☰ inserts a numbered list. ▮☰ inserts a bulleted list.
	Format Paragraph	This formats the current paragraph. This includes right, left, or center justifying the paragraph as well as indenting. You can also insert a line from this option.
	Highlight	This option allows you to highlight part of the message in a selected color.
	Background Color	This option sets the background of your message to a selected color.
	Insert a Link	Insert a link to another web location.

As you can see by the table, you have a great number of options for formatting a message. How you use these options is up to you. You can get pretty complex pretty fast.

WARNING *If you send a message to a person that uses an email reader that supports just text, then your fancy formatting will be stripped away. In general, you should avoid using too much formatting in a message.*

TIP *You should always spell-check your messages before sending them! Spell-checking is covered next.*

SPELL-CHECKING WITH THE SPELL CHECKER

There are a lot of formatting options and other options that you can use when creating an email message to send. There is one feature shown in Table 3.2 that you should almost always use. That is the spell checker. Using spell checker will help you look better as you'll be able to avoid spelling mistakes.

You can run the spell checker by clicking the icon shown in Table 3.2 or by selecting Spelling from the Tools menu. You can also press F7 to run the spell checker at any time. Once started, the spell checker will go through your message and verify the spelling of each word. If a misspelled word is found, you will be prompted, as shown in Figure 3.14. You can choose to ignore the misspelled word, change it, or if it is spelled correctly, you can choose to Add it to the dictionary.

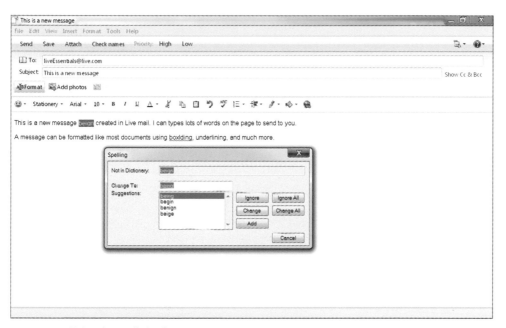

FIGURE 3.14 Using the spell checker

WARNING *While the spell checker will find words that are spelled wrong, it won't correct wrong words that are spelled correctly. For example, if you mean to say bear instead of bare, the spell checker won't help you because both spellings are correct!*

SAVING A DRAFT MESSAGE

After creating a message, you can either send it right away or you can choose to save it to send later. You save the message by clicking on Save in the menu of the email editor. When you do this, you'll be shown the message in Figure 3.15, and the email will be saved in your Drafts folder.

FIGURE 3.15 Saving an email

 After saving the message, you will remain in the message editor. You can choose to close the message by selecting File → Close from the menu or by clicking the Windows X button.

In the Windows Live Mail program, you'll now have the message stored in the draft folder on the left. You can click on the Drafts folder name to list all of your saved messages. To further edit or send the message, you can double-click on it to return to the message editor.

SENDING A MESSAGE

You can send a message from the new message editor. After creating your message, you can simply click the Send button to send it on its way. Once the message is sent, the message editor will be closed, and you'll be returned to the main Windows Live Mail program. Additionally, a copy of the message will be placed in the Sent items folder.

You can see a list of all your sent messages by clicking on the Sent items folder on the left side of the Windows Live Mail window. This will list all of the messages you've sent. You can actually double-click on a message to open it. Once it is open, you have the option to forward it or reply to those that were listed on the message.

Personalizing Your Email Messages

You've seen how to create and send a message. You've also been introduced to some standard formatting. There are a few features within Windows Live Mail that let you personalize your email messages. This includes adding stationery and using a signature.

Adding Stationery

Stationery in email is similar to stationery used for regular letters. While you can use formatting to add images, background colors, and other elements to an email message, by applying stationery, you can get a nice background on your email messages quickly and easily.

To apply stationery to an email message, you first need to create a new message. Once in the message editor, you can select Stationery from the toolbar or you can select Format → Apply stationery from the menu. Either way, you will be given the option to select either No stationery, which will remove the current stationery from the message, or More stationery, which will present you with a dialog similar to Figure 3.16.

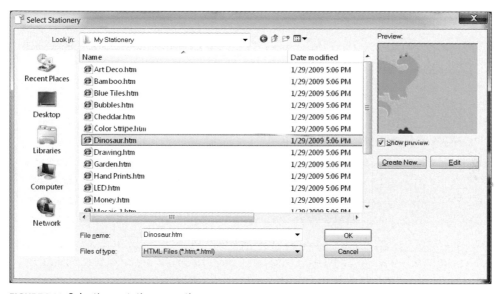

FIGURE 3.16 Selecting a stationery option

In Figure 3.16, you can see a number of different stationery files presented. These are simple HTML files that have formatting that can be applied behind your message. As you click on each of the items in the dialog, a preview will be shown on the right. In Figure 3.16, you can see that the Dinosaur stationery is currently highlighted.

Once you've found the stationery you'd like to use, you can click the OK button to apply it to your email message. In Figure 3.19 later in this chapter, you will see that the Money stationery was applied.

> **NOTE** *Once you've used a stationery type once, it will then be listed in the Stationery menu on the toolbar and on the Apply stationery menu. The assumption is that if you used it once, you'll likely use it again, so this saves you a step the next time you want to use it!*

Creating a Signature

Another way to customize your email messages is to create a signature. A signature is information that can automatically be added at the end of all your email messages. This can be as simple as your name or it can be as elaborate as pictures, formatted text, and more. In general, it is information you want to include on many of your messages.

You can actually create multiple signatures to use at different times. For example, you might want to create a personal signature to share with friends and family that includes your phone number and a nice quote. You could have a different signature for business associates that has a more formal name and your full address on it. Of course, what is actually in your signatures is totally up to you.

You create signatures from the main Windows Live Mail window. Select Tools → Options from the menu bar. This will display the Windows Live Mail options dialog. This dialog has a number of tabs on it and lots of settings. You should select the Signatures setting. The result should look like Figure 3.17.

You can see all of the signature settings in this dialog. You can set whether your signature is applied to all of your outgoing messages as well as determine if it should be applied to responses and forwarded messages.

In addition to determining when to use signatures, you can also create signatures on this dialog. The various signatures you have created will be listed in the middle box. In Figure 3.17 there were no signatures created. If there had been signatures, you could have selected them and used the Remove or Rename button to delete or rename them accordingly. You could also have chosen to edit an existing signature by double-clicking on its name.

To create a new signature, click the New button. This will activate the Edit Signature area. It will also list a default name for the signature in the signatures box. To create your signature, you can simply enter the text into the Text box as shown in Figure 3.18.

FIGURE 3.17 The Signature tab in the Options dialog

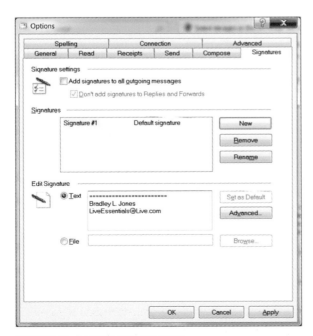

FIGURE 3.18 A simple text signature

Once you are happy with the text you've entered, you can click Apply to save the changes or to add the signature. Clicking OK will finish the editing and close the Options box, so if you want to add another signature or give your first one a better name, then use the Apply button and continue to make additional changes.

If you want to use more than simple text in your signature, then you will need to make the changes in a separate file and attach it using the File option. The file you attach can be a basic text file, or it can be a file containing HTML with fancy formatting and the like.

> **NOTE** *It is beyond the scope of this book to talk about HTML. HTML is a special way of marking up text with colors, fonts, and more. In fact, the messages and formatting you create in Windows Live Mail use HTML behind the scenes!*

Once you have more than one signature, you can choose which one is used by default. You can do this by selecting the signature in the Signature box and then clicking the Set as Default box.

Applying a Signature

Once you've created your signatures, you can use them in your email messages. If you choose to apply your signature to all outgoing messages, then when you create a new message, your default signature will automatically be added. If you don't have signatures applied automatically, you can still add a signature to your message by selecting one of your signatures from the Insert → Signatures menu. The names of your signatures will be listed on the menu for you to select.

In Figure 3.19, you can see the default signature that was entered in Figure 3.18 is being used. You should note that Windows Live Mail is smart enough to know that an email address was used. Thus, it converted the email address into a link. Figure 3.19 also uses stationery that was set earlier. One thing you should note about stationery and fancy formatting is that if you are not careful, it can get in the way of your message!

> **TIP** *In truth, a signature is simply text or a file that is stuck in your email messages. If there are quotes and other bits of text you use a lot and want to be able to stick into your emails, then you can create them as signatures and use the Insert → Signature menu option to add them into your messages. The "signature" will be inserted wherever the cursor is within the message.*

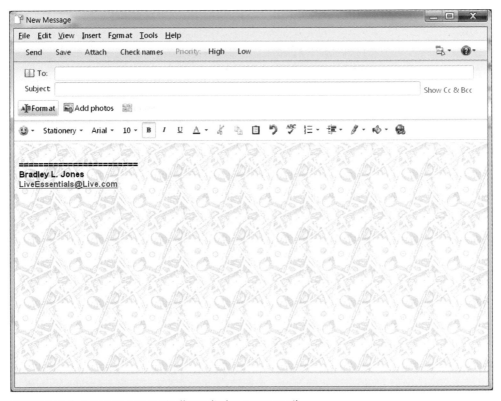

FIGURE 3.19 A signature automatically applied to a new email

TIP *If you want to remove a signature from an email message, simply select its text with the cursor and delete it from your message.*

Replying to and Forwarding Messages

Whether you read a message in the preview panel or the full message window, you will be able to reply to the sender or forward the message to other people. If you are in full message view, you will have options at the top to Reply, Reply all, and Forward.

If you choose to reply, you will be put into the email editor, where you'll be able to add to or change the existing message. This process will then operate just like creating a new message except that the subject line and To items will be filled in for you. The email will be addressed to the person that sent the original message.

Reply All is just like Reply, except that all the addresses that were in the To and the Cc lines will be included in the updated message you create. Anyone that might have been in the Bcc line will not be included, but then you won't know who those people were if they were included!

Whether replying or forwarding, you have the ability to modify the existing message or add to it. You also have the ability to change who you are sending the message to as well as add new people. In essence, once you've clicked on the option to reply or forward, you are then working with the message just as if you had created a new message. You have the ability to save a draft, send it, or simply throw away the changes you've made.

Working with Attachments

There are two features of email messages that were skipped over earlier. These are the ability to send files and the ability to send pictures. Doing either is relatively simple. In general, pictures are files; however, Windows Live Mail gives you added features when sending pictures, so they are covered separately.

SENDING FILES

To send a file, you simply need to attach it to your email message. This file can be a document, a video you create with Movie Maker, a picture, or anything else. There are two standard ways to attach a file.

 The first way to attach a file is to click on the Attach option when in the Message editor. This will present you with a Windows dialog box that you can use to search for and find a file. Figure 3.20 shows the File dialog box in Windows 7. Of course, the files you see will be those you have on your computer. You can use this dialog to navigate to and select the file you want to attach and send.

Once you've attached the file, its filename will be listed under the Subject box in your message. You can simply select it and press the Delete key on your keyboard to then remove it from the message.

The second way to attach a file is to use the Windows Explorer to find the file you want. Once you have found it, you can drag the filename from Windows Explorer and then drop it into the main part of the Message window. This will attach the file to the message.

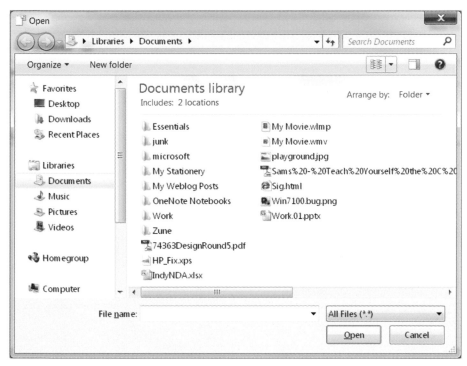

FIGURE 3.20 The Windows 7 Open dialog for selecting a file

NOTE *You should be aware that when you send a file to someone, you are sending them a copy of the file on your machine. Sending an attached file should not remove the file from your computer.*

SENDING PHOTOS/PICTURES

You can attach and send picture files exactly the same way that you attach and send regular files. You don't have to do anything extra or special. However, the file will be sent as a copy of what is on your computer and listed under the subject line as if it were any other type of file.

With pictures (including photos), you have additional options in Windows Live Mail. You can actually stick the pictures into your mail message. Not only that, but you can also adjust the layout, add borders, make some basic corrections, and more. To take advantage of these extra photo features, instead of attaching the photos in the manners discussed in the previous section, use the Add Photos button in the message editor. When you click this button, you will again be given an a Windows dialog for adding files, but this time it will be customized to adding photos and pictures, as shown in Figure 3.21.

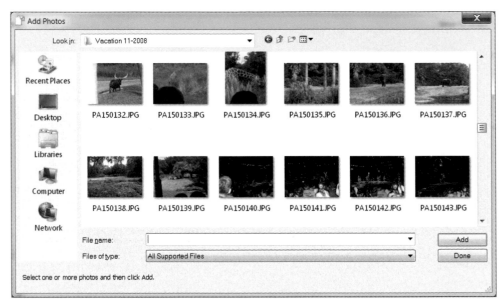

FIGURE 3.21 Adding photos

Once you find a photo you want to add, select it and click the Add button. This will add it to your message at the location where your cursor is. You can continue to add additional images. Once you are done, you can click the Done button to return to your message. As you can see in Figure 3.22, several photos were added to an email message.

 With photos added to the message, you can see in Figure 3.22 that you now have a new toolbar. You can see that there are a number of options on how the photos are displayed (such as with matting, a wood frame, as an instant photo, with metal corners, with a push pin look, as a spotlight, or with brushed edges). You also have other options for working with photos. To use the options, such as Autocorrect, Black & White, or Rotate, simply select an image then select the option. The selected photo will then be adjusted accordingly. As you'll see in Figure 3.23, the options you select are applied to the photos in the email.

 In addition to adjusting the photos, you can also adjust how they are laid out. You do this by clicking on the Layout button. This will give you options for how your photos are presented, as shown in Figure 3.23. The layout options include options for adjusting the size of the photos in the message.

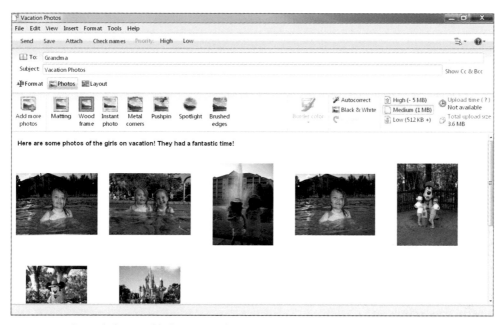

FIGURE 3.22 Several photos added to an email message

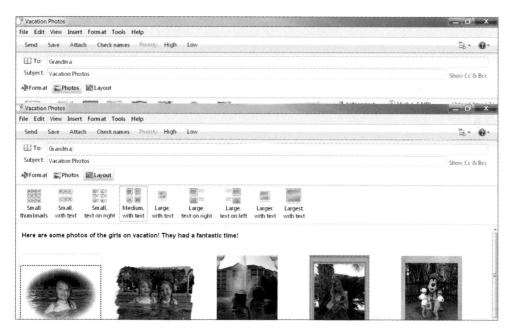

FIGURE 3.23 The photo layout options

TIP *If you want to replace a photo, simply double-click on it to open the Add Photo dialog again. If you want to remove one, select it and press the Delete key. The email message uses a copy of the photos, as opposed to the actual photos stored on your computer, so deleting one from your message won't remove the photo from your computer!*

NOTE *For more on working with Photos see Chapter 5 on the Windows Live Photo Gallery.*

Working with Folders

In Windows Live Mail's main window, you saw that there were a number of standard folders that are used. This includes the Inbox where your messages are delivered, the Drafts folder where your saved messages are placed, the Sent items folder where a copy of the messages you sent are located, the Junk e-mail folder where emails that are believed to be spam or junk are placed, and the Deleted items folder where things you delete are placed before being completely removed from the computer. There is also the Outbox that is used to put messages you are sending but have not yet been sent.

In addition to all of these folders, you can create your own folders to use. To create a new folder, select New → Folder from the toolbar. Alternatively, you can press Ctrl+Shift+D or right-click on an existing folder and select New Folder from the pop-up menu. Whichever way, you will be presented with the Create folder dialog, as shown in Figure 3.24.

To create the new folder, enter its name into the Folder name box. You can then determine where to place the folder by selecting an item in the lower box shown in Figure 3.24. If the location you selected is valid for creating a new folder, then the New button will be activated. Click OK to create the folder.

Once you've created a folder, you can start using it to place mail messages. From the main Windows Live Mail window, you can move listed emails from the middle section to a folder by dragging them to the left and dropping them into the folder. If you want to copy the email message instead of moving it, you can right-click on the message and select Copy to folder. This will display the list of folders for you to select from. The message will then be moved. Note that you can also right-click and choose Move to folder.

FIGURE 3.24 Creating a new folder

Using Contacts

When you mail letters, you likely open up an address book to find the address of the person you are going to send the letter. Rarely does a person memorize everyone's addresses. With Windows Live Mail, like having an address book with people's street addresses, you have an address book so that you don't have to remember everyone's email addresses. In this case, the address book is referred to as your contacts.

You'll be able to access your contacts by clicking on the Contacts option in the lower-right corner of the Windows Live Mail window. You can also press Ctrl+Shift+C or select Go → Contacts from the menu. Regardless of how you get there, you will be presented with your list of contacts. My contacts are shown in Figure 3.25, although I did modify their email addresses.

As you can see by the right side of Figure 3.25, there is a lot of information that can be kept on contacts. If you have already used Windows Live Messenger, Windows Live Groups, Windows Live Spaces, or one of the other Windows Live Services that uses contacts and people, then you will find that their information is also available here in Windows Live Mail for you to use.

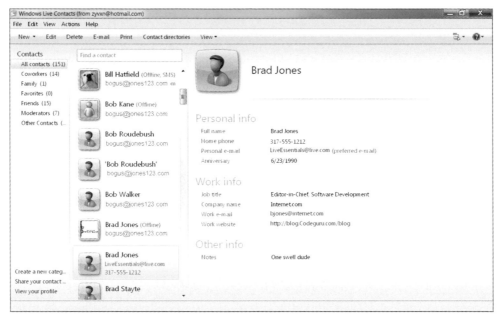

FIGURE 3.25 My contacts

 NOTE *If you have contacts that use one of the other Windows Live Services, then you will have information such as their avatar and their online status in your contacts list. For example, you can see that Bill has an avatar of a dog and that he is currently Offline.*

Creating New Contacts

 If a contact is not listed, then you might want to add them. You can add a new contact by clicking the New toolbar option on the Windows Live Contacts window. This will present you with the dialogs to enter information for the person. Figure 3.26 shows the initial window.

You can fill out the information in the dialog and click the Add contact button to add them. You should enter their name and Personal e-mail address at a minimum so as to be able to use them to send email to. Of course, you can also choose to add a lot of other information as well.

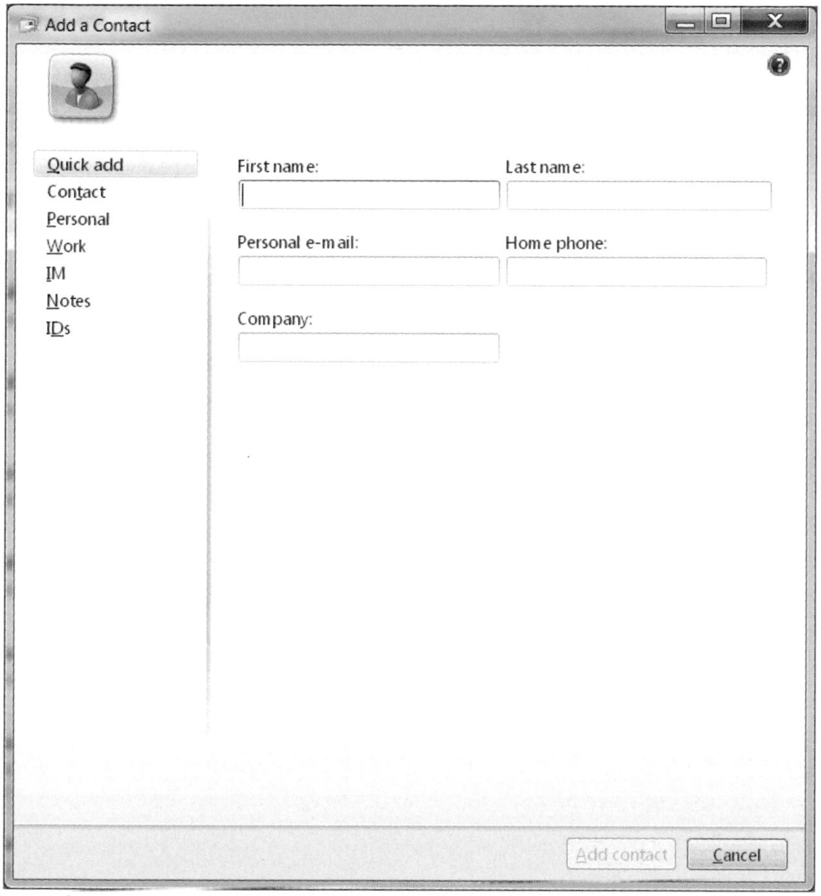

FIGURE 3.26 Adding a Contact

On the left side of the Add a Contact window are various categories of information you can choose to add for a person. This includes Contact, Personal, Work, IM, Notes, and IDs. All of this information is optional; however, once you enter it, you will be able to access it from your Windows Live account. You'll also find that some of the information carries over from one section to another. For example, Figure 3.27 shows the Personal options. The email address added in the Quick add section is carried into this section. If you change the email address in either place, it is updated in both places.

FIGURE 3.27 The personal information for a contact

TIP *You can also add a new contact directly from an email message. If you receive an email message from a person who is not a contact, there will be an Add Contact link next to their name when you are viewing the message in the Message editor. You can click on that link to open the Add contact window. The email address and name (if included) will be already added to the form.*

Organizing Contacts

On the main contact window (refer to Figure 3.25), notice that there are Contact groupings on the left side. These groupings work similarly to folders for emails. They allow you to organize your contacts. To categorize a contact, simply drag their name and avatar from the middle folder to the category you want to associate them to. For example, I can drag Angela Brown from the middle category to the Family folder on the left.

> **TIP** *You can add a contact to more than one contact folder. They will only show up in the All contacts category once though.*

The benefit of using the categories on the left is that I can click on them to filter the list of contacts. If I click on the Friends folder, I'll only see the people listed within it. If I want to see everyone, I click on the All contacts option.

Creating New Contacts Categories

In addition to adding contacts to the folders that are listed, I can create new folders as well. To create a new contacts folder, you can either click New → Category from the Contacts window menu, or you can right-click on an existing category and select Create a New Category from the menu that pops up. Once you've created a new category, you can add contacts by dragging and dropping them.

ADDING AND REMOVING CONTACTS IN A CATEGORY

You can drag and drop contacts to a category. There is a second way you can add contacts as well. This is by right-clicking on the category and selecting Edit category from the pop-up menu. This will display the Edit Category dialog similar to what is in Figure 3.28 where the Family category is being edited.

In this dialog you can change the name of the category in the top box. Additionally, by clicking on contacts in the list, you add them. You'll see their name added to the box on the bottom. In the figure, you can see that Angela Brown is the only member. As you click on names, those names will also be added.

If you have a name you want to remove from a category, then you can click on it again, and it will be removed from the box on the bottom. Alternatively, you can click on the name in the lower box and delete it from there.

Once you've made your changes and edits, you can click Save to save the changes you've made to the category.

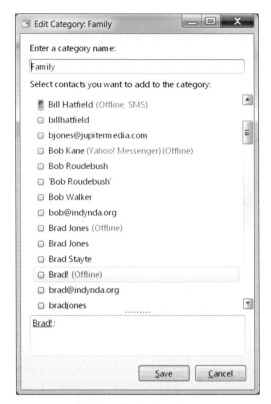

FIGURE 3.28 Editing a Contacts category

Blocking Spam and Unwanted Messages

It is unfortunate that when you start using email, you will start getting spam. Spam is unwanted messages that try to do things such as sell you unwanted stuff, get you to give away personal information, or steal from or trick you. Spam often includes inappropriate materials you might not want to see or have people using your computer see.

Windows Live Mail gives you the ability to mark an email message as junk. It also gives you the ability to mark all future mail from a person as junk. Junk email messages can be automatically moved to your Junk e-mail folder. If you get a message in your Inbox that you believe is junk, you can right-click on it to display a menu of options. One of the options will be Junk e-mail. Selecting it will give you a number of different options related to junk mail.

Selecting Mark as junk (or pressing Ctrl+Alt+J) will move the message to the Junk e-mail folder. This only impacts the current message. If you want to prevent the receipt of any future messages from the same person, which are likely to also be spam, then you can select the option to Add sender to blocked sender list. This will move any future email messages from that person to your Junk email folder. You can also choose to block all future email messages from anyone at the same domain.

Once you block a person or a domain, then all messages from them will be filtered. To change that, you need to remove them from the filtered list by marking them as safe again. You can do this from the same menu. You might, however, need to find the email in the Junk email folder.

Rather than dealing with junk messages one at a time as they come into your system, you can also set up a global junk email filter. You can set this filtering to a level where only those people or domains you specifically block are filtered out or all the way to the level where only those people or domains you say are safe will be allowed to reach your Inbox. To set up this global filtering, select Tools → Safety options from the Windows Live Mail menu. This will display the Safety Options dialog shown in Figure 3.29.

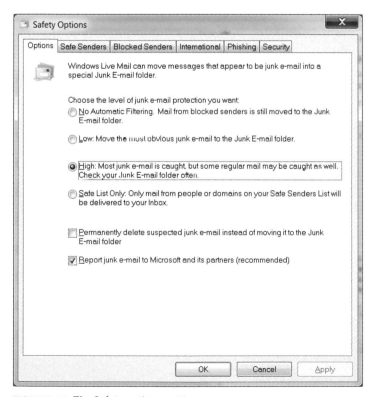

FIGURE 3.29 The Safety options settings

In the Safety Options dialog, you can choose the level you want. Your options are No Automatic Filtering, Low, High, or Safe List Only. Each of these options is defined in the figure. For most people, the default setting of High is appropriate. If you have children, you might want to set their email to Safe List Only and then approve the people they can receive messages from.

The options also include the ability to permanently delete suspected junk email instead of just having it moved to the Junk email folder. You set this option by checking the box. If you are using email filtering, then you can expect that at some point a valid email will be marked as junk; if you have the option selected to delete junk, you will never see such messages. It is, however, your choice to delete junk mail immediately or to have it moved.

Working with Senders

In the Safety Options dialog, there are several other tabs that you can use to help in making your email a bit safer. In the previous section, you saw that you could add people and domains to a blocked list. You can also add people to a safe list. These lists are also tabs in the Safety Options dialog. In Figure 3.30, you can see the Safe Senders option on the left and the Block Senders options on the right. The values that might be listed on your system will be different than those listed in the figure. If you have not blocked or approved any senders or domains, then your lists might be empty.

From these lists, you can click on names and choose to remove them or you can click the Add buttons to add new names or domains to the list.

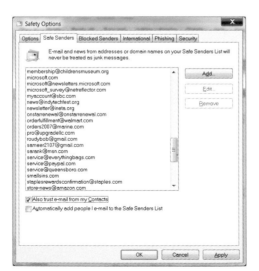
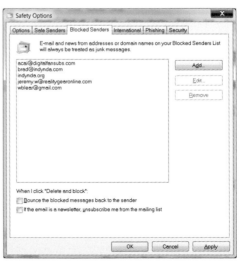

FIGURE 3.30 On the left is the Safe Senders Safety Options. On the right is the Blocked Senders.

Using RSS Feeds

There are a number of other features available in Windows Live Mail. In fact, Windows Live Mail is a large program that could be covered in a book of its own. There is one other feature that is valuable to know about. That is the ability to access RSS feeds.

RSS feeds are feeds that are available from sites that list the newest items to their site. For example, Microsoft's MSN site has a number of RSS feeds listed for its entertainment information. You can find the list of RSS feeds at entertainment.msn.com/rss/. Using Windows Live Mail, you could subscribe to any of the feeds on this page, or on any other page, by adding the addresses of the links to Windows Live Mail.

Adding a Feed

To add a feed, first select the Feeds page. You can do this by clicking on the Feeds link in the bottom-left corner of the Windows Live Mail window. Alternatively, you can select Go → Feeds or press Ctrl+Shift+K. Regardless of which method you select, you'll be taken to the Your feeds page within Windows Live Mail, as shown in Figure 3.31. Initially, you are not likely to have many, if any, feeds displayed.

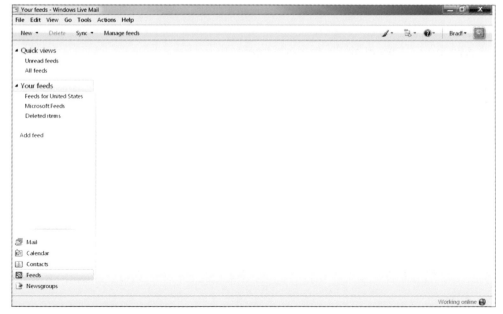

FIGURE 3.31 Your feeds within Windows Live Mail

As you can see, the overall layout is similar to the main Windows Live Mail page. You have categories on the left and a big open area to the right. When you select a feed, you will find that it is much more similar to mail.

To add a feed, click the Add feed link on the left side. This will present you with a prompt to enter a feed address as shown in Figure 3.32. You can enter the web address of a feed into this dialog.

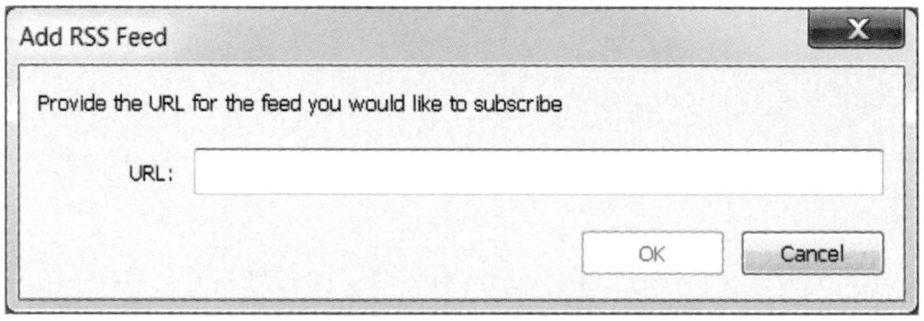

FIGURE 3.32 Adding an RSS feed

Once you enter a feed and select to add it, then the feed will be listed in Windows Live Mail. In Figure 3.33, you can see that several of the MSN feeds have been added. When you click on one of the feeds, you will see the list of feed items in the middle of the page, and a preview of the currently selected item will be presented on the right.

FIGURE 3.33 Several RSS feeds

NOTE *Managing and working with feeds and feed categories works in the same way as working with email folders and categories.*

TIP *You can use feeds to keep track of news and information. Instead of going to a bunch of sites to see the current news and articles, you can subscribe to the feeds in Windows Live Mail and see what is important from there.*

Using RSS Feeds

Of course, reviewing and reading your feeds can save you time; however, an RSS feed will generally only give you headlines and a brief description. If you find that you have an article or story you want to read, then you will still need to go to the site where the feed is from to read the story. Don't fret; each feed item will include a link to the original story. This is generally going to be in the preview window as a "more" link. Clicking on more should take you to the site and article.

In Conclusion

Windows Live Mail is a very robust mail program that provides access to RSS feeds, a calendar, contacts, newsgroups, and much more. While you might expect a free program to limit you to one account, with Windows Live Mail you can actually integrate a number of email accounts into the one program. If you don't have an email address or a mail account, you can tap into the Windows Live Hotmail email service for free. Additionally, the program includes security features as well as the ability to manage who can or cannot send you emails.

A lot of information was covered in this very long chapter. A book could be written just on Windows Live Mail. You should, however, be able to get the most out of Windows Live Mail from what was covered here. Feel free to poke around the menus and look at the other options. Many of the things that were not covered are pretty straightforward. For example, if you click on the Unread email view under Quick Views on the left, you will see all of the emails that are marked as unread.

Blogging and Writing with Windows Live Writer

IN THIS CHAPTER, YOU WILL:

▶ Learn about Windows Live Writer

▶ Set up a new blog on Windows Live

▶ Access Windows Live Spaces or other blog services from Windows Live Writer

▶ Write new blog entries

▶ Format blog entries using Windows Live Writer

▶ Add pictures and videos to your blog posts

▶ Publish your blog entries on the Internet

EVERYONE TENDS to have something to say. The way many people express their thoughts and opinions with others is to write them down and share them. The way to do this on the Internet is with a blog.

A blog is a web site where commentary or opinions are stated. A blog can also be a personal diary that you share with others. Regardless of what you write in your blog, you can use Windows Live Writer to create entries for your blog.

Of course, a lot of blogs already exist on the Internet. You can find blogs on virtually any topic. There is even a blog by the Microsoft Live Writer team at `windowslivewriter.spaces.live.com`.

What Is Windows Live Writer?

Windows Live Writer is a tool for creating blog entries. It is designed with many of the features of a basic word processor (such as Microsoft Word). The features included, however, are focused on allowing you to create blog entries. This includes the ability to add links to web pages, to embed images, to embed videos, and to format text.

More importantly, Windows Live Writer makes it easy for you to post what you write for your blog. If you are using one of the more popular blog services (a site that allows you to post your blog entries), Windows Live Writer can even upload your entries to that other site. Windows Live Writer supports blog services such as Windows Live, Wordpress, Blogger, LiveJournal, and TypePad. Of course, if you don't have a blog already, then Windows Live Writer can be used to set one up! Figure 4.1 shows the basic interface provided by Windows Live Writer.

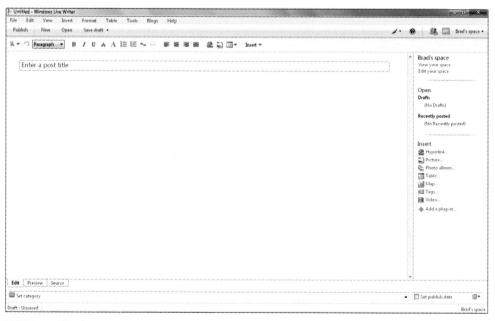

FIGURE 4.1 Windows Live Writer

Starting Windows Live Writer the First Time

In Chapter 1, you learned how to install the Windows Live Essentials Applications. If you installed Windows Live Writer, then it will be listed as one of the Windows Live Applications. When you start Windows Live Writer for the first time, you will be prompted to configure a few settings to set up your blog, as shown in Figure 4.2. After all, if you are going to write a blog entry, you'll need an area to post it.

FIGURE 4.2 Starting Windows Live Writer

NOTE *If Windows Live Writer has already been used on your system, then it might already be configured. If so, you might be taken directly into the Windows Live Writer screen shown earlier in Figure 4.1.*

The first screen you get, as shown in Figure 4.2, simply lets you know you need to configure Windows Live Writer. You can click Next to continue configuring Windows Live Writer. This will present you with Figure 4.3.

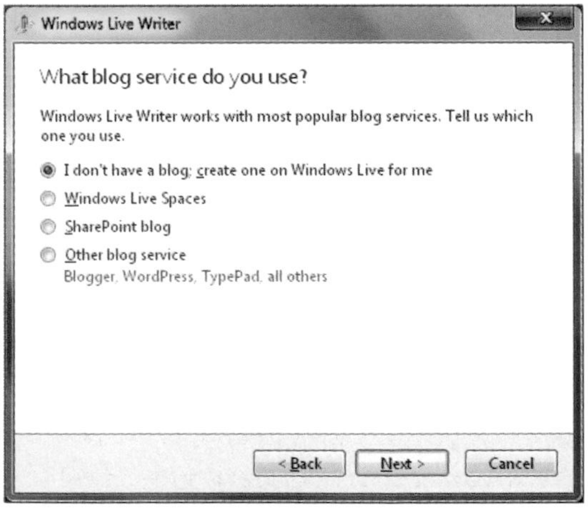

FIGURE 4.3 Selecting your blog service

If you don't have a blog service already, you'll be able to indicate that in this dialog. If you are already using Windows Live Spaces (covered in Chapter 8), you can select it. If you use a different blogging service, then you can select Other blog service. For the rest of this section, it is assumed that you will set up a new blog and that you'll let Windows Live do it for you. The following sections cover setting one up on Windows Live Spaces and posting to an alternative blogging service.

TIP *Note that if you decide you later want to associate or add a different blog to Windows Live Writer, you'll be able to do this. You'll be able to access these same dialogs from Windows Live Writer by selecting Add blog account from the Blog menu item in Windows Live Writer.*

Setting Up Your Own Blog Area

To create a new blog using Windows Live Writer, select the "I don't have a blog" option from the previous dialog and then click Next. This will present you with the dialog in Figure 4.4.

FIGURE 4.4 Signing In to Windows Live

Because your blog is online, you will need to be online. The dialog you are prompted with is requesting that you log in to your Windows Live account. Enter your Windows Live ID and password and click next. At this point, Windows Live Writer will begin setting up your blog account on Windows Live Spaces. You'll see the status of this, as shown in Figure 4.5.

NOTE *Chapter 1 covered setting up a Windows Live ID.*

FIGURE 4.5 Creating the blog account on Windows Live

Once your blog area is created, you'll be prompted, as shown in Figure 4.6, to give your blog a nickname. This nickname will help you identify your blog, plus it will provide an overall title. You'll also use the nickname to tell different blogs apart if you have more than one.

FIGURE 4.6 Adding a blog nickname

At this point, you've set up your blog. You are now ready to start using Windows Live Writer. You should now see a screen very similar to Figure 4.1 shown earlier, except that instead of saying "Brad's Place" on the upper-right side, it will have your blog's nickname!

> **TIP** *As you can see in Figure 4.5, I gave my blog a light name of "Brad's Place." If you are going to focus your blog on a given topic, then you might want to adjust the name accordingly. For example, if I were blogging only about movie reviews, then I might call my block "Brad's Movie Review Rants" or something similar that indicates that the blog is reviews. If I were talking about technology, the nickname could be "Tech Rants." Overall, it never hurts to add a little personality to your blog's nickname, while also being descriptive.*

Using Windows Live and Windows Live Spaces

The second option for setting up a blog is to create one on Windows Live Spaces. If you select this option, the program will walk you through the same process that was described in the previous section.

> **NOTE** *Windows Live Spaces is covered in Chapter 8. Windows Live Spaces is one of the places you can post a blog—and it is free!*

Using another Blog Service

You can also connect Windows Live Writer to a blog on a different blogging service. To do this, start by choosing to add a new blog. You can set up a new blog by selecting Blogs → Add blog account from the Windows Live Writer menus. This will display the same dialog you saw in Figure 4.3.

Select Other blog service and then click Next. This will start the process to connect Windows Live Writer to one of the non-Microsoft blogging services. The dialog shown in Figure 4.7 will be presented.

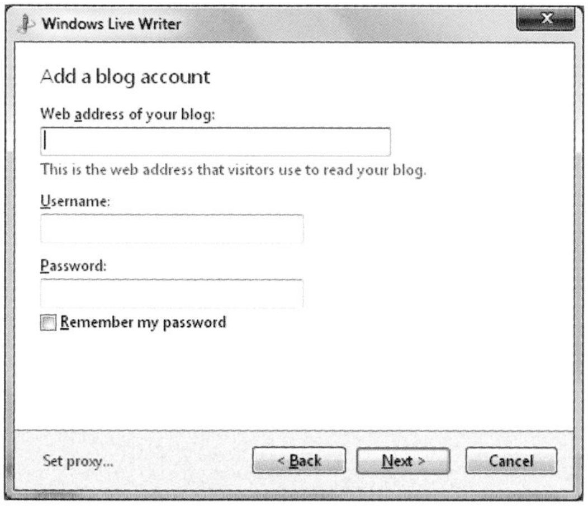

FIGURE 4.7 Adding a blog account

You'll need to enter the address of your blog as well as the login information for using the blog service. If you use a standard blogging service, then hopefully Windows Live Writer will be able to automatically configure what you need to use your blog. If not, then you might also be prompted, as shown in Figure 4.8 to select the blog type as well as to enter the URL for posting to your blog. This prompt will occur if Windows Live Writer could not figure out your blog settings based on the prior prompts.

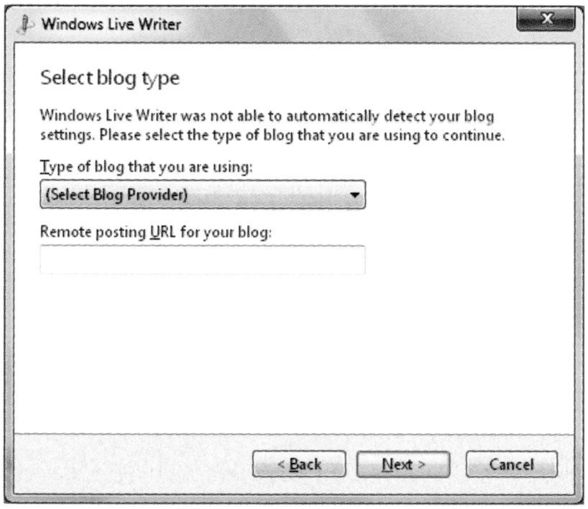

FIGURE 4.8 Setting the blog type

Once you've entered the information for setting up your blog, if you entered it correctly, your blog should now be listed in the upper-right corner of Windows Live Writer. There is a chance you will be prompted to enter a temporary post to configure Windows Live Writer with your blog's theme.

WARNING *Setting up another blog service might not be easy. If Windows Live Writer can't figure out your blog service automatically, then you'll be prompted, as shown in Figure 4.8, to enter additional information. You might need to consult your blog documentation or ask your blog provider to provide this information. This includes providing the host name, which is the name of the server where your blog is hosted. You might also be asked for the web address or path for your blog.*

Creating a Simple Blog Entry

Once you have a blog service set up, you are ready to start writing your first blog. Windows Live Writer won't do the writing for you, but it will help you make it presentable! You'll be able to enter your text, preview it, and then you'll be able to publish it directly to the blog you set up.

Before entering text, it is worth noting a few things about the Windows Live Writer interface. Figure 4.9 shows you various parts of the editor that you may or may not see when you first start it.

There are several key areas of the interface that you should note. These are identified in Figure 4.9. Many of these items will be referenced throughout this chapter. A few should be a bit obvious, such as the menu. It is possible that you might not see the taskbar on the right side. You can turn the Taskpane on and off by selecting View → Taskpane from the Windows Live Writer menus or by pressing F9.

You might also see colors around the work area that match the theme of your blog. A theme is a color scheme or design within Windows Live Spaces or your blog. In Chapter 8, you'll see how to set themes for Windows Live Spaces. If you are posting your blog to Windows Live Spaces, then your blog will use that theme.

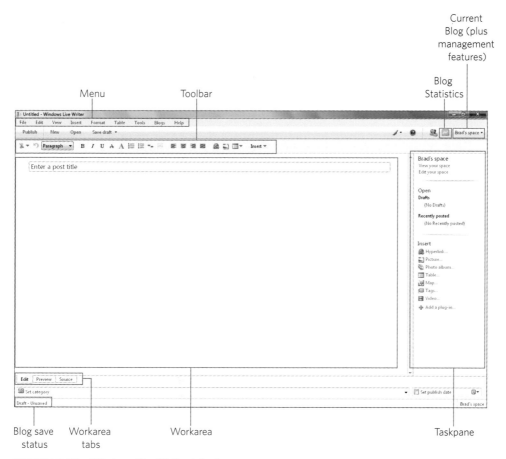

FIGURE 4.9 The Windows Live Writer interface

Entering Text

You saw in Figure 4.1 the basic Windows Live Writer window. If you click into the center area of the Windows Live Writer window, you can begin entering text, as shown in Figure 4.10.

NOTE *You might see a different style background than what is shown in Figure 4.10. If so, don't fret. You'll learn about themes a little bit later.*

FIGURE 4:10 Entering blog text

As you can see, you can simply type any text you want. You can press Enter to add spaces between paragraphs. For the most part, entering blog text is just like entering text into a word processor program.

In addition to entering the main text, you can also enter a title for your blog post. In fact, you should enter a title so that you can differentiate each post you make. To enter a title, simply click on the Enter a post title text in the Windows Live Writer window. This will remove that text and allow you to enter a title for your blog post.

Previewing Your Entry

Once you've entered your blog post, you'll want to publish it to the Internet so that others can read it. Of course, it is always best to review your post first. You can preview how your blog post will look in one of several ways. On the bottom of the entry window is a Preview tab that you can click to see the preview. Alternatively, you can select View → Preview from the Windows Live Writer menus. Of course, the easiest way to see the preview is to simply press the F12 key.

When you view the preview, it will display the text in a sample of your blog layout. You'll be able to see the formatting and other elements that you use. In Figure 4.11, you can see that I added a title to the blog entry that was shown in Figure 4.10.

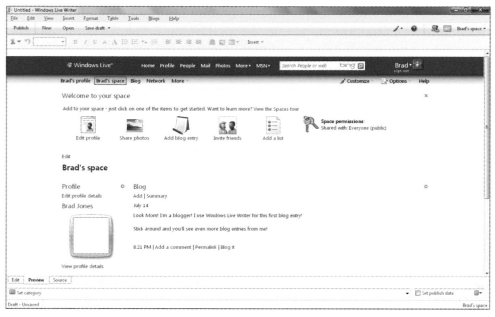

FIGURE 4.11 Previewing a blog entry

If you find that you need to make changes, you can return to the editing mode of
Windows Live Writer. There are several ways to do this. You can select the Edit tab at
the bottom of the editor, you can select View → Edit from the Windows Live Writer
menus, or you can simply press F11. Regardless of how you do it, you'll be returned to
the Edit window where you can make changes.

IF YOU UNDERSTAND HTML

If you are techie and understand the Hypertext Markup Language (HTML), you can
actually edit the HTML for your blog entry. You can do this by selecting the Source
tab at the bottom of the editor window. You can also get to the source by selecting
View → Source from the menus. Pressing the Shift+F11 keys will also take you to the
HTML code.

The nice thing about Windows Live Writer is that there is absolutely no need for
you to mess with the techie HTML code if you don't want to. You can do all the
formatting without ever looking at the HTML. If, however, someone were to give
you HTML code to post in your blog, you could go to the Source area and simply
paste or write the HTML code there.

Saving Drafts

You don't have to immediately publish entries that you make for your blog. You can save draft versions and come back and edit them or publish them later. To save an entry, select a save option from the File menu or from the Save draft option on the secondary toolbar.

If you select Save a local draft (or press Ctrl+S), then a copy of the current blog entry will be saved to your computer. When you save the entry, it will be saved using the entry's title. For example, Figure 4.12 shows an entry that was saved locally. You can see at the bottom of the figure that the entry was saved at 12:01 AM on 7/15/2009. You can also see in the Taskpane on the right that the entry is logged with the tile that is used for the entry.

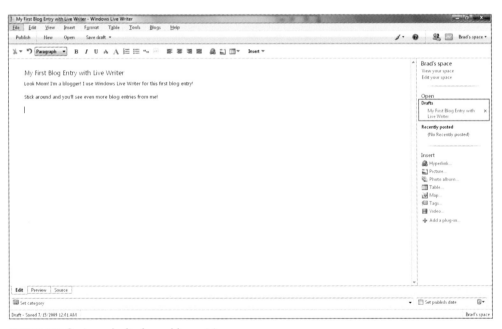

FIGURE 4.12 Saving a draft of your blog entries

In addition to saving an entry locally, you can also choose to save the draft to your blog online. Because this is online, you are posting the draft to your online blog. You can do this by selecting either Post draft to blog or Post draft and edit online. Either way, you will post a draft online.

Once you've saved a draft, you'll be able to retrieve it later. The Taskpane on the right will list some of the more recently used blog entries. If the entry is listed there, you can simply click on it to open it for editing.

You can also retrieve a previously saved blog entry by selecting Open from the File menu. You can also press Ctrl+0 to open a file. Either way, a dialog will be presented, as shown in Figure 4.13.

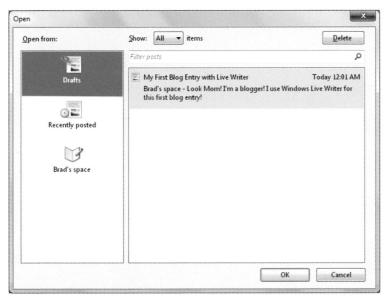

FIGURE 4.13 Opening a blog entry

This dialog will list your most recent drafts. As you can see in Figure 4.13, only one entry has been done from Windows Live Writer. As more are created and saved, they will be listed. If you have too many listed, you can select to show only the first 25 by modifying the Show option from the top of the dialog. You can also filter what is displayed by entering words to match in the Filter posts area of the dialog. As you enter text into the filter area, any blogs that don't have matching text will be immediately removed. This will make it much easier for you to find a specific blog.

NOTE *You can choose to delete a blog entry by clicking on it in the Open dialog and then clicking the Delete button. You can also click the list X icon to the right of an entry name in the Taskpane.*

Publishing Your Entry

 Once you are happy with your entry, you can publish it to your blog on the Internet for the world to see. You can do this by clicking the Publish button on the secondary toolbar. You can also publish the blog by selecting Publish to blog from the File menu or by pressing Ctrl+Shift+P. If you are not logged in to your blog account, you will be prompted to log in. Once you are logged in, you will see the status of the blog being posted, as shown in Figure 4.14. Once the posting is complete, your entry will be published.

FIGURE 4.14 Publishing your blog entry

 TIP *Before publishing your blog, you should always check your spelling. This is easily done using the spell checker built into Live Writer. To run the spell checker, Select Tools → Check Spelling or press F7.*

Setting a Publish Date

 It is worth noting that your blog will be published with the current date and time. If you want to change the date and time that is associated with your blog entry, you can. In the bottom-right corner of Windows Live Writer there is a box to set the publish date. If you click the little calendar icon, a calendar will be displayed that can be used to select a date. If you select a past date, it will look as if your entry posted on that date. If you pick a future date, your article will not actually be posted on the live site until that date.

Adding Fancy Formatting to Your Blog Entry

Now that you know how to enter, save, and publish your blog entries, it is time to see how to make them look fancier. Windows Live Writer gives you lots of tools to format and add features to your entries. Many of the features you can use to format your entries are identical to what you would find in a word processor program. Table 4.1 presents many tools you can use to format your text. These tools are available from the toolbar in Windows Live Writer as well as from the Format menu option.

TABLE 4.1 The Formatting Options

ICON	ITEM	DESCRIPTION
B	Bolding	Bolds the highlighted text.
I	Italicize	Italicizes the selected text
U	Underline	Underlines the selected text
A	Strikethrough	Draws a line through the selected test
A	Font	Allows you to change the font characteristics of the selected text. If text is not selected, then it will set the font for new text entered. You can set the font, the style, the size, and the color.
	Number list	Creates a numbered list.
	Bullet list	Creates a bulleted list of items,
	Block quote	Creates quoted text.
	Left justify	Left-justifies text.
	Center	Center-justifies text.
	Right justify	Right-justifies text.
	Justify	Justify text on both right and left sides.

Using the items listed in Table 4.1, you can make your text much more presentable. Most of these are straightforward. The Font option is the most complex in that it displays a standard font dialog that, in turn, will allow you to make a number of selections. Among the selections is the ability to change the font's color.

In addition to the items in Table 4.1, there is a Paragraph option. This option allows you to set the text style to one of the standard Internet heading styles or to the paragraph setting. Figure 4.15 shows the seven different sizes of headings that you can select from the Paragraph menu. It also shows the standard paragraph format relative to the headings.

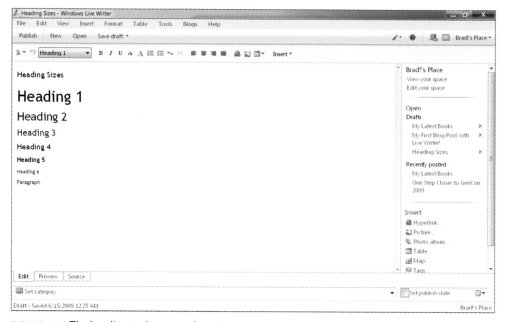

FIGURE 4.15 The heading and paragraph settings

TIP *When creating headings within a blog post, you should use the Paragraph heading tags. Search engines on the Web will look at the text in these tags closer than the rest of the text in your blog post, so it is good to put key descriptive information (words) in your headings.*

I've briefly presented the different formatting options in this chapter; however, the best way to see what each does is to create a blog entry and start playing. Figure 4.16 shows a new entry that uses several of the above features. Of course, it is always good to limit the amount of formatting you do in order to avoid overwhelming those trying to read what you've written.

In addition to the fancy formatting, you can also insert a number of items into your blog entries. These include:

▶ Hyperlinks

▶ Tables

▶ Maps

▶ Photos and pictures

▶ Videos

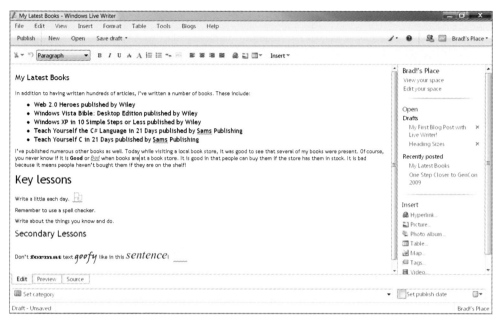

FIGURE 4.16 A formatted blog entry

Adding Hyperlinks

In simple terms, a hyperlink is a connection you add into your blog that links to another page or an object on a different page. To add a hyperlink, click on the hyperlink icon in the toolbar, or select Insert → Hyperlink. You can also press Ctrl+K. The result is that the Insert Hyperlink dialog will be displayed, as shown in Figure 4.17.

FIGURE 4.17 Inserting a hyperlink

You'll be able to enter the web address that you want to link to in the URL field. If you highlight text before clicking the Insert hyperlink button, the highlighted text will show in the Text to be displayed area. If you didn't highlight text, then you can enter text. This text will be put back into the blog entry as the link to the URL you enter.

You can also choose a couple of additional options. You can choose to open the item at your link in a new window. There are even a few additional options that you can access by clicking on the Advanced button. This includes the ability to enter a title as well as set relationship (Rel) options on the link.

 In addition to being able to enter a specific URL, you can also click the Link to button. This will show you options. The first is to link to a previous blog post. You'll be shown a list of the previous blog posts, and you'll be able to choose one of them to link to.

 The second option is to link to an Auto link entry. This option will show you text links that have been saved. You can save a link to this list for future use by checking the Automatically link this text option.

Once you've made your selections for your link, you can click Insert to add it to your blog entry. Your blog entry will then show the link. If you find you need to change or remove the link, you can right click on it to see a pop-up menu with several options. This will include an option to open the hyperlink, which will open the link in your default browser. There is also an option to edit the hyperlink, which will take you back to the dialog you saw in Figure 4.17. The Remove hyperlink will remove the link from your blog entry. Removing the link will not remove the text within the link.

> **NOTE** *The Auto links list will include a Windows Live Writer Blog entry. This is the URL of the blog from the Windows Live Writer team.*

Adding Maps

There is a Maps service that is a part of the Windows Live Services that you can use. This service allows you to add maps directly into your blog. To insert a map, select the Insert button on the tool bar and then choose Map. This will present the Insert Map dialog, as shown in Figure 4.18. Alternatively, you can choose Insert → Map from the menus in Windows Live Writer.

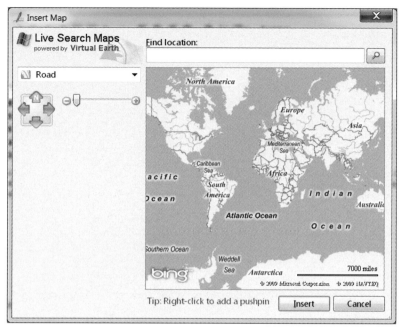

FIGURE 4.18 The Insert map dialog

On the Insert map dialog that is presented, you can enter a place into the Find location box. For example, you could enter a city and state to zoom into that location. Once you have a location in the center, you can click with the mouse and drag the map around. You can also click on the arrows to the left and move the map. If you want to zoom in, you can click on the plus sign on the left. Clicking on the minus sign will zoom out.

In addition to moving and zooming a map, you can switch the view of your map. The default view that you see is the road view. You can also switch to an aerial view and a birds-eye view. The bird's-eye view gives you a real view of what a location looks like. In Figure 4.19, you can see that two maps have been inserted into a blog entry. The one on the left is a simple map that is zoomed in a little bit. The image on the right is the same map zoomed in a little closer and shows a bird's-eye view. As you can see, this is the Wiley building in Fishers, Indiana.

You can insert as many maps into your blog entry as you would like. You can also click on the map in a blog and drag one of the corners or sides to increase or decrease its size.

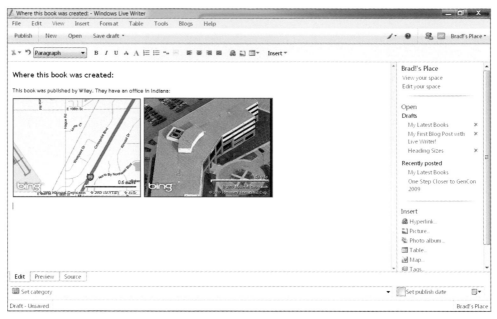

FIGURE 4.19 Two map images inserted side by side

WARNING *You can use the maps to find your home and other locations, but you should use caution giving out too much personal information. Showing where you live is not necessarily a safe thing to do.*

Adding Photos and Pictures to Your Blog Entries

You can also add images into your blog. The easiest way to add a picture is to click on the Insert Picture icon. This will result in a Windows file dialog being shown for you to select a picture to insert. The dialog from Windows 7 is shown in Figure 4.20.

You can navigate this dialog like any other Windows dialog. When you find the picture you want to insert into the blog, click Open. This will insert the selected image into the blog in the location where the cursor originally was.

NOTE *To insert a picture, you can also select Insert → Picture from the Windows Live Writer menu or from the Toolbar. Selecting Ctrl+L also works for inserting a picture.*

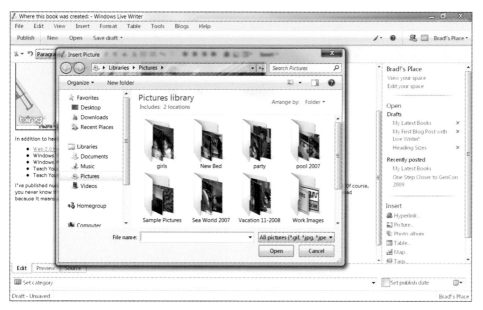

FIGURE 4.20 Inserting a picture into your blog

In Figure 4.21, you can see that an image has been inserted. More importantly, you can see on the right that when the picture is selected, the Taskpane is changed to contain controls that relate to manipulating the image.

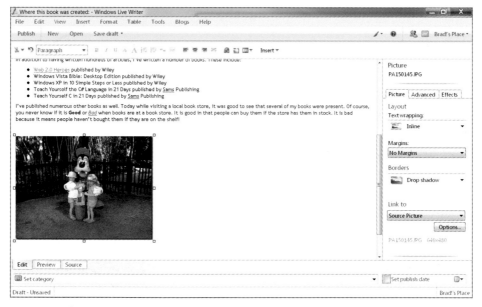

FIGURE 4.21 Inserting a picture into a blog

In the Taskpane, you can see three tabs. The Picture tab will let you set features on how the picture is laid out. You can modify the settings to change how text is wrapped around the picture, you can adjust margin values, and you can adjust the border style. If you want to link the picture to another site or address, you can use the Link to drop down and select URL option. This will display a dialog, as shown in Figure 4.22.

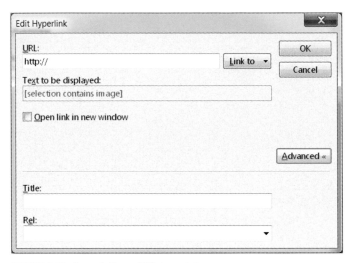

FIGURE 4.22 Associating a URL to a picture

In this dialog, you can enter the URL you want to link the picture to, and then click OK. This will associate your image to the picture.

You can also click on the Advanced tab in the Taskpane. This will give you a number of additional options for manipulating the images. You can pick a standard size for your image as well as perform picture manipulations, such as rotate, adjust contrast, crop, tilt, or add a watermark. For more information on working with these features, see Chapter 5 on using the Windows Live Photo Gallery.

WATERMARK YOUR IMAGES

The one feature that is unique in the advanced tabs is the watermark option. Clicking the watermark option will display the dialog in Figure 4.23. This will let you enter and format text that will be placed on top of your image (watermark it) to help keep others from copying it.

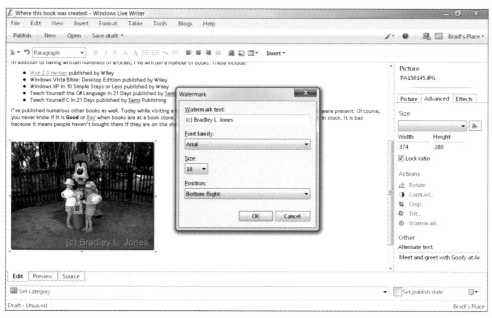

FIGURE 4.23 The dialog for watermarking an image and an image with a watermark

Adding Photo Albums

In addition to inserting a single image, you can also insert a photo album, or group of images. This is done by selecting Insert → Photo album from the Windows Live Writer menus or toolbar. This will present you with the dialog for inserting a new album, as shown in Figure 4.24.

In this dialog, you can create a title for your photo album as well as drag and drop images or pictures into the box within the dialog. Once you've added all the images you want to include, you can click OK to insert the album into the blog entry. Figure 4.25 shows an album added to a blog entry.

The album inserted into Figure 4.25 uses the Spread style. In the Taskpane, you can change the layout of the images in the album to one of a variety of options. These include Spread, Grid, Scatter, and Fan. You can also change which pictures are used in the layout by clicking on the Change cover pictures link. This will randomly choose images from those in your album. There are other values you can also set within the Taskpane for customizing your album.

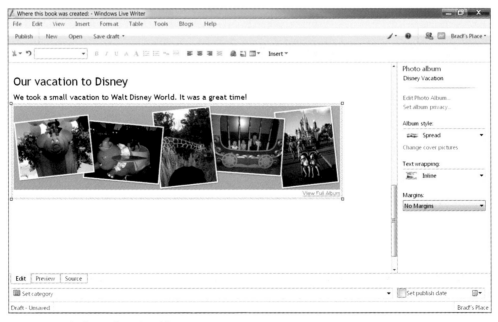

FIGURE 4.24 Adding a photo album

FIGURE 4.25 A photo album in a blog entry

Adding Video to Your Blog Entries

Adding a video to your blog entry works in much the same way as adding a picture or an album. You select Insert → Video from the Windows Live Writer menu or toolbar. This displays the dialog for adding the video. From this dialog, you can select the option to add a video from the Web, from a file, or from a video service. If you select the From File tab, you'll see something similar to Figure 4.26.

FIGURE 4.26 Inserting a video from your computer

You can use this dialog to select a video on your machine. You should note that while you are adding a video from your machine, you will need to put the video on the Web in order for it to be accessible from your blog. To load the video to the Web, you need to include the information requested on the File tab. If you chose a video on your machine that was created with Movie Maker, then any information included with it will be presented once you've selected the file. For example, Figure 4.26 shows the title, description, and tags that were associated with the vacation video that was selected. You'll have to provide the rest of the information on the dialog before you will be able to add the video. For example, you will need to select the category and state that it is okay to use the video.

> **TIP** *You can learn about creating and using videos in Chapter 6 on using Windows Live Movie Maker. You'll also learn about placing your own videos on SoapBox in Chapter 6.*

If you want to use a video that is already on the Web, it is much simpler. You simply need the URL of the video. In this case, you can select the option to insert a video and then select the From Web tab in the dialog that is presented. You can then copy the URL from the video and paste it into the Video URL or Embed box in the dialog. If you click the preview button, the video will be displayed in the dialog, as shown in Figure 4.27.

FIGURE 4.27 Inserting a video from the Web

Once you are happy with the video, you can click Insert and the video will be placed into your blog entry.

Adding Tables to Your Blog Entries

 Windows Live Writer gives you the ability to add tables to your blog. A table is basically a grid that helps you align items in rows and columns. A table is composed of rows and columns, which intersect to form cells, as shown in Figure 4.28. Within each cell, you can place any type of item you'd like including text, pictures, videos, and more.

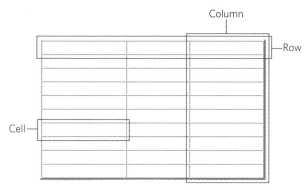

FIGURE 4.28 Parts of a table

You choose to insert a table in a number of ways. You can click on the Insert table icon or you can select Table → Insert table. You will then be prompted, as shown in Figure 4.29, to indicate how many rows and columns you want to have in your table.

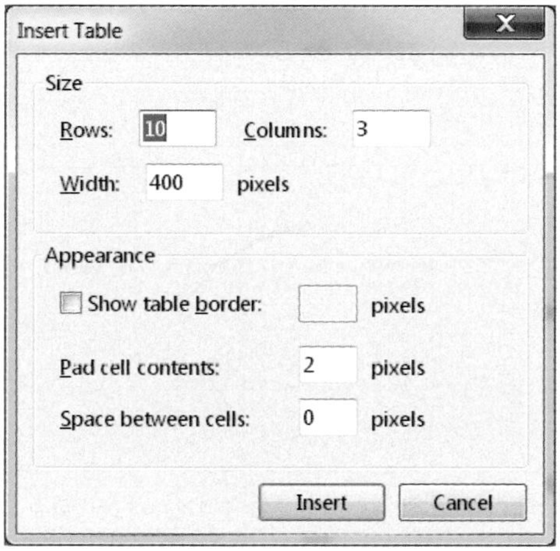

FIGURE 4.29 Inserting a table

The Insert Table dialog will also allow you to set how wide you want the table to be on the page. The default value you see in Figure 4.29 is 400 pixels. A pixel is simply a dot on the screen. If you are not sure how wide you want your table, just take your best guess or leave the default value. You'll be able to change this value later.

If you want a border to show on your table, you can click the Show table border option and then set a width for the border. The border will actually be displayed around the edge of the table and around each cell. You can increase the width of the border around the edge of the table by increasing the number of pixels to a value greater than one.

Once you've selected your settings, you can click Insert to place the table into your blog entry at the location where the cursor was. Figure 4.30 shows a table inserted with ten rows and three columns. No border was selected; however, the dotted lines are displayed in Windows Live Writer to make it easy for you to see the table to add information.

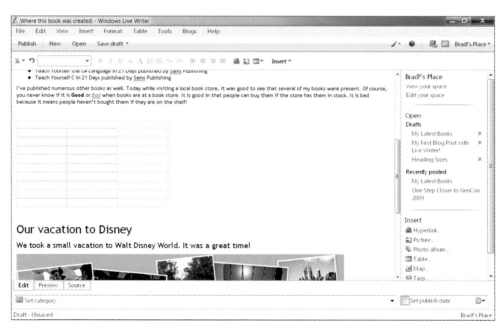

FIGURE 4.30 An inserted table in Windows Live Writer

With your table in place, you can now start adding information to it. You can simply click in a cell and start adding text, images, videos, or anything you want. If you chose to add something that is wider than a cell, the cell's width will adjust. This might also adjust other cells. If you find that you need your table to be wider, or that you want to adjust the original settings, you can modify the table's properties. You can do this by clicking on the table and then selecting Table → Table properties from the Windows Live Writer menu. You'll see the same dialog you saw in Figure 4.29 earlier. In Figure 4.31, you see a table being used to organize text and images. Note that the various text formatting features can be used on the text within cells to align, color, or otherwise change things.

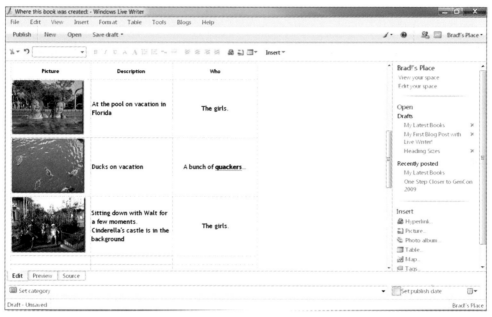

FIGURE 4.31 A table with content

If you look at the Table menu item, or if you click on the Table icon, you will see a large number of options for working with a table. These include options for changing properties on rows, columns, and cells, as well as options for manipulating columns and rows. If you want to move or delete a column or row, you should select it with the mouse and then choose the option you want from the Table menu.

WARNING *If you create a table without a border, then you will still see dotted lines around each cell in the table in Windows Live Writer. When you preview your blog entry, those lines will not be there. The lines are there to help you see and set up the information in your table.*

NOTE *You can add color and other features to a cell in a table. Windows Live Writer doesn't have settings to do this; however, you can do it by directly modifying the source on the Source tab. Doing this, however, is beyond the scope of this book. There are a number of good books on modifying HTML.*

TIP *Tables can seem complicated. The best way to understand all the features and formatting you can do is to simply play around with the options in the Table menu. Some will pop up prompts for you to enter formatting. Spending 10 minutes playing around will teach you quite a bit about what you can do with tables!*

Organizing Blog Entries

You've learned how to create and post a blog. You've even learned how to insert a number of different items into your blog entries. You are ready to go write lots of blog entries and post them to the Internet for the world to see.

Of course, with time, you will build up a large number of entries. You'll likely want to organize or group them in some way that allows them to be found easily. To make it easier to organize your blogs, you can categorize them.

Categorizing Your Blog Entries

 A category is simply a grouping that you can use. To assign a category, click the Set category option at the bottom left side of Windows Live Writer. This will display a list of categories similar to what is shown in Figure 4.32.

You can select any of the categories that are listed by simply clicking on it. If you want to create a new category, you can type the new category name into the Add Category box and then click the Add button. This will add the new category to the list of categories. When you click a category, or add a new one, it will immediately be displayed in the Windows Live Writer window on the status bar in the bottom left.

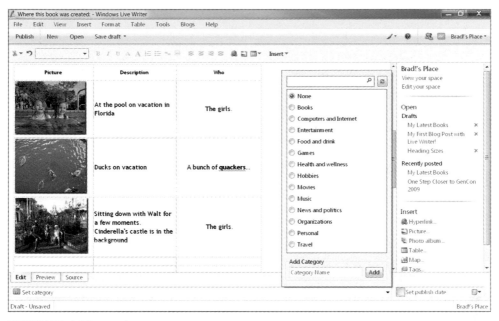

FIGURE 4.32 Adding a category

Once you're satisfied with your choice, simply click anywhere in the Windows Live Writer window to close the category box. If you decide you want to remove the category, simply click on the category that is listed and the list will be shown again. You can choose None to remove the category.

> **TIP** *It is easy to create new categories; however, you should only create them when one of the existing categories doesn't work.*

Tagging Your Blog Entries

Another popular way for information to be categorized on the Internet is to use tags. A tag is simply a word that is associated with your blog entry. People can use a tag to then get back to your content. For example, if you wrote a blog entry about a new recipe you found, you could tag it as a "recipe" or "cooking" or any other word that people might associate with the entry. Many major sites use tags as a means of navigating to content.

You can add tags to your blog by selecting to Insert → Tags from the Windows Live Writer menu or from the toolbar. This will display the dialog shown in Figure 4.33.

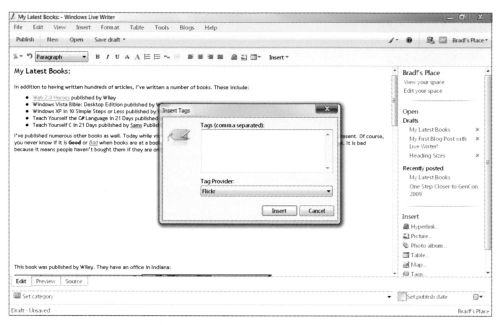

FIGURE 4.33 The Insert Tags dialog

In this dialog, you can enter the tag terms you want to associate with your blog entry. You also tie these tags to other sites. For example, to associate tags to Flickr (a photo site), you can select Flickr as the Tag Provider. In Figure 4.34, you can see that I've done exactly that. I've entered a number of tag words (each separated by a comma) and associated it to Flickr as the provider.

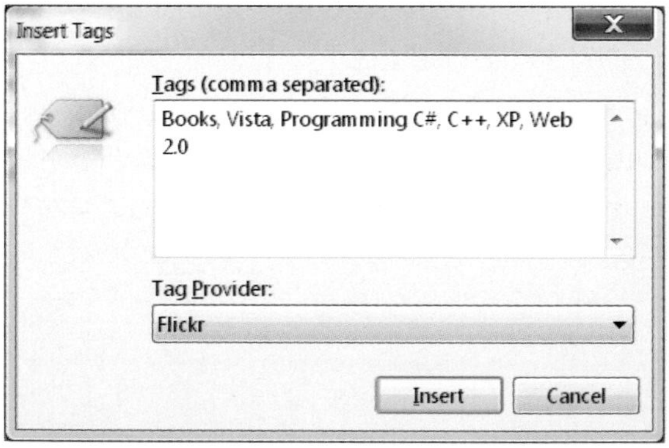

FIGURE 4.34 Adding tags

When Insert is clicked, these tags will be added to the blog entry with a link to the provider. The keywords will be viewable by you and by anyone reading your blog. Figure 4.35 shows how the keywords from the dialog in Figure 4.34 are shown in the blog entry.

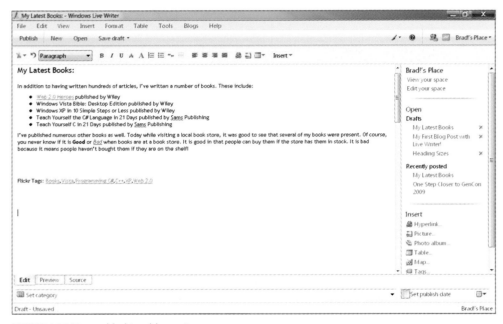

FIGURE 4.35 Tags added to a blog entry

Doing More with Plug-Ins

Finally, by using plug-ins in Windows Live Writer, you can extend what you can do. To add a plug-in, click on the Add a plug-in link in the Taskpane. This will open up a web site that will list the various plug-ins similar to Figure 4.36.

You can search through the list of items. When you find one you like, you can click the download button to download the plug-in. This will start the processes of downloading and installation. You'll want to read the dialogs that are presented and chose the option to Run the program to install it.

WARNING *You should note that when downloading and installing items from others, you risk getting a virus (malware). You should only download items created by people or companies you are comfortable with.*

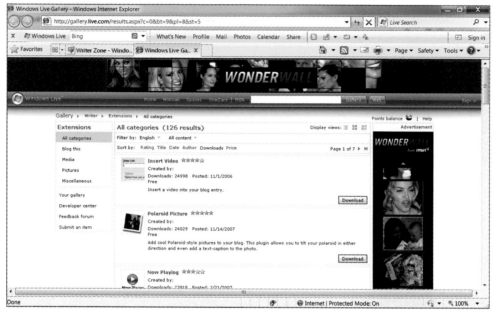

FIGURE 4.36 List of plug-ins

TIP *One of the more valuable plug-ins is Blog This for Firefox. This plug-in gives you a button that lets you launch Windows Live Writer from Firefox. When Windows Live Writer opens, it will have information about the current page already in the blog entry.*

In Conclusion

In this chapter, you learned about Windows Live Writer. Using Windows Live Writer, you can create blog entries and post them to your favorite blogging site. You learned how to use Windows Live Writer to create a new blog on the Internet if you don't have a blogging service already.

In addition to creating basic blog entries, you also learned how to insert pictures, videos, photo albums, tables, and more. The end result is that you can create entries for your blog that look pretty cool!

Managing Pictures with Windows Live Photo Gallery

IN THIS CHAPTER, YOU WILL:

▶ Discover the power of Windows Live Photo Gallery

▶ View the photos and videos that are on your computer

▶ Rotate images to the correct orientation—even rotate videos

▶ Discover how to fix a variety of issues with your images ranging from red eye to color saturation

▶ Organize your images and videos by tags, ratings, people, and more

▶ Understand how to email photos to others

▶ Collate your images and videos into a slide show or a screen saver

▶ Learn how to share your photos on your Windows Live account, with Windows Live Groups, or on online services such as Flickr

▶ Discover how to print multiple images at the same time

WITH THE proliferation of digital cameras and the ability to take hundreds of pictures before needing to offload the images, it is no surprise that it is easy to end up with thousands of pictures on your computer. While you can purchase a variety of programs to organize and manipulate your photos and pictures, an alternative is to use Windows Live Photo Gallery. Using this simple program, you can organize, manipulate, tag, and even print your pictures.

In Windows Vista, Windows Photo Gallery is included. A photo gallery program is not a part of Windows XP or Windows 7. You can, however, download it as part of the Windows Live Essentials. Once it is downloaded, you'll be able to view and manipulate your digital photos and other pictures.

 Windows Live Photo Gallery comes with a viewer for looking at your pictures. It also has several easy-to-use tools that enable you to do common fixes and adjustments to photos. In fact, this program is all you need to fix most photos. If you find that you need more features to meet your photo-editing needs, then you always have the option of purchasing a more robust photo-editing software package.

In Chapter 1, you learned how to install the Windows Live Essentials, including the Photo Gallery. Once it is installed, you'll find the Windows Live Photo Gallery application on your Start menu. The first time you run the program you might be asked—as shown in Figure 5.1—if you want to also view pictures of file types other than those that will be displayed. If in doubt, and if you have not installed other photo-manipulating software on your machine, then I recommend that you click the Yes button. The recommendations are simply other types of pictures that might be on your computer.

FIGURE 5.1 The prompt the first time you run Windows Live Photo Gallery

NOTE *Windows comes with a program called Microsoft Paint that can be used to draw pictures. While Paint can be used to manipulate and print photos and pictures, it is really only intended to be a drawing program.*

Viewing Photos and Movies

While you can use Windows Explorer to view pictures on your computer, Windows Live Photo Gallery provides you with additional features and viewing options. When you run Windows Live Photo Gallery, your photos and videos will be displayed similarly to Figure 5.2.

The Windows Live Photo Gallery allows you to see thumbnail icons and some details for the images and videos on your system in most of the common folders, including your picture and video folders as well as the public picture and video folders. More importantly, it will allow you to sort, search, or filter images based on a number of criteria. In short, you have a page that lists the images and videos on your computer in a categorized format.

FIGURE 5.2 The Windows Live Photo Gallery main page showing all images and videos

When in the gallery view, you can adjust the appearance of the main page. For example, you can select the top item, "All photos and pictures," to see a representation of all of the pictures and videos. These will be listed in the center area of the gallery as thumbnail images. You can vary what is displayed in the center in a variety of ways. You can:

▶ Display more or less in the display area.

▶ Select what is displayed using folders and tags.

▶ Filter what is displayed based on ratings

▶ Sort and arrange the items seen

The following sections will show you how to change what is displayed, but first, it is worth mentioning that you can select an individual image to work with it. You can use the Windows Live Photo Gallery viewer with a photo by either right-clicking on it and selecting Preview photo (or Preview video) or by double-clicking on the item's thumbnail. The viewer will be covered in more detail later.

Displaying More (or Less) in the Photo Gallery Display Area

Before talking about ways to change the specific selection of pictures and videos in the middle section of Windows Live Photo Gallery, you should know that you can change how the icons are displayed as well as what size the icons are.

There are two primary display presentations, a detailed view and a thumbnail view. The thumbnail view gives you a small representation of the picture. Figure 5.2 earlier showed the thumbnail view on the display page. If you hover over an image in the thumbnail view, a pop-up will display information about the picture.

The detailed view presents you with a small representation of the picture in the form of an icon along with some details about the image, including its filename, the date taken, its file size, its resolution, its rating, and any caption, you might have added. Figure 5.3 shows the Windows Live Photo Gallery, using the Details view.

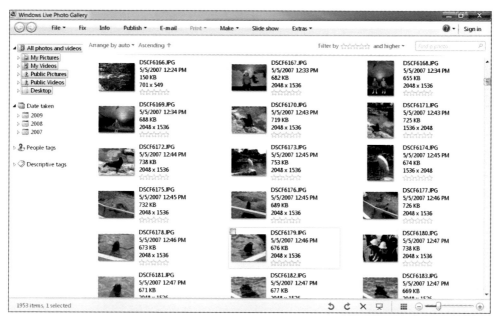

FIGURE 5.3 The Windows Live Photo Gallery showing images and videos in the Details view

You can switch between the Detailed and Thumbnail views by clicking on corresponding icons. The location of these icons is highlighted in Figure 5.4, which shows the toolbar at the bottom of the gallery. The item marked "Change View" toggles between the two different views.

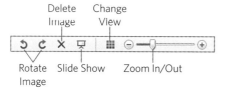

FIGURE 5.4 Tools for manipulating images or the Photo Gallery view

A few other controls are available in the toolbar. The Zoom In/Out control will allow you to increase the size of the icon images displayed by clicking on the plus sign or by sliding the handle in the middle to the right). You can decrease the size, and thus display more items, by clicking on the minus sign or by sliding the handle to the left. As you can see in Figure 5.5, you can zoom the icons to a very large size. If you want to see such large images, it is best to click into the viewer as mentioned earlier.

FIGURE 5.5 Zooming to a larger view of the icons in thumbnail view

Selecting What Is Displayed Using Folders and Tags

Now that you've seen how to manipulate the size of the items in the middle of the display page as well as how to toggle the added information on and off, you'll likely want to reduce the number of items displayed so that it is easier to find what you want. If you want to narrow down the images displayed, you can select a folder location, a date range, People tags, or Descriptive tags from those listed on the left side of the Photo Gallery. Once you make a selection, the images within the center location will be filtered based on your selection.

The folders you can select from are based on the folders on your computer that have been included in your gallery. Depending on how you've organized your folders, you might have a lot or just a few. You can navigate to different folders by clicking on them in the Photo Gallery. If you click on the little triangle to the left of a folder that has subfolders, it will expand to show the subfolders when you click on it. Note that the triangles will only show when your cursor is hovering over the folders, as shown in Figure 5.6.

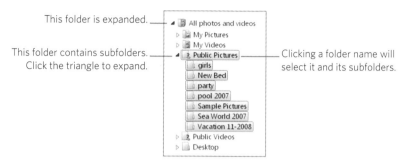

FIGURE 5.6 The folders on my computer for finding items

In addition to the folders, you can also expand the Date taken options, the People tags, and the Descriptive tags. If you've not added People or Descriptive tags, then there won't be much to see. As you'll learn later, these tags can really make it easier to organize and find your photos. You'll learn how to add these tags to your photos and videos later in this chapter. For now, know that you'll be able to pull images based on those tags. That alone should give you an idea of their value!

When you click on a folder or other container, it will be highlighted, and the items within it will be displayed in the gallery. For example, if you select Public Pictures, then only the items in your Public Pictures folder will be displayed. Similarly, if you select a specific date under the Date taken area, then only photos from that date will be shown.

WHAT IF A FOLDER ISN'T LISTED?

If you don't see a folder listed that you know contains pictures or videos, then you can tell Windows Live Photo Gallery to add that folder. To add the folder, select "Include a folder in the gallery" from the File menu. This will pop up a Windows dialog that will let you navigate to and select a folder on your computer. The folder will then be listed in Windows Live Photo Gallery.

Filter What Is Displayed Based on Ratings

In most cases, you'll use the folders on the left side to filter what you want to see. You can, however, also filter by rating. A rating is simply a number of stars you assign to an image, from one star to five stars. Unrated images have no stars. If you like an image or video, you give it a lot of stars, so a five-star item is one you really like.

☆☆☆☆☆ If your images aren't already rated, then you'll learn how to rate them later in this chapter. If they are rated, then you can use the filter option near the top of the Windows Live Photo Gallery display area to select a star rating. You'll then be able to state whether you want to display all items with that rating, those that are at that rating and higher (the default), or those at that rating and lower. You do this by clicking on the start image at the level you want, then selecting the option from the drop-down shown in Figure 5.7.

FIGURE 5.7 Showing items based on ratings

Sorting and Arranging the Items Seen

You've seen how to change the display area, how to select items from different areas, and how to filter what is shown. If doing these actions still results in a large number of items being displayed, then you will likely want to sort them.

You'll find that if you click on the Arrange by option, you can then choose to sort by one of the following options:

▶ Name

▶ Date

- ▶ Rating
- ▶ Type
- ▶ Tag
- ▶ Person

You can also let Photo Gallery automatically sort the items based on the other options you've selected. Once you pick an option to arrange your items by, you can also choose to organize them in either ascending or descending order. The options for arranging the icons are to the left of the options to filter by ratings. You can see in Figure 5.7 that the items are arranged automatically and in ascending order.

There are also additional sorting options you can use in the Photo Gallery. These include sorting on the following:

- ▶ Date taken
- ▶ Date modified
- ▶ File size
- ▶ Image size
- ▶ Rating
- ▶ Caption
- ▶ File name

To sort by one of these options, you need to right-click in the main Photo Gallery area and then select Sort by. This will display a menu of the above options. You can also select either Ascending or Descending for these options as well.

Rotating Images

Nearly everyone turns their camera sideways to take a portrait picture. Unfortunately, this means that your picture is presented sideways on the computer, as shown in the left side of Figure 5.8. The Windows Live Photo Gallery makes it easy to rotate your images so that they are presented correctly. This is done with the rotate controls presented in the bottom-right portion of the Windows Live Photo Gallery window. These controls were shown earlier in Figure 5.4.

FIGURE 5.8 A figure before and after being rotated

To rotate an image, first select it in the gallery by clicking on it. This will highlight the image by putting a box around it. You can then click one of the two rotation controls. This will rotate the image 90 degrees clockwise or counterclockwise, depending on which of the two controls you click. The right side of Figure 5.8 shows the image after it has been rotated.

Be aware that, once you click to rotate the image, the image will be immediately rotated. The image stored on your computer will be updated with the new profile. If you find that you clicked to rotate an image and didn't actually want it rotated, you can click the opposite rotation icon to rotate it back.

 NOTE *If you were to click one of these icons four times, you'd end up with the picture being in the same position it was when you started.*

 NOTE *You can also double-click or open an image in the Photo Gallery viewer before rotating it. You'll find that the rotation controls are available in the viewer as well.*

 NOTE *Yes, you can rotate a video. Try it!*

Fixing Pictures

No matter how good you are at taking pictures, there is likely to come a time when you need to fix one. This might be an adjustment to the exposure, a change in the color, or removing red eye. In addition to making fixes, you might choose to simply manipulate a photo or picture for the sake of seeing what you can do. This could be changing from a colored picture to one that is black and white or even tinting with other colors. You can even do a few professional effects such as adding sepia coloring. Of course, if you happened to scan in an image, you might just need to straighten an image or crop it.

FIGURE 5.9 The Windows Live Photo Gallery Fix options

All of these tasks are made very simple in Windows Live Photo Gallery. Each can be done with just a few steps. You start by selecting the image you want to manipulate or fix as shown earlier in this chapter. Once you've selected it, you can select Fix from the menu in Windows Live Photo Gallery. This will display the Fix menu, as shown in Figure 5.9. From this menu, you can select any of the following options:

▶ Crop photo

▶ Auto adjust

- ▶ Adjust exposure
- ▶ Adjust color
- ▶ Fix red eye
- ▶ Straighten image
- ▶ Adjust detail
- ▶ Black and white effects

In addition to the preceding fixes, you might also want to make one of the following changes to an image:

- ▶ Resize
- ▶ Change time taken

Each of these fixes or changes is covered in the following sections.

 WARNING *The features for fixing photos will not work on videos.*

Cropping Photos

One of the most common fixes or changes made to a picture is to crop an image. This is especially true as the number of pixels captured in the average camera continues to increase. By taking a picture at a higher resolution, you are able to cut out a portion of the image and still get a high-quality print from it.

To crop a picture, select the image as shown earlier and then select the Fix menu option in Windows Live Photo Gallery. From the Fix menu, click Crop. This will display a proportion option. The proportion option will allow you to select the shape of the area you want to crop. If you plan to print an image from the cropped selection, then you should pick a corresponding proportion option. For example, to print a standard photo, you can select the 4x6 option. This selection will present a frame on the image that you can then adjust as shown in Figure 5.10.

 NOTE *Some image types might not allow you to make changes and fixes in Photo Gallery. Specifically, you might need to convert a png file to a different file type before you can fix it.*

FIGURE 5.10 Cropping an image

Once you've placed the frame on the image, you can adjust its size using the mouse and dragging the corners of the image in or out. You can also rotate the frame so that it is vertical as opposed to horizontal by clicking on Rotate frame text in the Fix menu. Once you have the area marked that you want to crop, click the Apply button. The cropped image will then be displayed as shown in Figure 5.11.

In addition to selecting one of the preset proportion sizes, you can also choose to create a custom selection area. This will add additional handles to the selected area so that you can stretch the selection area's width and height independently of each other.

> **NOTE** *By default, Windows Live Photo Gallery makes a copy of your picture so that you can revert to the original at any time, if necessary. Later in this chapter, you'll learn how to revert to the original or undo any other changes you make.*

FIGURE 5.11 The cropped image

Auto-Adjusting

There are times when you need to make adjustments for poor lighting or for a slightly blurry image. You can make these changes individually or you can choose to let the Photo Gallery make the adjustment for you. This automatic adjustment is done by selecting the Auto adjust option from the list of fixes. When you select Auto adjust, the corresponding menus will expand to show you the finalized setting. Figure 5.12 shows the image in Figure 5.9 after it has been auto-adjusted.

While the changes are slight in this example, the new image has slightly crisper colors. If you look closely, you'll also see that the image was straightened as well. This was all done by simply clicking on the Auto adjust option.

You'll see that the Fix options menu expanded to shows the resulting adjustments that were made to the image. Auto adjust will actually fix the brightness, contrast, and color as well as automatically straighten the image. You can choose to adjust the setting even more if you decide you don't like the adjustments that were made.

FIGURE 5.12 An Auto-adjusted image

Adjusting Exposure

If you decide that you want to make individual adjustments to an image, then one of the options for fixes is to adjust the exposure by selecting Adjust exposure. Clicking Adjust exposure will expand a variety of options. Most of these are relatively straightforward. You can adjust:

- ▶ Brightness
- ▶ Contrast
- ▶ Shadows (This will not affect midtone or highlight details.)
- ▶ Highlights (This will not affect midtone or shadow details.)
- ▶ White Point and Black Point

You adjust the white point and black point by adjusting the little white and black arrows on the bottom of the histogram. The white point and black point are the lightest and darkest areas of the photo, respectively. By adjusting them, you adjust the other characteristics of the image.

Adjusting Color

The option for Adjust color will allow you to change the color temperature, the tint, and the saturation in your image. The best way to see what these do if you are unfamiliar with them is to pull up an image and adjust the settings. You'll be able to create interesting color effects ranging from making a picture black and white to increasing different color intensities. For example, in Figure 5.13 the saturation has been increased to make the colors more vivid. Likewise, the saturation could have been reduced to zero (the bar moved all the way to the left) to make the image look black and white.

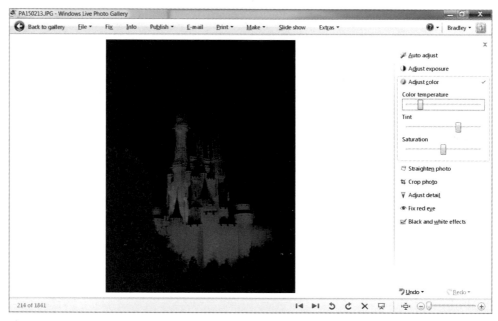

FIGURE 5.13 Increasing the saturation to make the colors more vivid

Fixing Red Eye

One common problem with photos is red eye. Red eye is an effect in a photo whereby a person's eyes appear red. Many cameras have special flashes to help avoid red eye, but even with red eye reduction, it still happens.

Red eye is generally fixed in a photo by making the areas of the eyes black instead of red. The black looks more natural, like the black in the pupil of your eyes. While you could open a paint program to fix red eye by hand, Windows Live Photo Gallery makes it as simple as selecting options and clicking.

To fix red eye, select the image and then select Fix from the menu. Within the Fix options, select Fix red eye to start the process. This will expand the red eye option, as shown on Figure 5.14.

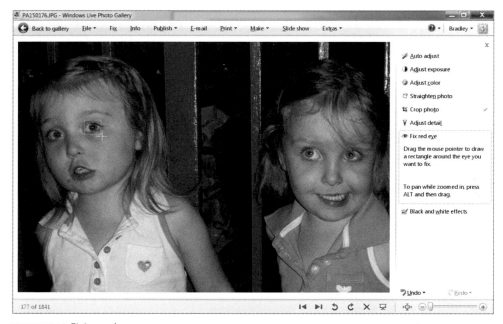

FIGURE 5.14 Fixing red eye

As the red eye option states, you can use the mouse pointer to drag a rectangle around an eye that you want to fix. You can only fix one eye at a time, so you'll do this more than once if there is more than one red eye in a picture. Once you've drawn the rectangle (as shown in Figure 5.14), the red area of the eye will be immediately changed to black. You should note that if there isn't a red eye within the rectangle, then obviously it will not be removed.

WARNING *Note that if you draw the red eye rectangle around a red area within your image, that area could be changed to black even though it might not be an eye.*

Straightening

When you take a picture with a camera, it is relatively easy to keep the camera straight. When you scan images into a computer from existing pictures, it isn't always as easy to keep them straight. Regardless of whether you've obtained the images from a camera, scanner, or other means, Windows Live Photo Gallery will help you straighten them if you happen to have them a bit crooked.

 Figure 5.15 is an image that was taken at an angle. You can tell it was an angle because it is within a pool and the water is at an angle. This image is a prime candidate for straightening.

FIGURE 5.15 A crooked image

To straighten a photo, you once again start by selecting the image and then going to the Fix options. Selecting Straighten photo will provide a slider control that will allow you turn a photo right or left. Lines will be presented across the image to help you. Additionally, the first time you select Straighten photo on an image, the slider for straightening the image will automatically be adjusted, as will the image. You can either choose to keep the adjustment that is made or move the slider to make more (or less) adjustment. Figure 5.16 shows the initial results of having selected Straighten photo on Figure 5.15.

FIGURE 5.16 Straightening the previous image

Adjust Details

If you want to sharpen an image or reduce the noise that might be within it, then you can select Adjust detail in the Fix options. This will provide you with a slider to sharpen your image, as well as a slider to reduce the amount of noise in the image. In addition to the sliders, you'll also be presented with an Analyze button that you can use to attempt to automatically adjust the noise (bad pixels in your image).

> **NOTE** *When you choose Adjust detail, the image will be zoomed in so that you can get a better view.*

Adding Black and White Effects

Windows Live Photo Gallery provides a limited number of filter and tone effects that you can add to an image. These are provided under the Black and white effects option in the Fix menu.

When you select the Black and white effects option, you will be shown six different filters you can apply to your image. Figure 5.17 shows an image that has had each of the six filters applied. Of course, several of the filters are a bit hard to differentiate when looking at a picture in a book. The best way to see what the filters do is to try them.

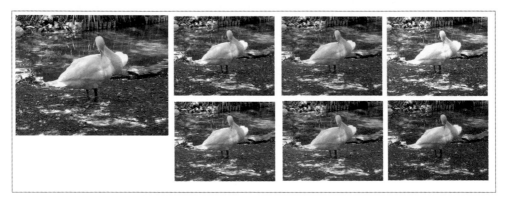

FIGURE 5.17 The various filters applied to an image

To apply a filter, simply click on it in the Black and white effects box. The filter will be immediately applied.

Undoing Changes

The previous sections showed you a number of ways to change and fix your images. As you are making changes in the viewer with the Fix options, you have the ability to undo them. If you look at the previous figures, you'll see that an Undo option is listed at the bottom of the Fix options area. If you click on Undo, you will be shown a list of all the changes you've made to the image. You can select any of them to undo the change. You can select Redo to reapply a change.

 TIP *You can also press the Ctrl key along with the letter Z to undo the last change. Ctrl+Y will redo the last option.*

Once you've made the changes, you can return to the gallery, and your changes will have been saved. The changes will be saved to the original file. Even though the changes are made to the file at this time, you are not stuck with them. You can select the image and return to the viewer to revert the image back to the original. When you return, the Undo button will be labeled Revert. Clicking Revert will return the image to its original state. You can also press Ctrl+R to revert the image.

When you choose to revert the image, you will be prompted to confirm that you really want to do this. Once you revert to the original image, all changes will be lost. You won't even be able to select Redo to get the changes back.

Resizing a Picture

Cropping chops a part out of an image; however, there will be times when you want the entire image to simply be made smaller, or even larger. Windows Live Photo Gallery makes it easy to resize an image.

> **NOTE** *Making an image larger or smaller involves changing the image's resolution. The resolution is the number of pixels that make up the height and width of your image. When you reduce the resolution, you are reducing the width and height of the image.*

Resizing an image is not done from the Fix options. Rather, to resize an image, right-click on it in the main gallery view. This will display a pop-up similar to Figure 5.18 that will provide you with options to resize your image.

FIGURE 5.18 Options for resizing an image

From the resize dialog, you will be able to select a standard size to resize you image. You'll also be able to select the location where you want to save the resized image. If you don't want to use a standard size, you can choose Customize from the Select a size drop-down menu and then enter a maximum width in the Maximum dimensions box.

Once you've selected a width for your image, you can then choose the Browse button if you don't want to save the image in the same folder as the original. If you do save the new image in the same folder, then it will be renamed with the new dimensions added to the end of the name. For example, resizing an image called "MyPic" will result in its being renamed "MyPic (640x479)."

When your choices have been made, click the Resize and Save button to resize and save the image. If for some reason the image can't be resized, you will be given an error message. Some of the general reasons why an image can't be resized include being out of hard drive space or usable memory, having a problem reading the original file, or being unable to write to the new location. There might be an unknown error as well, in which case Windows Live Photo Gallery is likely to state that there was a general resize failure.

Creating a Panoramic View

Microsoft did a commercial on television showing how easy it is to take a bunch of pictures and "squish" them into one big picture. They had a seven-year-old girl show how to create such a panoramic view within the commercial. Like many tasks, creating a panoramic view is easy once you know how. In this case, it is so easy that even a seven year old can do it!

To create a panoramic view, start by taking or obtaining a number of pictures that overlap. Load these images onto your computer so that you can access them. Once they are on your computer, you should be able to locate them in Windows Live Photo Gallery by navigating to the folder or other location where you placed them. Once there, select the images that will compose your panoramic image.

I've uploaded half a dozen overlapping pictures of my own. In Figure 5.19, you can see that I am using the mouse to drag a box over the six images to select them.

I could also have selected the images by clicking on the check box in the upper-left corner of each, or by clicking on each while holding down the control button. Selecting images was covered earlier in this chapter.

 Once you've selected your images, click on the Make option at the top of Windows Live Photo Gallery and choose Create panoramic photo. This will start the process of creating the new image. You'll be presented with a pop-up that will show you the status of the creation process, as shown in Figure 5.20.

FIGURE 5.19 Selecting a number of images that overlap

FIGURE 5.20 Creating the panoramic photo

If you watch the dialog, you'll see that several steps are involved in creating the panoramic view. This starts with reading the image files and may include solving photo alignments, compositing photos, and then saving the photo. When the process is complete, your new photo will be presented. My photo created with the images from Figure 5.19 is presented in Figure 5.21.

If you look at the resolution of the resulting image, you'll see that it is much larger than that of the original images. This should make perfect sense. After all, the new image is basically the other images laid next to each other with a bit of overlap and combined to create one large image.

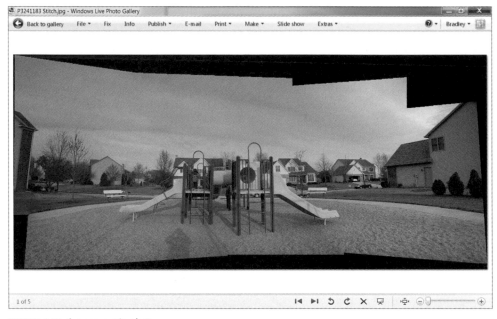

FIGURE 5.21 A panoramic photo

TIP *As you can see in Figure 5.21, the resulting photo has odd edges. This is because the various images were stitched together. This does not necessarily result in a perfectly rectangular photo. You can always crop the image to eliminate the odd edges.*

Managing Photos

If you have a large number of images and photos on your computer, you'll quickly realize that managing photos by dates and folders alone is just not good enough. As mentioned earlier, you'll want to start using other means for finding or filtering the photos you see. This might be ratings, tags, people, or more. Of course, to find these characteristics, you need to start assigning them to your photos. In addition to assigning these ratings and tags, you might also find that you need to adjust some other characteristics. Have no fear, Windows Live Photo Gallery makes managing your photos and their characteristics easy.

In general, to add or modify characteristics to a photo, you will use the Info option. This information can be displayed for a photo in either the primary gallery, or the viewer when looking at an individual image. In either case, you display the information by clicking Info in the menu options at the top of the gallery. The information will be displayed to the right, as shown in Figures 5.22 and 5.23. As you can see from the two figures, the information is displayed in the same way, regardless of whether you are in the gallery or the viewer.

FIGURE 5.22 Info displayed in the gallery

FIGURE 5.23 Info displayed in the viewer

Rating Photos

One easy thing to start doing with your photos is to rate them. As mentioned earlier, you choose to display only items with certain rating characteristics. A rating is a score from one star to five stars that you can give an image.

 Once you've chosen to display a photo's Info, you will have an option to rate the photo. You do this by selecting one to five stars from the Rating option. If you look at either Figure 5.22 or 5.23, you'll see five outlined stars are included in the rating within the information about the shown photo. You can use the mouse to actually hover over and click on the stars to set or change the rating. Initially, these stars are just outlines. Once you select a score, you'll notice the color change to yellow to show that there is a score set. If you change your mind on a score, simply hover over the stars and click to reset the value.

> **NOTE** *Generally, you would use a five-star rating for an image you like. You'd use a one-star rating for an image you don't like.*

Tagging Photos

Tagging is set similarly to ratings in that you go to the Info area to set or change them. Tags, however, are at the top. You can see in Figures 5.22 and 5.23 that there are two different types of tags, People tags and Descriptive tags. People tags let you identify people in a photo, including yourself. Descriptive tags allow you to assign any words to an image that might be helpful later in sort or searching for an image.

As an example of Descriptive tags, you can add words like "Vacation" or "Wedding" to a photo. You can also add any other word. If you decide later the word doesn't work, you can always change or remove it. You can always come back and add more words later as well. You might want to add dates to tags; however, that isn't really necessary, since the date the photo was taken is already a part of the information stored with the photo.

Adding Descriptive Tags

To add Descriptive tags, click Add Descriptive tags in the Info area. You'll then be prompted to simply start entering words or phrases one at a time. If you've entered tags on your computer before, then a drop-down list of those tags will be presented that you can simply select one. This helps to keep your tags consistent. Once you've added tags, they will be listed in the Info box.

Adding People Tags

People tags operate a little bit differently from the Descriptive tags. When you add a People tag, you actually identify the person in the photo. You do this by using the mouse to draw a small box over the location in the photo where the person is.

Windows Live Photo Gallery is actually smart enough that it will also try to find faces within a photo. If it does, it will list "Person found" under the People tags option. Clicking on the Person found text will highlight a box over the face or location where Windows Live Photo Gallery found the person. You can then identify who the person is by clicking the Identify word next to the Person found text.

When identifying a person, you will be prompted to enter their name, as shown in Figure 5.24. You will be given the names of contacts in your Windows Live account as well as the names of people you've identified in other photos and of course yourself. Once you select or enter the name, it will be displayed in the information box.

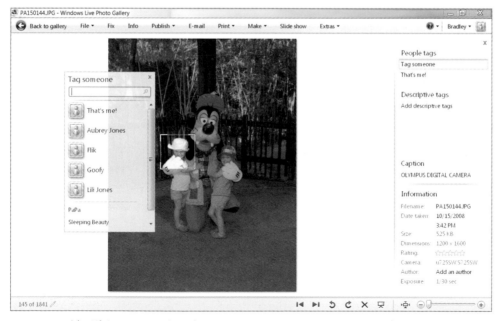

FIGURE 5.24 Identifying a person in a photo

If Windows Live Photo Gallery didn't find someone automatically, you can click on the Tag someone text to identify them yourself. This will change your mouse cursor to a plus and allow you to draw a rectangle around a person (or their face) on the photo. Once you've drawn the rectangle, then just as you saw in Figure 5.24, you'll get the dialog to select or enter a person's name.

The other option for tagging a person is for identifying yourself. This is done by clicking the That's me! text in the Info area. As when identifying a person, this will change your cursor to a plus and allow you to draw a rectangle over yourself or your face. Instead of being prompted to select a name, your name will simply be assigned and listed in the Info. As you can see in Figure 5.25, I've identified three people in the photo shown in Figure 5.24.

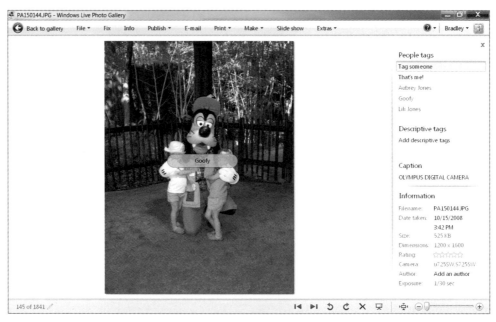

FIGURE 5.25 A photo with the people identified and Descriptive tags added

If there are People tags listed in the Info area, you can hover over the person's name. This will show the box that was drawn on the picture to allow you to see which person the name belongs to. Additionally, if you hover over the areas you marked in the photo, the name you selected will be displayed, as shown in Figure 5.25, where the cursor was over Goofy. If you find that you don't want one of the tags, you can simply click the X that is shown to the right of the tag when you hover the mouse cursor over it. This will remove the tag.

> **NOTE** *If you use the Info pane from the Photo Gallery rather than from the Viewer, then when you select to tag people, you will only be able to select or state a name. To identify the specific people by selecting them in a photo, you'll need to be in the viewer. After all, the Photo Gallery doesn't show a large enough image for you to work with in selecting people most of the time. An image will be opened in the viewer if you do try to identify more than one person.*

> **NOTE** *With videos, you can add tags for people, but you won't be able to select them within the video.*

Adding a Caption

In addition to tagging people and descriptive terms, you can also add a caption to your photos. Add a caption by clicking the Add caption text in the Info area and then entering the information in the box presented.

Changing Date/Time

Included with the information on a photo is the date and time that the picture was created or taken. This is identified in the Information in the bottom half of the Info page. You can see the Date taken in Figure 5.25 was 10/15/2008 at 3:42 PM. While there generally isn't a reason to do so, you can actually change this date and time if you so desire.

To change either, simply click on them in the Information area within the Info panel area. This will then allow you to enter a new date or time. If you chose to change the date, when you click on the date to edit it, a little icon will be displayed. You can click on it to get a calendar to appear, as shown in Figure 5.26. You can select a date from the calendar or simply enter one by hand.

FIGURE 5.26 Selecting a new Taken date

Adding an Author

It is always nice to give credit to the person who took or created a picture. You can do this by clicking on the Add an author text next to the Author option listed in the information area. A simple text box will be displayed where you can type in the name of the author. If you later want to change the author, simply click on the information you had entered and replace it with your new information.

> **TIP** *The author information is like a lot of the other information within the Info panel in that you can later search for pictures by a given author.*

Renaming Items

You've learned how to add or change a lot of descriptive information related to your photos, pictures, and videos. The one additional process that you should know how to do is to rename your items.

There are two ways you can rename your items within Windows Live Photo Gallery. Within the Info panel, you can change the Filename within the Information section by clicking on it and then entering the new filename. You'll notice when you do this, that you only change the base name—you can't change the extension.

The second process to change the name of an item is performed within the gallery itself. Rather than selecting the Info option and then changing the name in the Info panel, you can also right-click on an image. This will cause a pop-up menu to be displayed. You can then select Rename to rename the item. Doing this will actually open the Info panel in the gallery with the name highlighted.

Producing Output with Photos

Once you have photos on your computer, you are likely going to want to share them or to do something with them. You saw earlier how you could manipulate pictures by cropping, resizing, or even combining for panoramic views. Once you've invested some time in getting your pictures clean, sharp, and just the way you want them, then you are likely to want to start doing something with them. Windows Live Photo Gallery gives you a number of options for doing things with your pictures and videos. This includes emailing them to others, creating a movie (using Windows Live Movie Maker), publishing them to your blog, or creating a slide show.

Emailing Pictures

If you choose to email one or more items, then you can do it directly from Windows Live Photo Gallery, if you have an email program set up on your computer. You start by selecting one or more images that you want to send. Then, click the E-mail option in the menu at the top of Windows Live Photo Gallery. When you do this, if you are sending a picture, you will be prompted to set a size for the photos you are sending, as shown in Figure 5.27

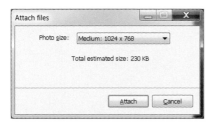

FIGURE 5.27 Emailing photos

Picture files can be very large. The higher the resolution, generally, the larger the file will be. As you can see in the dialog that is presented in Figure 5.27, you are given a rough estimate of the size the image file will be when you send it. This is a rough estimate because the image will be resized when it is sent. If you click on the size button, you'll be able to select from various resizing options. As you change your choice, you'll see that the total estimated size will change.

Once you've made your selection, you can click the Attach button to do the actual resize and have your email program open.

> **NOTE** *You'll need to have a mail program set up or you will get an error when trying to attach the images to an email.*

Make a Movie

Window Live Photo Gallery will also allow you to produce a movie from a selection of items. It is really just a matter of a few steps to have a video clip that highlights the images. The production is accomplished by working with Windows Live Movie Maker.

Start by selecting the images you want to include. Once they are selected, click on Make in the Windows Live Photo Gallery menu, then select Make a movie, as shown in Figure 5.28. Windows Live Movie Maker will open with the selected images.

FIGURE 5.28 Selecting images to make a movie

WARNING *You must have Windows Live Movie Maker installed to make a movie from your photos in Windows Live Photo Gallery.*

Once the images are opened in Windows Live Movie Maker, you can generate a movie using them. Do this by selecting Output in the toolbar. You can then select the option to create a WMV movie file from the options listed. For more on adjusting transitions between images, changing display times, and other options within your movie, see Chapter 6.

Publishing to a Blog

The previous section shows you how to use Windows Live Photo Gallery to create a movie by interacting with Windows Live Movie Maker. Windows Live Photo Gallery can interact with other Windows Live applications as well. In fact, you can interact with Windows Live Writer and, thus, post images directly into a blog post from Windows Live Photo Gallery.

To post images from Windows Live Photo Gallery to a blog entry, start by selecting them within the Windows Live Photo Gallery. Then select Make from the menu followed by the Make a blog post option. This will open the selected images in Windows Live Writer, as shown in Figure 5.29. Note that you will need to have Windows Live Writer installed on your computer.

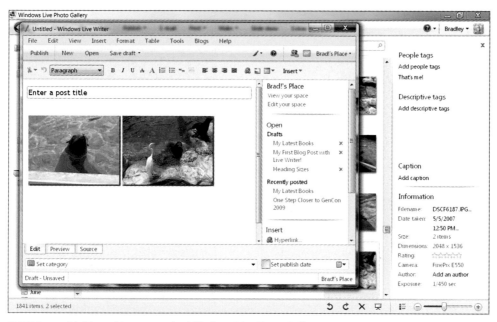

FIGURE 5.29 Making a blog post using Windows Live Photo Gallery items

You can continue to edit the blog post in Windows Live Writer and publish it to your blog. The specifics of using Windows Live Writer are covered in Chapter 4.

Create a Slide Show

Windows Live Photo Gallery provides the ability for you to organize your photos into a slide show that you can view on your computer. Additionally, you can set the screen saver on your computer to a slide show.

There are a variety of ways to start a slide show when you are in Windows Live Photo Gallery. You can simply click on the Slide Show option in the menu, you can click on the slide show icon near the bottom of the Windows Live Photo Gallery, you can press Alt+S, or you can press F12.

When the screen saver loads, your screen will initially go dark before showing your images. Your images will be shown one after the other in standard slide show fashion.

You might be wondering what images will be shown in the slide show. You can control this by either selecting individual images in the gallery or by selecting a group of images. In other words, whatever images you currently have displayed in the gallery will be used unless you have individually selected images.

Once you start the slide show, you will have a number of options that you set to adjust the speed that the images are displayed and how they are displayed. You can also skip to the next or previous image as well as pause on the current image. This is all controlled by controls displayed when you move your mouse over the screen saver, as shown in Figure 5.30.

FIGURE 5.30 The slide show controls

Before covering specifics about the slide show, you should know how to exit it. To exit, either click on the Exit option in the controls, or press the Escape key. Either way you will be returned to the gallery.

Moving between Slides in a Slide Show

You can use the controls in the middle to navigate to the previous or next image. You can use the control in the circle to pause. These three controls are shown in Figure 5.31.

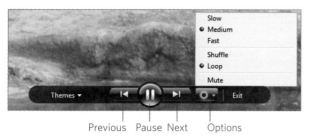

FIGURE 5.31 Controls for moving between slides

You can also change the speed that each image is displayed as well as the order by using the menu next to the control on the right. Table 5.1 shows what the controls identified in Figure 5.31 do.

TABLE 5.1 Slide Show Navigation Controls

CONTROL	FUNCTION
Previous	Shift to previous item in slide show.
Pause	Stop on the current item in the slide show. The pause button will change to a play button. Clicking the Play button will restart the slide show.
Next	Shift to the next item in the slide show.
Slow/Medium/Fast	Set the speed of the slide show. The default is Medium. Slow will display items for a longer period of time. Fast will display items for a shorter period of time.
Shuffle	Selecting Shuffle will cause images to be displayed in a random order. If this is not selected, then images will be displayed sequentially. The default is sequential.
Loop	If Loop is selected, then once the last image is displayed, the slide show will automatically start displaying the images again. If Loop is not selected, then once all the images are displayed, the slide show will end. By default, the slides will Loop.
Mute	If Mute is selected, then sound will not be displayed. While pictures don't have sound, videos do. If Mute is selected, then sound from videos will not be heard.

NOTE *Slide shows can contain pictures, videos, or both.*

Setting a Theme in Your Slide Show

In addition to controlling how the slide show moves between items, you can also control the theme used for the slide show. A theme is a layout and background to give your slide show more pizzazz as well as adjust how transitions occur between images. You can see the various themes by selecting Themes from the slide show controls. This will list all the available themes you can use. By default, you'll see the following items listed:

- ▶ Classic
- ▶ Fade
- ▶ Pan and zoom
- ▶ Black and white
- ▶ Sepia
- ▶ Album
- ▶ Collage
- ▶ Frame
- ▶ Glass
- ▶ Spin
- ▶ Stack
- ▶ Travel

It is worth pointing out what a few of these items do. The easiest way to see what each does is to start the slide show and switch between themes. You'll find that Classic simply switches between items in the slide show with no transitions. Fade provides a smoother switching between items by providing a fading transition from one item to the next. Pan and zoom adds a little motion to the items in your slide show by zooming in and out of items that are displayed.

The Black and white as well as the Sepia options don't deal with transitions, but rather cause a change to the items. Black and white changes the items displayed to black and white, Sepia changes them to sepia, which is a bit "classier."

The rest of the options provide much more visually interesting displays. Figure 5.32 shows a scene from the Collage theme. Figure 5.33 shows the look of the Travel theme. Themes can adjust how things are displayed as well as transitions between items.

FIGURE 5.32 The Collage theme

FIGURE 5.33 The Travel theme

Using the Slide Show Screen Saver

One final thing about the slide show deserves mention. You can set your Windows screen saver to use the Slide Show from the Windows Live Photo Gallery. You can set this using the Windows display properties, or you can set the screen saver directly from Windows Live Photo Gallery.

To set the Windows screen saver from Windows Live Photo Gallery, select Screen saver settings from the File menu in the gallery view. This will launch the Windows Screen Saver Settings dialog. Figure 5.34 shows this dialog from Windows 7. If you are using a different version of Windows, then this dialog might be slightly different.

FIGURE 5.34 Screen Saver Settings dialog from Windows 7

You can select the Settings if you want to change the options for the screen saver. As you can see in Figure 5.35, there are a number of options you can set such as where to pull images from, what ratings or tags should (or shouldn't) be used, the speed of the display, whether the slides should be shuffled (randomly displayed), and what theme should be used. You can also set the theme to Random to allow the screen saver to randomly decide the theme.

Once you have selected your settings, you can click Save to save them. This will save the Slide Show as your Windows screen saver.

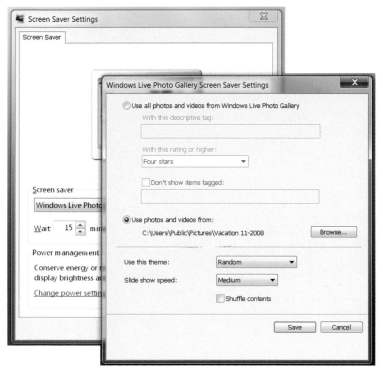

FIGURE 5.35 Screen Saver Settings specific to the Windows Live Photo Gallery screen saver

> **NOTE** *If you need more information about Windows screen savers, see your Windows documentation.*

Burning Images to a Disk

Because blank DVDs and CDs are relatively cheap, they make a great way to back up your images and videos. They also make a great way to share your images and videos with others who don't want to spend time downloading them or viewing them online. Windows Live Photo Gallery makes it easy to copy your files to disks assuming that your computer has a DVD or CD burner.

Burning a DVD

 If your computer has a DVD burner, then you can use Windows Live Photo Gallery to write your videos and images to it. Windows Live Photo Gallery uses the Windows DVD Maker software to create a DVD. This program comes on Windows Vista Home Premium, Windows Vista Ultimate, and versions of Windows 7. If you have the right version of Windows, then when you will see an option to Burn a DVD under the Make menu of Windows Live Photo Gallery. Selecting this option will run the Windows DVD Maker program. Windows DVD Maker is covered in Chapter 6 along with the Movie Maker program.

If you don't see the option to Burn a DVD in the Make menu, then you don't have the Windows DVD Maker software. As such, you'll need to find and likely buy software for burning a DVD. If your machine comes with a DVD burner, then it likely came with software as well. You'll want to check your computer's documentation to verify if you have software and how it works.

 WARNING *Not all DVD players can write DVDs. You should verify that your computer has a DVD burner. If it doesn't, you won't be able to create a DVD no matter how you try!*

Burning a CD

Most newer computers include a CD drive that can write a CD as well as read them. If yours has one, then from the Windows Live Photo Gallery, you can copy your images and videos to CDs for backup or for sharing.

To copy items to a CD, first select them in the Photo Gallery. You can then select Burn a data CD from the Make menu. This will start the process of creating a CD by prompting you to insert a blank CD into your CD drive. You should insert an appropriate disk into your CD drive. After you do, the process will resume within a minute or two.

From this point, the process of burning a CD might vary depending on what version of Windows you are running. In fact, the process of creating a CD is actually a part of Windows and not a part of Windows Live Photo Gallery. As such, the specific steps will vary depending on the version of Windows you are using. For the most part, you should be able to follow the steps as you are prompted. If you need more help, consult the help files in your copy of Windows.

Publishing Photos

If you have an online Windows Live account, then you can publish your photos and videos online. By publishing them online, you can allow others to have access to your images. You can share items by posting them to your online Windows Live account, to Windows Live Groups (which is covered more in Chapter 9), to your online events, as well as to online services such as Flickr and SoapBox.

Creating an Album on Windows Live

To share items online using the Windows Live Services, you would create an album. You can create a photo album in Windows Live or in Windows Live Groups.

To create an online album, you start by signing into Windows Live. You can sign in directly from Windows Live Photo Gallery by clicking the Sign in option in the upper-right corner. Note that if you are already signed into Windows Live, your Windows Live ID will be displayed. If you are not signed in, click the Sign in option and sign in, as shown in Figure 5.36, using your ID and password.

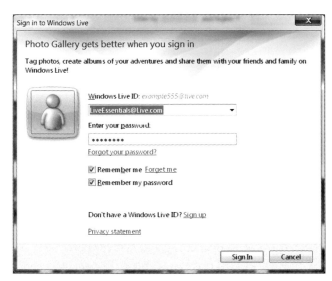

FIGURE 5.36 Signing into Windows Live

Once signed in, you will be able to use the Publish option on the Windows Live Photo Gallery menu to publish an album. You should start by selecting the images you want to publish online. To publish an album to your Windows Live account, select Online album from the Publish menu. This will allow you to create a new album group on Windows Live, as shown in Figure 5.37.

FIGURE 5.37 Publishing photos and videos to Windows Live

As you can see in the dialog in Figure 5.37, you can give your new album a name. You can also select who has access to the photos. You can see that the default is to give public access to Everyone. You can change this by clicking on the drop-down menu. You will be shown the available sharing levels such as to share just with your network or just yourself (Just me). In addition to these options, there might also be an option to change the size of the images as they are uploaded. This is done using the control labeled Upload size. In Figure 5.37, you can see that the images are being uploaded in the Large size of 1600 pixels. This can be adjusted to a smaller size, which also reduces the bandwidth required to upload and download the images. Once you've made your choices, click Publish to start the uploading process.

The status will be shown as each image is uploaded. Once all the images are placed in the album, you'll be given a confirmation message, as shown in Figure 5.38. You can close this message when you are done reading it, or you can click View album to view your images online. Figure 5.39 shows icons for images that were just uploaded to Windows Live from Windows Live Photo Gallery.

FIGURE 5.38 Confirmation that your photos are on Windows Live

FIGURE 5.39 Photos on Windows Live

Publishing to Windows Live Groups

Publishing to your online Groups is similar to publishing to Windows Live in general. The difference is that your images will only be shared with those people in one of your Windows Live Groups. Again, you will need to select the images you want to publish. You can then select Group album from the Publish menu to publish to a Windows Live Group. This will display a list of your Windows Live Groups. You can then select the group where you want to publish the items.

Once you've selected a group, you will see a dialog similar to the one you saw in Figure 5.38 for publishing items to Windows Live. This time, however, you are creating an album within the group, so instead of setting permissions to everybody, your network, or yourself, you are instead able to allow members of the group that you selected. You can choose to allow members to either edit the images or just view the images. All the other settings are the same as for setting up a Windows Live album—you can set a name and an upload size. Click Publish to again upload the images. The results will be very similar to uploading to Windows Live.

NOTE *You can learn more about creating and using Live Groups in Chapter 9.*

Publishing to Online Services

In addition to publishing to Windows Live, you can also publish to online services such as Flickr. To publish to Flickr, select the images you want to post, then select Publish on Flickr form the Publish menu. If you don't see this option on the Publish menu, then select More services from the Publish menu. You should find Publish on Flickr on this submenu.

WARNING *You will be required to log in to Flickr in order to post items there. You will need to create a Flickr account to use for your items. Flickr can be found at* www.Flickr.com. *You can create a basic account for free.*

Before Windows Live Photo Gallery can post items to Flickr, you will need to provide authorization for Windows Live Photo Gallery to interact with your Flickr account. Because of this, the first time you select to publish to Flickr, you will see a dialog like the one in Figure 5.40 requesting you to enter your authorization information.

FIGURE 5.40 Authorizing Flickr for your images

This will be followed by additional dialogs and a request to log in to Flickr. Once you've logged in to your Flickr account, you'll have to choose to allow Flickr and Windows Live Photo Gallery to be linked. Clicking the OK, I'LL ALLOW IT button on the Flickr page, as shown in Figure 5.41, will do this.

FIGURE 5.41 Linking Windows Live to Flickr

You will get a confirmation message once you've succeeded in linking Flickr to your Windows Live Photo Gallery. Now when you select Publish to Flickr, you will be prompted with a dialog similar to Figure 5.42. You'll be able to select the Flickr accounts you've authorized, the photo set from Flickr you want to add the images to (or leave as Don't add to a set if you don't want to add to a set), the upload size (Photo size), and the type of permission you want to give the images on Flickr. Once you've made your selections, click Publish to start the uploading and publishing of the items.

FIGURE 5.42 Uploading photos to Flickr

TIP *If you want to remove the authorization you created on Flickr for Windows Live Photo Gallery, then you will need to go to Flickr and revoke the permission in the Account settings.*

Printing Photos

As you've seen, there are plenty of ways to use and share your pictures electronically, but sometimes it is nice to simply print pictures to have and to hold. You can print your photos in Windows Live Photo Gallery by selecting Print from the menu. This will display the print dialog, as shown in Figure 5.43.

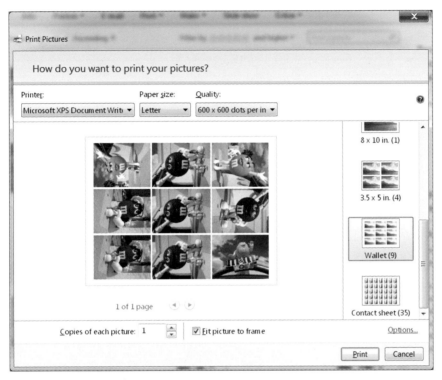

FIGURE 5.43 Printing a Photo

From the print dialog, you can select standard print options such as which printer to use, the paper size, the resolution, how many copies of each picture to print, and whether to fit the pictures to the frame size. On the right side of the dialog, you will also be able to select the number of images that are printed and their size. For example, in Figure 5.43, you can see that letter size paper is being used. You can also see that wallet sized images are being used, thus printing nine images on a single page. If you had selected fewer than nine images, then you'd see them all on the page. If you selected more than fit on a page, then multiple pages would be printed.

Once you are happy with your selections, you can click the Print button to start printing the images. From this point, the printing should follow the same steps as printing anything from Windows.

> **TIP** *In general, you should not print at a resolution lower than 300x300 for photos. The higher the resolution, the crisper the pictures should be.*

In Conclusion

In this chapter you learned about Windows Live Photo Gallery. You learned how it can be used to manipulate, fix, or simply view the images and videos on your computer. Additionally, you learned how you can share your media files with others as well as learned that you can use your media files within blogs using Windows Live Writer, within movies using Windows Live Movie Maker, and much more.

Creating Movies with Movie Maker

IN THIS CHAPTER, YOU WILL:

▶ Learn about Windows Live Movie Maker

▶ Discover the different components of Windows Live Movie Maker

▶ Learn how to add photos and videos to a movie

▶ Add transitions and video effects to your movies

▶ Incorporate music and background sound in your productions

▶ Add text and titles to your movie

▶ Use the Mixer to modify sound

▶ Publish your movie productions to your computer or a portable device

▶ Create a DVD of your movie

▶ Post your movie to online sites such as YouTube

NEARLY EVERYONE has had a time where they've been forced to sit through home movies of family or friends. Some are entertaining, but most are not. One of the reasons home movies are often monotonous is that they are primarily the raw video clips people took with their camera. These clips are often filled with unbearably dull moments as well as repetitive scenes.

With many video cameras being inexpensive today, with the ability of most digital cameras to take short videos snippets, and with the ability of many cell phones to record video, it is not surprising that you could end up with a lot of video clips. If all you do is show these raw clips of video, then there is a good chance you are going to create your own repetitive, monotonous moments!

One way to make the clips more entertaining is to use video software to edit your video and knit the clips, together with photos, into something more organized. Adding background music, transitions, and other effects can go a long way toward turning home video into something much more interesting and entertaining.

One of the applications you can download as a part of Windows Live Essentials is Windows Live Movie Maker. This free program will allow you to start making your own movies not only from your video clips but also from any photos or pictures on your system. Windows Live Movie Maker makes it easy to get started with your own video production.

> ### THINK SHORTER IF YOU WANT TO ENTERTAIN
>
> One of the biggest mistakes people make in producing a home movie is to simply show the raw videos they take with their video camera. While this might be entertaining to you, if you allow scenes to go too long, you will likely bore everyone else. You'll learn how to shorten clips as well as how to knit clips together in this chapter. With Windows Live Movie Maker, you should find it very easy to create your own masterpieces that don't put people to sleep!

Knowing Your Movie Maker

Before you get started, it is important to make sure that you are using the right version of Movie Maker. This chapter covers the Windows Live Movie Maker that you can download from Windows Live, as shown in Chapter 1. There is actually a different Movie Maker that was included with Windows XP and Windows Vista. Figure 6.1 shows the original Movie Maker

Let me repeat that the Windows Live Movie Maker is not the same as the Windows Movie Maker shown in Figure 6.1. For one thing, Windows Live Movie Maker is only supported on Windows Vista and later versions of Windows, including Windows 7. More importantly, Windows Live Movie Maker has been simplified to make it easier for you to produce videos. This chapter will only focus on the Windows Live Movie Maker.

FIGURE 6.1 The original Movie Maker. This is not Windows Live Movie Maker.

NOTE *Windows Live Movie Maker requires Windows Vista or later. It is not supported on earlier versions of Windows.*

The Windows Live Movie Maker Workspace

When you first pull up Windows Live Movie Maker, you will see a very simple interface, as shown in Figure 6.2. In fact, its streamlined interface couldn't be much simpler.

You'll notice in the interface a number of areas that will be referenced later in this chapter. This includes the menus, the storyboard, the preview area, and more.

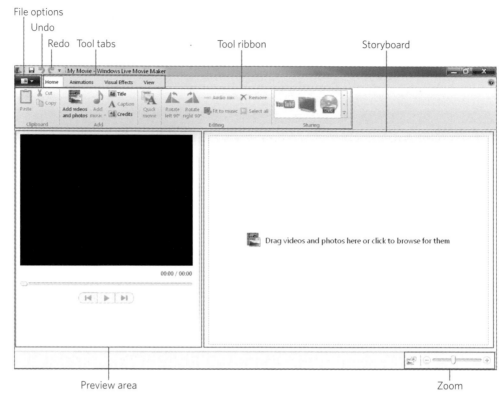

FIGURE 6.2 The streamlined Windows Live Movie Maker

Getting Content for Movie Maker

In order to make a movie, you will need to start with video clips or images. You can pull these directly into Windows Live Movie Maker from a digital device or you can pull items that are on your machine. In this section, you will see how to pull content into Windows Live Movie Maker so that you can then manipulate it and produce a video. You'll first see how to pull in items from your machine, and then you'll learn to pull them from devices. In later sections, you will learn how to manipulate these items.

SUPPORTED GRAPHIC FILE TYPES IN WINDOWS LIVE MOVIE MAKER

Windows Live Movie Makers supports a number of file types. This includes the following:

- ▶ Windows Media Video (.wmv)
- ▶ Unprotected Windows Media Files (.asf, .wm)
- ▶ AVI files (.avi)
- ▶ Microsoft Recorded TV Show files* (.dvr-ms)

- ▶ MPEG-2 Movie Files* (.mpeg, .mpg, .mpe, .m1v, .mp2, .mpv2.mod, .vob)
- ▶ Bitmap (.bmp)
- ▶ Graphics Interchange Format (.gif)
- ▶ Joint Photographic Experts Group (.jpg and .jpeg)
- ▶ Portable Network Graphics (.png)
- ▶ Tagged Image File Format (.tif, .tiff)
- ▶ HD Photo (.wdp)

*Not supported on all operating systems.

Adding Video and Photos from Your Computer

If you have videos or pictures on your machine or your local network, you can use them within any new video productions you create. The process to add an item to a production is the same whether it is a video you are adding or an image.

To add an item, select the Add videos and photos icon on the left side of the tool ribbon. This will open the Add Videos and Photos dialog window that you can use to select video and picture items to add to your movie. Figure 6.3 shows the dialog as seen in Windows 7 with a number of folders and files available. This is a standard Windows Explorer dialog that you can use to navigate to any of the folders on your computer or network. Because it is a standard Windows dialog, if you are using Windows Vista, then the dialog will appear slightly different, but most of the functionality will be the same.

To add the item, first click on the item. This will put the item's name into the file-name entry box. You can then select the Open button to add it to your movie. You can actually select more than one file at a time by holding down the Control button while clicking on selections.

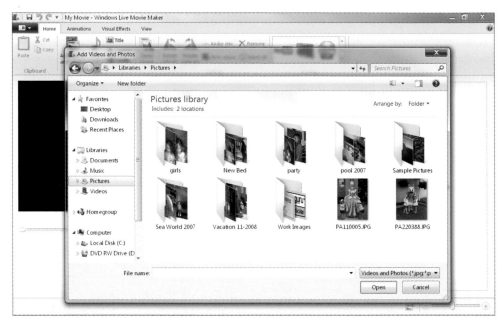

FIGURE 6.3 Selecting videos and pictures to use in your movie

Once you've opened and added the item, it will be placed into Windows Live Movie Maker. Figure 6.4 shows a single video clip added.

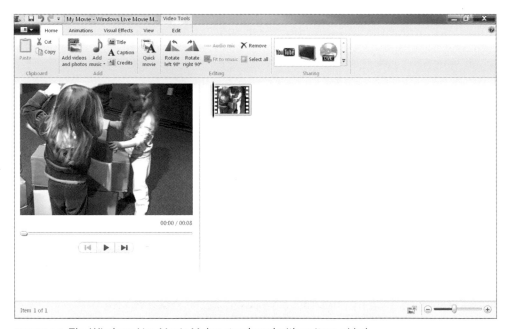

FIGURE 6.4 The Windows Live Movie Maker storyboard with an item added

As you can see, the preview area shows the start of the video clip. An icon of the clip is added into the storyboard area as well. You can continue to add additional items by selecting the Add button again. Each new item will be added after the others in the storyboard. Figure 6.5 shows Windows Live Movie Maker with several clips and photos added.

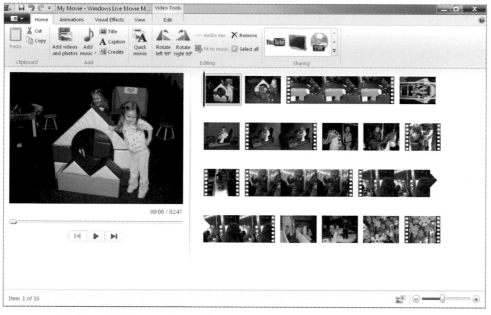

FIGURE 6.5 Windows Live Movie Maker with several items added

> **TIP** *You might want to add an item more than once. This will put the item into your movie more than once, but as you'll find out later, there are reasons to do this. For example, if you want to place a few photos in the middle of a movie clip, then add the movie clip, add the photos, and then add the movie clip again. Later you'll see how to then trim the two movie clips to show the first part and the last part.*

Limiting Selections in the Add Movies and Photos Dialog

Within the dialog for adding videos and photos, you can limit what is displayed to just videos or just images. You can also choose to show all files. This is done with the drop-down list in the dialog as shown in Figure 6.6. Again, this is shown for Windows 7; however, the same functionality is available in Windows Vista.

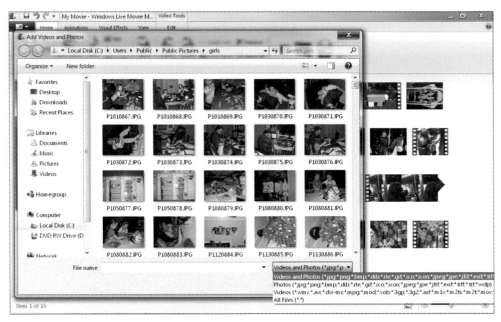

FIGURE 6.6 Changing what is displayed in the dialog to add videos and photos

Showing a Preview in the Add Movies and Photos Dialog

While you can adjust the Add Movie and Photo dialog to show different-sized icons and display information, in Windows 7 you can also show a preview of a selected item. To show a preview in the Windows 7 dialog, simply click the Preview Pane button shown in Figure 6.7. The preview lets you see a larger view of an image or it lets you play a video that is selected.

For videos, you can actually play the video directly in the dialog by pressing the Play button, or you can choose to open the video in Windows Media Player. Either way, it lets you see the video without having to add it to your movie production first.

You can turn off the preview by clicking the Preview Pane button a second time.

Removing Items from the Storyboard

Once you've added items to Windows Live Movie Maker, their icons are added to the storyboard. At this point, they will be part of your movie. If you decide you don't want a picture or a photo in your movie, you can remove it.

Show and Hide Preview Page

FIGURE 6.7 Previewing photos and videos before adding them

There are three ways to remove an item. You can click on an icon of an item in the storyboard to select it. Once you select it, you can click on the Remove icon to remove it.

Remove

You can also simply press the Delete key on your keyboard, and a selected item will be removed. The third way to remove an item is to right-click on the icon and select Remove from the menu that is displayed, as shown in Figure 6.8.

FIGURE 6.8 The menu from right-clicking a storyboard item

It is important to note that when you added an item to the storyboard, you did not do anything to the original item. In the same way, when you delete an item from your storyboard, you are also not doing anything to the original item. It still resides on your computer or network in the same location it was in before using Windows Live Movie Maker. If you remove something by mistake, you can simply add it back from its original location.

NOTE *When you remove the item from the storyboard, you are not removing it from its original location. The item still exists; it is simply no longer a part of your movie.*

Previewing Your Movie

At this point, you are likely curious to see what you've created. In truth, what you've created is not a huge production if all you've done is add raw clips or videos. Never fear, Windows Live Movie Maker can change all that, as you'll learn later in this chapter. Regardless, you'll likely want to see what you've created to this point.

NOTE *When you inserted a photo, it was given a duration for which it will be displayed. In essence that will allow a video to be displayed in your movie rather than simply flashing by too quickly to be noticed.*

You can preview what is in your storyboard at any time. As you saw in Figure 6.2, the left side of the Windows Live Movie Maker is the preview panel. This contains the movie you are building. The preview panel also contains a time line for the current video or picture as well as buttons for playing the clip. At any time, you can click the play button (the triangle that points to the right) to play your movie. To play the movie from the beginning, you should click on the first icon in the storyboard and then click the play button. Alternately, you can drag the slider on the play bar to the left with your mouse (see Figure 6.9) to the beginning (left side). You an also press the Spacebar to play the movie.

One other benefit of the preview panel can be seen in Figure 6.9. The preview panel tells you the total time of your movie based on the current items you've added. In the figure, you can see that my movie is currently two minutes and eighteen seconds long. If you are trying to limit the size of your movie, then you can keep an eye on the time as you make adjustments to your video. Such adjustments can be trimming videos as well as setting how long photos are displayed.

Start of movie · Previous frame · Play/ Pause · Next frame · Current location in movie · Total length of movie

FIGURE 6.9 The play bar for previewing your video

When you press the Play button, the preview will begin, and the Play button will change to a Pause button. Additionally, if you watch within the storyboard area, you will see a black bar moving through the icons. This black bar shows you the current location being played in your movie.

There are two other controls in the preview pane. These are the arrows with the lines next to them. While you might expect these to take you to the beginning or end of the movie, that is not what they do. They actually take you to the next frame or previous frame within the movie. This gives you the control to see exactly what is happening in your movie frame by frame.

Arranging Movie Clips

When you add an item to Windows Live Movie Maker, it will be inserted to the right of the current position within the movie. The current position is marked by the black bar that moves through the movie as it is playing. While this is nice, there are times when you end up adding something to the wrong location or there are times when you simply want to rearrange your items.

To rearrange the clips and photos in your storyboard, simply use your mouse to drag them to the location where you want them. You'll know where the item will be placed from the vertical line that is displayed, as shown in Figure 6.10.

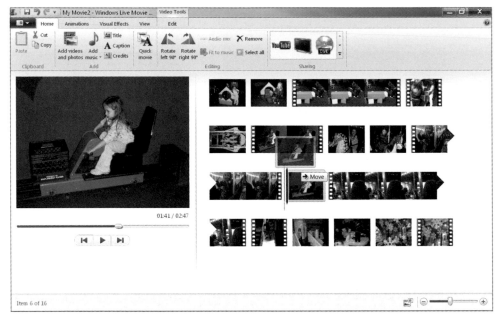

FIGURE 6.10 Dragging an item to a new location

You can also cut or copy items and paste them elsewhere as well. You can do this using the following steps:

Step 1: Select the item and right-click to show a pop-up menu (as was shown in Figure 6.8).

Step 2: Select the option to either cut or copy. Cutting will move the item, Copying will create a duplicate in the new location.

Step 3: Select any other item in the storyboard. The item you are cutting or copying will be placed after the item you select. To place it at the beginning of the movie, you'll need to drag the item and drop it there.

Step 4: Right-click to present the pop-up menu.

Step 5: Select Paste from the pop-up menu.

Windows Live Movie Maker and Windows Live Photo Gallery

At this point, you've seen how to add items to the storyboard, how to arrange them in the order you want, and how to remove the items you don't want. This gives you the basis for producing a video. You still need to manipulate the items on your storyboard to make them flow; you might also want to manipulate background information or even add effects. Before covering these features, it is worth mentioning one other way to add items to Windows Live Movie Maker.

In Chapter 5, you learned how to manipulate images, photos, and even videos on your computer. From Windows Live Photo Gallery, you can add items directly to Windows Live Movie Maker. You do this by selecting the items in Windows Live Photo Gallery. Once the items are selected, choose Make a Movie from the Make menu, as shown in Figure 6.11.

> **NOTE** *If you already have Windows Live Movie Maker open, then when you select Make a Movie from Windows Live Photo Gallery, the items will be added to the end of your existing movie.*

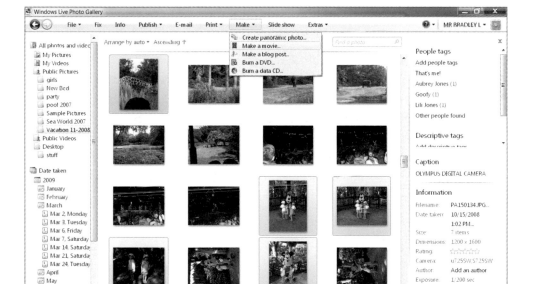

FIGURE 6.11 Adding items to Windows Live Movie Maker from Windows Live Photo Gallery

Getting Movies from a Camcorder

Of course, your raw video footage most likely started in a camcorder, digital camera, or cell phone. While it would be great to directly import videos from your device into Windows Live Movie Maker, this is unfortunately not supported. Rather, you will need to import them from your device to the computer and then import those files.

 Windows Live Movie Maker does, however, make this easy by including an option on the file menu for importing videos onto your computer. You can select Import from device from the File menu to start the Windows import functionality. This will import the video into Windows Live Photo Gallery. You can then use the video files as you would any other video file on your computer.

 NOTE *You can also use Windows Live Photo Gallery for importing files from devices to your computer.*

Movies versus Movie Projects

If you've added a bunch of items to Windows Live Movie Maker, then you will probably want to save your work. Windows Live Movie Maker can save your work as a movie project. A movie project is not the same thing as a movie.

A project is not a file that you can give to others to really watch. Rather, it is what Windows Live Movie Maker stores to keep track of your storyboard, the videos, the photos, the images, the music, the text, the transitions, the effects, and all the things you've done with all of these pieces in Windows Live Movie Maker. You can use the project to generate an actual movie file that you can give to others. You'll learn how to generate movie files later in this chapter.

 To save your storyboard as a project file, select Save from the File menu. This will present you with a dialog similar to Figure 6.12. Note that this is the dialog from Windows 7. In Windows Vista, this will be slightly different.

Enter a name for your project in the File name entry box, then click the Save button. Windows Live Movie Maker will save your project file. This is a standard save dialog, so you can use it to save your file in another location if you want.

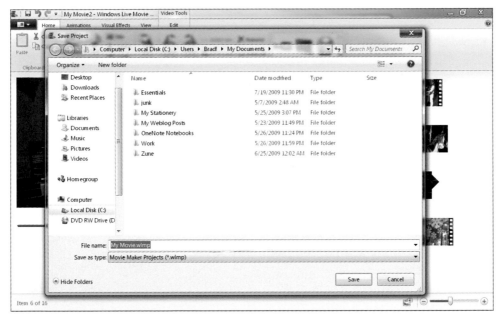

FIGURE 6.12 The Save Project dialog window for saving your project

NOTE *Windows Live Movie Maker files are stored with a file extension of* .wlmp.

Spicing Up Your Movie

Once you have videos and images added to your movie project, you are well on your way to creating your movie production. You still, however, will want to clip and trim some of your raw footage. You might also want to add transitions, effects, a soundtrack, and much more. The following sections will walk you through the options Windows Live Movie Maker offers that will help you to spice up your movie.

Trimming Scenes

One of the common errors people make when creating a movie—especially a home movie—is to use video clips that are too long. You will often make something much more entertaining if you keep your video clips short. Many times, the raw video clips you have can go on for long periods of time. Even 15-second clips from a cell phone can seem long if it is something repetitive or if it has even just a few seconds where nothing is happening.

Windows Live Movie Maker provides tools for allowing you to trim or edit the length of your video clips. You can choose to trim any of the video clips you've added to your movie project. You can cut the beginning, end, or both ends of your clips.

When you trim a clip, be aware that you are not affecting the original video file that is stored on your computer. Rather, Windows Live Movie Maker simply keeps track of the changes you've made to the video clip within the application. This means that if you decide that you want to add back footage that you cut, you can.

To trim a video clip, start by selecting the video clip you want to trim on the storyboard. Once the item is selected, click on the Edit tab near the top of Windows Live Movie Maker. This will show the Edit tool ribbon and its options as shown in Figure 6.13. You'll see the trim options within the Video section of the ribbon. You'll also see the Split option, which also comes in handy when trying to trim video clips.

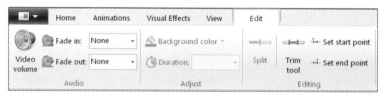

FIGURE 6.13 The Edit tool ribbon options

 The easiest way to trim a video clip is to start by selecting the Trim tool icon. Once the Trim tool icon is clicked, the preview pane of Windows Live Movie Maker will change, as will the items displayed in the Edit tool ribbon, as shown in Figure 6.14.

Under the video preview image is a play bar that contains a handle on each end. You can use the mouse to drag these handles. Dragging the handle on the left will move the starting point of the video clip farther into the video. Dragging the handle on the end of the play line (on the right side), will clip the end of the video. You can choose to move both handles or only one. You can also adjust the starting and ending point by changing the values on the toolbar. You can use the up and down arrows to the right of the time in the Start point and End point boxes, or you can type in a value of your own.

 Once you've adjusted the handles or times, you can click the play icon to preview the trimmed clip. You can continue to adjust and play the video clip as much as you want.

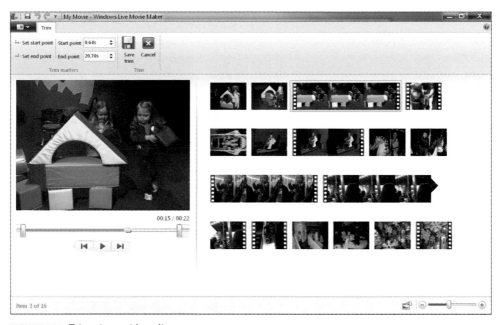

FIGURE 6.14 Trimming a video clip

TIP *You should also notice that in addition to the Play button, you also have the previous and next frame buttons. Therefore, you can snip a video down to a single frame if you want! Of course, a single frame video will fly by quickly in your movie!*

Once you have trimmed the clip as you want, you should click the Save Trim and close icon in the ribbon at the top. This will save your trim settings and return you to the standard storyboard. If you decide you don't want to trim the item, you can click the Cancel icon instead.

WARNING *If you click on an item in the storyboard, you will leave the Trim options and lose any changes you have made but not saved.*

Once you have saved your trimmed clip, you will be returned to the storyboard. If you look closely, you'll see that your total movie time will be adjusted in the preview to reflect the fact that you just clipped a video.

If you want to remove a section from the middle of a single video clip, there is an easy solution. Simply split the video into two separate pieces and then trim the end of the first piece and the beginning of the second piece. To split a video, select it in the main storyboard. Then press the play button in the preview window to start playing the clip. Play the clip until you get to the point where you want to clip the video. At that point, press the pause button to stop the playback. You can then click on the Split icon in the Edit toolbar. This will break the current clip into two separate pieces at the point where you paused.

In Figure 6.15, you can see that I've split one of the clips. You can see this in the top line if you compare the storyboard in Figure 6.14 to the one in Figure 6.15. With the split video, you can now trim the beginnings and ends of both pieces. The splitting allows me to rearrange the video into the order I want as well as to add transitions between pieces of the raw video.

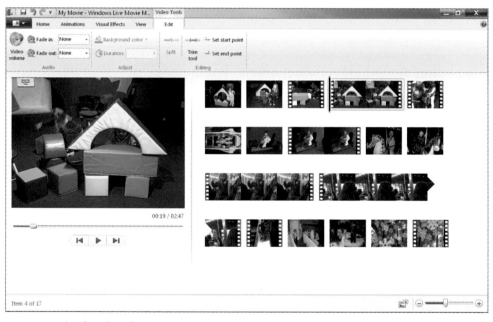

FIGURE 6.15 A split video clip

TIP *While watching your kids do goofy stuff for 10 or 15 minutes might entertain you, most other people will be bored after just a minute or two. You should take this into consideration if you are creating videos for others. Lots of shorter clips that transition from one to another can often be more entertaining to others. You'd be surprised at how much you can show with just a few seconds of video. Reducing vacation video down to 10 or 15 minutes of highlights will likely be more entertaining than the hours of raw footage and possibly hundreds of photos you likely captured. If you can get it down to five minutes, then you might actually get your family to watch the whole thing!*

Adding Transition Effects to a Movie

If you have more than one item in your storyboard, then there is a good chance that you will want to add a transition between the items in order to make your movie flow smoother. Windows Live Movie Maker provides several transitions you can place between scenes and photos. These transitions are available for you to place between any two items in your storyboard.

The transitions that are available can be found on the Animations tab in Windows Live Movie Maker. When you select this tab, you will find Transitions as well as panning and zooming options, as shown in Figure 6.16.

FIGURE 6.16 The Animations ribbon

As you can see in the ribbon, there are a number of options for transitions. These options can be used to add a transition between any two items in your storyboard. To add the transition, do the following:

Step 1: Decide which two items you want to set a transition between.

Step 2: Click on the second of the two items to select the item.

Step 3: Click on the Animations tab in Windows Live Movie Maker to display the Transitions options, as shown in Figure 6.16.

Step 4: Click on the transition effect that you want to place between the two items. Alternatively, you can select the first transition icon to remove the transition between the two items. There are a lot more transitions than what is shown in Figure 6.16. You can actually click the arrows on the right to show more of the transitions.

At this point, you will have added the transition. If you want, you can also adjust how long the transition will take to occur. This can be set in the Duration box to the right of the transitions. In general, you might want to speed up the duration by picking a different value from the drop-down list.

You can preview transitions as you are adding them. The preview will start with the prior item in the storyboard. You can preview the transition by using the preview area and playing your video, or you can simply hover over a transition icon in the toolbar to automatically see the preview of that transition. Figure 6.17 shows you the wide variety of transitions you can choose to use. The easiest way to see what they do is to apply them and preview the video.

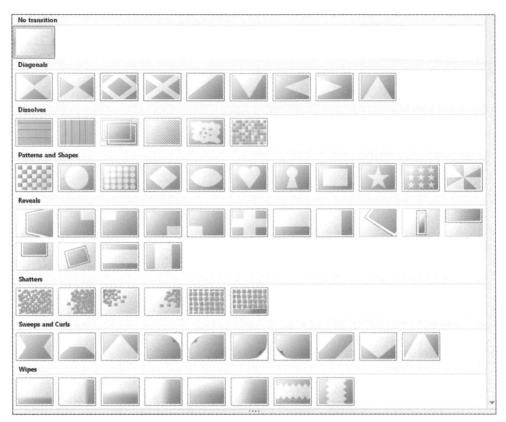

FIGURE 6.17 The standard transition choices

If you would like to add a transition to all the items at once, you can select all the items in your storyboard and then click the icon for the transition you want to apply. This will apply the transition before each of the selected items.

TIP *To select all the items in the storyboard, you can click in one corner and drag the mouse cursor to the other corner of the storyboard. Other ways to select all the items are to press Ctrl+A or right-click on a blank area of the storyboard and choose Select All from the pop-up menu.*

Adding Panning and Zooming

Transitions help make the change from one item in your storyboard to another happen smoothly and in a more animated manner. This can give your movie character. Another type of animation that can really give your movie a much more professional feel is the addition of panning and zooming to any photos or still images you've added to your movie.

Generally, a photo in your movie is simply displayed for a given period of time. Unlike a video, there is no movement in a picture, so the image would simply appear. You can, however, give the appearance of movement to a still picture by panning across the image or by zooming in or out of the image.

To add panning or zooming, click on the Animation tab as you did for transitions. On the Animation tab (which was shown in Figure 6.16), you can see that there are Pan and zoom options on the right side. If you click on an image in your storyboard, the Pan and zoom options will become active. You can hover over the icons on the toolbar to see what they will do to your image. You can also click on the arrows to the right of the icons shown in the toolbar to see even more pan and zoom options, as shown in Figure 6.18.

> **NOTE** *If you select a video in the storyboard, the Pan and zoom options won't be accessible. They only apply to photos and still images.*

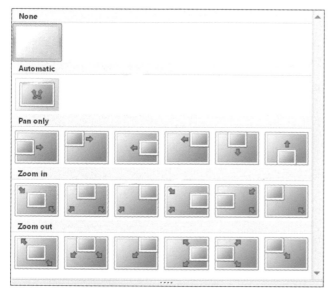

FIGURE 6.18 Pan and zoom options

Adding Visual Effects

Transitions are added between items in your storyboard. Panning and zooming give photos movement. Another option you have for spicing up your videos is effects. Effects can be added to a video clip or picture in your storyboard in order to change their appearance or to add odd visual effects—as its name implies!

Effects change the appearance of the item in your movie. This can be by adding warping and movement to the item, or by messing with the color palette that is used. You can dither an item, you can fade it to a color such as black or white, you can add ripples, you can view it in sepia, or you can do a variety of other cool things.

You can access the visual effects options by selecting the Visual Effects tab. This will display the Visual Effects toolbar, as shown in Figure 6.19.

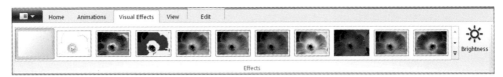

FIGURE 6.19 The Visual Effects toolbar

An effect can be applied to any of the items in your movie. To apply an effect, select the item in the storyboard, and then click on the effect in the Visual Effects ribbon. To remove the effect, click the No effect item from the Visual Effects ribbon. Figure 6.20 shows the default effects available in Windows Live Movie Maker.

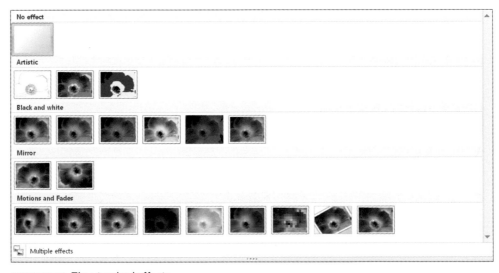

FIGURE 6.20 The standard effects

As with transitions, to add a single effect to all of the items in your storyboard, simply select all of the items and then click the effect to apply. You can select all of the items by either using the mouse, by pressing Ctrl+A, or by right-clicking on an open spot in the storyboard and choosing Select All. Of course, you can also select multiple items by holding down the Ctrl key while clicking each item.

> **TIP** *One neat effect to add to photos in your movie is to place two copies of the photo together. On the first photo apply one of the effects such as black and white or sepia. Between the two photos add a crossfade transition. The result is that you end up with color fading in your photo.*

You can add multiple visual effects to an item as well. To do this, click on the More arrow to the right of the displayed effects in the toolbar. This will display a drop-down list showing more icons of the different visual effects. At the bottom of the drop-down will be a Multiple Effects option that you can click. This will open the Add or Remove Effects dialog shown in Figure 6.21.

FIGURE 6.21 The Add or Remove Effects dialog

From this dialog, you can click on items on the left to select them. Clicking the Add button will then shift them to the right side of the dialog and thus include the effect. If you add something by mistake, you can click on it in the right side to select it, then click the Remove button to take it off. Once you've selected all of the effects you want to add, you can click the Apply button to add them to the item in your movie.

You'll also notice that there are Move Up and Move Down buttons that you can use. This will allow you to change the order that effects are applied to the item. Do be forewarned that if you add conflicting effects, generally the top effect will be applied. For example, an item can't be both black & white and sepia.

TIP *Double-clicking on an item in either list within the Add or Remove Effects dialog will cause the item to shift to the other list (thus removing or adding it without needing to click the buttons in the middle)!*

TIP *There is also a brightness option on the Visual Effects toolbar. You can use this to lighten videos or images.*

Manipulating Photo and Picture Timing

You've added videos and pictures to your storyboard and thus to your movie. Up to this point, however, all of the pictures or photos you've added are displayed for the same amount of time. There are times when you might want to move quickly through a bunch of pictures, and there are times when you might want to take a little extra time on a picture.

You adjust the timing by selecting the image or images that you want to affect. You then select the Edit tab at the top of Windows Live Movie Maker, as was shown in Figure 6.13.

To adjust the timing, you can adjust the value for Duration. You can enter a new value directly into the Duration box or you can use the drop-down list to display possible duration values, as shown in Figure 6.22.

The value displayed is in seconds, so 5.00 would be five seconds. You can enter values that are different than those in the list. You can also enter longer amounts than what is displayed in the drop-down; however, you should consider that looking at a single picture for more than 30 seconds can become rather boring within a movie!

NOTE *You can hover over an item in the storyboard to get information about its duration, whether it has been clipped, and more. The information will be displayed in a pop-up like the following:*

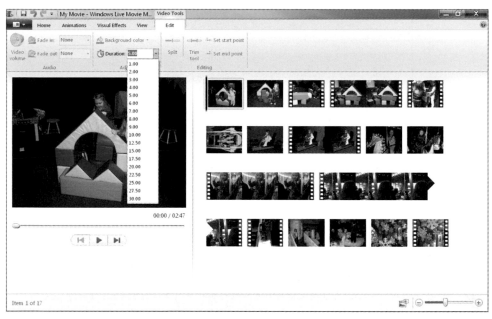

FIGURE 6.22 Selecting a value for Duration (in seconds)

Adding a Title and Credits

At this point, your movie should be starting to come together. Of course, to add some finishing touches, you'll likely want to add a title to the beginning of your movie and credits to the end.

Movie Maker provides you a way to add a title to the beginning of your movie, credits at the end, and even to add text on top of any item within your storyboard. Not only can you add text, but you can also adjust its font, color, size, and whether it is bold or italicized.

To add text, you can choose either Title, Caption, or Credits from the Home tab. The Title option will add a text box before the current item in the storyboard. The Caption option will add text that will display on top of the current item. The Credits option will add a text box to the end of your movie.

There are a few options that are the same regardless of which type of text element you decide to add to your movie. For example, when you add a text element, then a new tab will be displayed in Windows Live Movie Maker that will show Text tool formatting options. This toolbar is shown in Figure 6.23

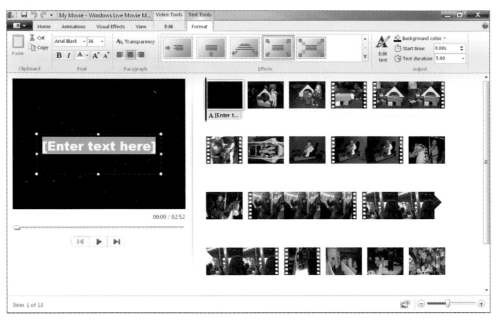

FIGURE 6.23 The Text Tools Format tab and toolbar

As you can see in this toolbar, there are options for setting the font style, size, color, justification, and more. These are the same standard text formatting options and tools you see in most Windows programs that work with text. There is also a Transparency option that will set whether the text is solid or whether the background will show through. If you click on the transparency option, a slide control will be displayed that will allow you to adjust the level.

Other controls for text include the ability to indicate when within the current item the text should be displayed as well as how long it should be displayed. For example, you can set the Start time to 1.00 seconds from the beginning of the item, and you can have it last for 3.00 seconds. If this is a title or credit text item that would normally last five seconds, then you would see the blank background for a second, the text would appear for three seconds, and then for the last second, the background would be blank again. If this were a caption, then the text would appear over the background photo or video for the time settings you select.

NOTE *The Start time is the time from the beginning of the movie, not the time from the beginning of the current element. When you first select to add a text item, the start time will initially be set to the start time of that element. If you want to wait until the element has played for a second, then simply add 1.00 to the initial Start time displayed.*

The other option you have when showing text is an effects setting. When using text effects, the text is manipulated. Effects include scrolling, zooming, or flying across the screen. Figure 6.24 shows the options listed when you click the More area for the text effects on the Edit toolbar. You can select any of these to control how your text is displayed or moved while it is on the screen.

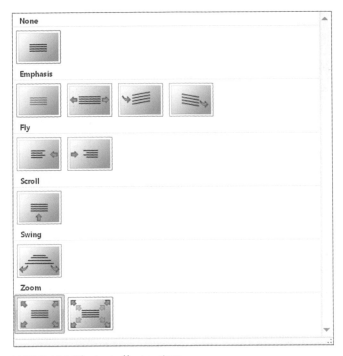

FIGURE 6.24 The text effect options

If you add a text item and then move to a different item in your storyboard before actually adding the text, then it might seem like you are unable to find where the text is located when looking at the preview window. You can get back to the text by first clicking on the storyboard item, then clicking in the preview pane to show the editable text, or you can click on the Edit text icon. Either way, you will then be able to see and edit either the placeholder text, or the last text you entered. In Figure 6.25, you can see that text is being added to a caption. You can also see that the color, font, and other settings have been adjusted.

Once you've added a text item to your movie, you will be able to see it in the storyboard. Windows Live Movie Maker adds a text indicator under the storyboard item. You can see in Figure 6.25 the pinkish text bar in the storyboard.

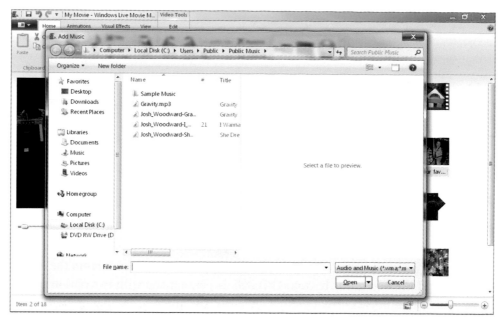

FIGURE 6.26 Adding a music or sound file

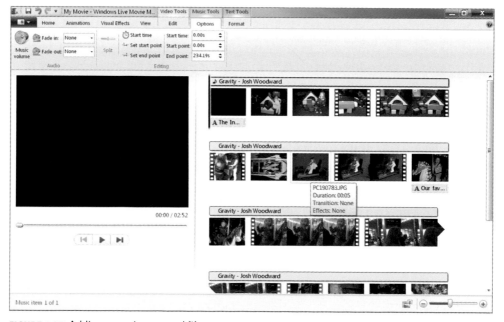

FIGURE 6.27 Adding a music or sound file

Muting Clips

When you add a sound clip, it will play on top of the audio within a video clip. Thus, you could end up with two different soundtracks competing with each other. One of your options is to mute the sound that was originally within your video clip. Whereas you can only apply one music file and it applies to your entire movie, you can control the muting of video clips individually within your project.

To mute a video clip, you can use the following steps:

Step 1: Select the video clip in the storyboard that you want to mute.

Step 2: Click the Edit Tab

Step 3: From the Edit Tab's ribbon, select the Video volume button within the Audio section. This will display a slider. Move the slider all the way to the left to mute the video clip. To unmute the video clip, do the same thing, but move the slider all the way to the right.

> **TIP** *Instead of muting a video clip, you can adjust its volume up or down. This will allow you to compensate if you have video clips that have varying sound levels.*

Mixing Sound

Windows Live Movie Maker comes with a Mixer. The Mixer allows you to set a balance between the audio within all of the video clips of your project (as a group) as opposed to the audio files you have added to your movie. If you turn up the sound on your audio file, it will turn down the sound on your video clips. If you turn up the sound on your video clips, it turns down the sound on your audio file.

Step 1: Select the Home Tab near the top of Windows Live Movie Maker.

Step 2: Within the Home tab's ribbon, select the Audio Mix button in the Editing section. This will display the Mixer control:

Step 3: Adjust the slider within the Mixer control to determine whether the video clip's audio or the added sound file gets priority for sound. Slide it toward the video icon to give the sound in your video clips higher priority. Slide it toward the musical note icon to give your soundtrack file more priority.

> **TIP** *If you only want to hear the soundtrack file, move the slider all the way to the right toward the musical note icon.*

Getting Music to Fit the Movie

If you are lucky, the length of your soundtrack will fit the length of your movie. Of course, it is rare you'll be that lucky. If the movie you are creating is composed entirely of pictures, then Windows Live Movie Maker will adjust the duration that each picture is displayed so that it fits the length of your audio file. This only works if your movie is entirely composed of pictures. If you have any video clips in your movie, then you will not be able to use the Fit feature in Windows Live Movie Maker.

To fit your photos to fit the audio file, select the Home tab. On the Home tab, click the Fit to Music button in the Soundtrack area of the displayed ribbon. Each of the images will have their durations adjusted so that they end when the sound file ends.

Creating Movies Automatically

Up to this point, you have learned how to create a movie and how to set up each aspect of it. Windows Live Movie Maker can actually make creating a movie much easier. This is with the Auto movie option.

You still need to add your images and video clips to the movie as you were shown how to do earlier. Once you've added these, you can click the Auto movie icon on the Home tab's toolbar. You will be given a prompt asking if you want Movie Maker to make a movie for you quickly. If you click OK, then transitions, fades, and other effects will automatically be added to your storyboard. Music, if it has been added, will also be adjusted within your movie. If you've not added any music files, you will be asked if you want to add a file. Finally, the movie will be updated in your storyboard, and you'll be on your way. You can simply use the features that were automatically added, or you can begin to adjust them as you learned how to do earlier in this chapter!

Publishing and Sharing a Movie

At this point, you've seen how to enter video clips and pictures, you've seen how to add a soundtrack, and you've seen how to modify settings for your movie including mixing sounds and setting durations. You've seen how to add text to items in your storyboard to add a title and possibly credits. At this point, you should be able to create a complete movie. If you use the preview, you can even watch your completed movie.

It would be wise to save your final movie project as shown earlier. More importantly, you might want to generate a movie file that you can share with others. While you could share your Windows Live Movie Maker project file that would require the people you share with to have Windows Live Movie Maker installed. That is not really the right way to share a movie. Rather, it makes a lot more sense to create a movie file you can share with others that they can use on their own computer or DVD player.

You can produce a movie file to store on your computer for your own use, a file you can copy to a DVD for others to use in a DVD player, or a file that gets copied to a digital device, or even a file you can upload to an Internet video service like YouTube. In the following sections, you'll see how to produce a movie file for each of these instances.

> **NOTE** *In Movie Maker, publishing a movie indicates generating a movie file that is then placed in a location on the Internet where people can access it. This would include YouTube and similar sites. Sharing a movie refers to creating a file that others can access and use. You learn more about both of these in the following sections.*

Setting Your Movie's Aspect Ratio

Before jumping into how to share or publish your movie, it is important to consider your movie's aspect ratio. In a world of widescreen televisions and computer monitors, it makes sense that we should cover aspect ratios for the movies you generate. Windows Live Movie Maker gives you the ability to select between standard 4:3 ratio and widescreen 16:9 ratio. If you have standard ratio clips, then black bars will be added to the right and left sides if you choose to use widescreen.

To set the aspect ratio, you can go the View tab and select the Aspect ratio icon as shown in Figure 6.28. This will display two options: one for standard and one for widescreen. Your storyboard icons will change to reflect your choice.

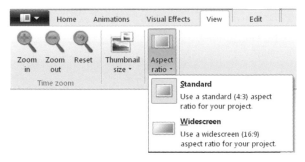

FIGURE 6.28 Setting your movie's aspect ratio

Publishing to Your Computer

The easiest thing to do to produce a movie is to save a movie file to your local computer. Publishing a movie file to your local computer is the same as saving a movie file to your local computer. Once it is on your computer, you can use a program like Windows Media Player to watch your movie.

Unlike a Windows Live Movie Maker project file, the movie file you generate will be a single file that contains everything about your movie. You'll also be able to share that one file.

To produce a movie file on your computer, you can proceed in one of two ways. You can click on the File icon and choose Save movie or you can click on the Home tab, which contains options for Sharing. If you use the Sharing options, you can click on the More and select the Output option in the Make Movie section on the tool ribbon. This will give you options for publishing your movie, as shown in Figure 6.29.

FIGURE 6.29 Options on tool ribbon for Sharing (creating) movie files

To publish a movie to your machine that is similar to what you'd watch on a standard television, select the icon for standard definition. Alternatively, you can select one of the high-definition resolutions or one of the lower-definition resolutions that are good for mobile devices or sending in emails.

In most of these cases, you will be creating a Windows Media video (.wmv). When you click on one of the icons in Figure 6.29 or on the Save movie menu, you will be prompted to enter a filename for your movie. Enter a filename and click the save button to start generating a movie. As the movie generates, a dialog as shown in Figure 6.30 will be displayed to show you the current status of the generation.

FIGURE 6.30 The status of generating a movie

Once the generation has completed, a dialog similar to Figure 6.31 will be displayed. You can choose one of three options. You can choose to open the file to play it in your default movie program. You can also choose to view the folder where the file was generated. If you wanted to share the file, then you could open the folder and then copy it from there. Your third option is to simply close the message and go back to working in Windows Live Movie Maker.

FIGURE 6.31 The status showing the movie is completed

Publishing to a Mobile Device

In addition to creating a standard movie file, you can also generate a movie file that can be used on mobile devices such as iPods and Zunes. Generally, the movie files used on these devices use a smaller resolution (screen size) than a standard movie file. Additionally, these movies are smaller in size than a standard movie file.

 To generate a movie file of the right size for these devices, you'll follow the same process as you did to create a movie on your computer with one exception—you'll choose For portable device or mobile phone (.wmv) from the Output options. Once you've generated the file, you can then follow the instructions from your portable device to transfer your generated movie file to the device.

Copying a Movie to DVD

 Windows Live Movie Maker will also integrate with Windows DVD Maker to allow you to generate a DVD. To do this, select the option to burn your movie to DVD. When you select this option, you will generate a movie file just like what was shown in the previous section; however, after the movie is generated, Windows DVD Maker will open with the saved movie file, as shown in Figure 6.32.

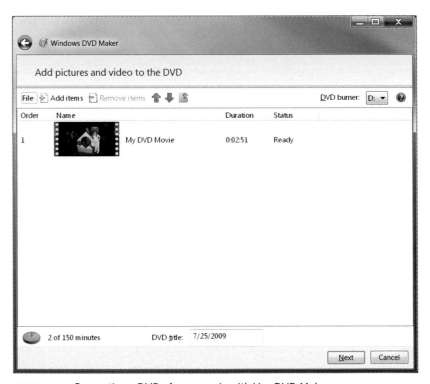

FIGURE 6.32 Generating a DVD of your movie with Live DVD Maker

Clicking Next in Windows DVD Maker will walk you through generating a DVD. In the next screen within Windows DVD Maker, you can create a menu or simply progress to burning the DVD by clicking the Burn button. This will begin the process of creating the DVD as shown in Figure 6.33.

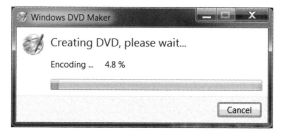

FIGURE 6.33 Burning a DVD with Windows DVD Maker

NOTE *There is a lot more to using Windows DVD Maker. Check your Windows help to learn more about this program.*

WARNING *If your video contains family members, especially children, you should use caution before making it public. Often names are spoken and a lot of other personal information can be given in a family video. This personal information can be used for identity theft or other bad things.*

Publishing to YouTube

Of course, the most popular site today to post a video to is YouTube. To post a video to YouTube, you can generate a file to your disk, as shown previously, and then use the YouTube site to upload the file.

Alternatively, you can choose the YouTube icon from the Sharing options on the Home tab ribbon or you can select Publish movie → Publish to YouTube from the File menu. This will start the process of publishing to YouTube. The first step will be for you to log in to YouTube using the presented dialog, as shown in Figure 6.34.

FIGURE 6.34 Logging in to YouTube

After logging in to YouTube through Movie Maker, you will be prompted as shown in Figure 6.35 to enter information about your movie, including a title, description, descriptive tags, a category, and a permissions level. Once you've entered all the information, click the Publish button to save the movie to YouTube. It will take a bit of time to save and publish it. Status bars will be shown so that you know how much progress has been made.

FIGURE 6.35 Entering information into YouTube

NOTE *The more that you do in your movie and the longer your movie is, the longer it will take to produce and publish your movie.*

WARNING *You can't publish a movie to YouTube if you are not connected to the Internet!*

STORYBOARD VIEW OPTIONS

If you begin making a movie with lots of items on the storyboard, then you might find it hard to see everything. Windows Live Movie Maker provides you with a few options to adjust how things on the storyboard are presented. This includes the ability to zoom in and out from a time perspective as well as to changing the size of the icons presented. You can make these changes on the View menu. Specifically, you can zoom into or out of the storyboard. Zooming in allows you to see more details on what is happening in your storyboard. Zooming out reduces what you see but allows you to see more on your screen.

You can also choose the Thumbnail size icon on the View toolbar to adjust the size of the icons presented in the storyboard. You can adjust them from extra small to extra large. Again, this is just a way to see more details on your clips or to see more clips. For example, as shown in Figure 6.36, adjusting to Extra large icons, let's you see the details of your clips better.

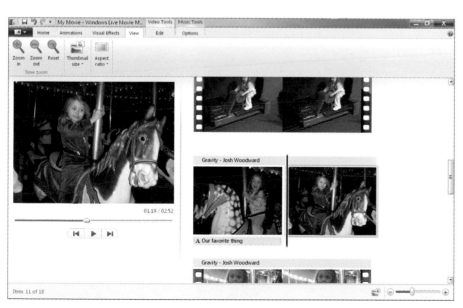

FIGURE 6.36 Using Extra large icons for the storyboard

Using Windows Live Movie Maker Add-Ins

Want to post your movie to Facebook, Flickr, Drupal Publisher, or a variety of other services? Then you can either generate a movie as shown earlier and use those services to upload the movie, or as was possible with YouTube, you can add a plug-in to Movie Maker that helps make the process easier. Add-ins can also make a variety of other uploading and other tasks easier as well.

 To add on an add-in, go to the Home tab and select Add a plug-in from the bottom of the More menu for Sharing. You will need to be connected to the Internet, as this will launch a web page with a list of plug-ins that are available. You'll be able to click on any of the plug-ins to begin the process of obtaining and installing them.

Because each plug-in can be different, it is beyond the scope of this chapter to explain each one. You'll need to follow the instructions on the web site to see what is necessary to install each.

In Conclusion

In this chapter, you learned about Windows Live Movie Maker. You saw how to import videos and pictures into Windows Live Movie Maker. Once they were imported, you learned how to add transitions, effects, sound, and other features so as to turn your clips into a full-fledged movie production. You wrapped up the chapter by learning how to produce and share your productions both online and off.

CHAPTER 7

Organizing with Windows Live Calendar

IN THIS CHAPTER, YOU WILL:

▶ Learn about Microsoft's Windows Live Calendar versus Windows Calendar

▶ Discover different views to look at a calendar

▶ See how to work with more than one calendar

▶ Learn how to schedule meetings, appointments, and events on your calendar

▶ Examine how to set up and use reminders

▶ Print your schedule or calendar

WINDOWS MAKES it is easy to use a calendar to keep track of appointments, meetings, events, or even birthdays. Not only can you track events and special occasions, but you can also track items that you need to do and keep track of your schedule. Even more interesting, you can set up multiple calendars to keep track of different things. You can have a calendar for your work events and a different one for your personal events. You can view the calendars individually or in combination. If you have an Internet connection, then you can also share your calendar with others by using the online Windows Live Calendar service, which makes it easy to coordinate schedules and more.

Using Windows Live Calendar and Windows Calendar

There are two calendar programs that are part of the Windows Live Applications and Services that you can use. This chapter will primarily focus on the Windows Calendar, which is a part of the Windows Live Mail program in the Windows Live Downloads. The other calendar program is the Windows Live Calendar that is a part of the online Windows Live Service you can use while connected to the Internet. Figure 7.1 shows these two calendars.

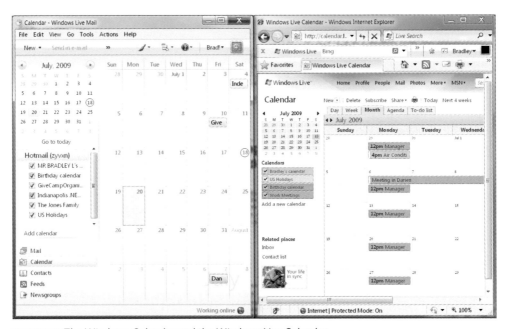

FIGURE 7.1 The Windows Calendar and the Windows Live Calendar

While there are two different calendar programs, you can actually synchronize these two calendars so that you can use either one and still have all your appointments and events in both programs.

To use the Windows Calendar on your computer without needing to be on the Internet, you should install Windows Live Mail as a part of the Windows Live Applications, as shown in Chapter 1. Because Windows Calendar is a part of the Windows Live Mail program, you can get to it by running Windows Live Mail from your computer's Start menu. Once the mail program is running, you will see an option on the lower left side for selecting the Calendar. Click on the Calendar option, and you will see a calendar similar to what is shown on the left side of Figure 7.1.

If you want to use the Windows Live Calendar service on the Internet, you can go to `calendar.live.com` and sign in with your Windows Live ID. Once you sign in, you'll see a calendar similar to what is shown on the right side of Figure 7.1.

While these are two separate calendars, if you log in to both with the same Windows Live ID, then the events and calendars within them will automatically be synchronized. You do, however, have to sign in with the same Windows Live ID for this to work.

> NOTE *In most of this chapter, the focus is on the calendar that is a part of Windows Live Mail that you can download, as shown in Chapter 1. Most of the features, however, will operate similarly on both the local and the online calendars.*

Viewing Calendars

The first time you display the calendar in Windows Live Mail, it will appear similarly to what is shown in Figure 7.2. This is a simple calendar view with few things listed on it.

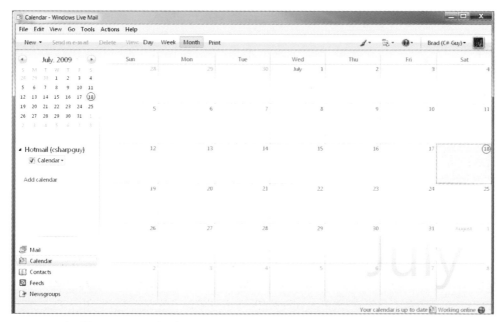

FIGURE 7.2 Looking at a new calendar

While you can begin working with a calendar immediately, you should go ahead and log in to your Windows Live ID. You can log in by clicking the Sign In option in the upper-right corner. You'll be prompted to enter your Windows Live ID and password. This will then display any calendars associated with your account. When you are signed in, your ID will be shown in the upper right. It will also be shown on the left side above your calendars. You can see in Figure 7.1 that the Windows Live Essentials ID is logged into Windows Live Mail. When you log in, you'll see your own ID.

Checking Day, Week, and Month Views

By default, you see the monthly calendar. You can actually change the view to make it easier to see details. You can switch between a Day, Week, and Month view. The easiest way to change the view is to click on Day, Week, or Month in the toolbar across the top of the calendar. Figure 7.2 shows the Month view. Figure 7.3 shows the Day and Week views.

FIGURE 7.3 The Day and Week calendar views

You can also change the views by selecting Day, Week, or Month from the View menu. There are keyboard shortcut keys for each, too. You can press Ctrl+Alt+1 for the Day view, Ctrl+Alt+2 for the Week view, or Ctrl+Alt+3 for the Month view.

Customizing Your Calendars

When you first start working with Windows Live Mail's calendar, you'll likely have a generic calendar similar to what you see in Figure 7.3. You can customize this calendar with a new name, color scheme, or description. To do so, click on the name of the calendar in the list of calendars on the left side. This will display a menu of options, as shown in Figure 7.4.

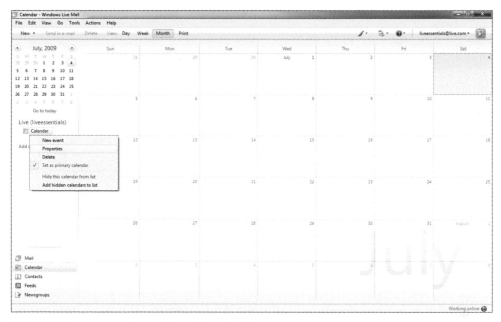

FIGURE 7.4 Pop-up menu for working with a calendar

Select Properties from the menu. This will display the dialog shown in Figure 7.5. You'll then be able to customize the calendar. You can enter a new name in the Calendar name. You can also enter a description for the calendar. In between these two are a number of colored squares. Clicking on one of the colored squares will assign that color to the calendar. This color will be used to identify the calendar and its events. If you create or use more than one calendar, then you'll be able to assign a different color to each in order to tell them apart

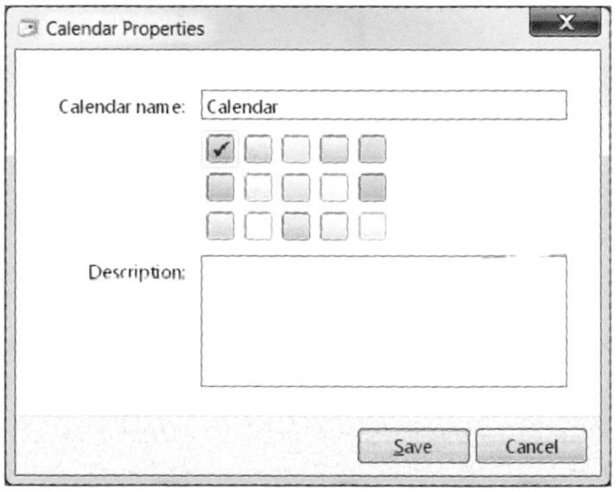

FIGURE 7.5 Setting calendar properties

TIP *The name of a calendar is used to select, display, and hide a calendar, so you should create one that is descriptive. As you'll learn in the next section, you can actually create and use several calendars at once.*

Creating New Calendars

You can create new calendars for tracking different things. For example, you can have a personal calendar and a work calendar. You can set up a separate calendar for birthdays as well. The Windows Live Calendar will allow you to select which calendars you want to display. You can even show multiple calendars at the same time. As you learned in the previous section, you'll be able to tell events and appointments apart in your different calendars based on the color you associate to the calendar.

To create a new calendar, you can simply click on the Add calendar link in the left pane. Alternatively, you can select New → Calendar from the toolbar. In addition to these two, you can use the File menu option and select New → Calendar from there. Before the calendar is created, you'll be prompted as shown in Figure 7.6 to provide some information.

TIP *You can also create a new calendar by pressing Ctrl+Shift+D.*

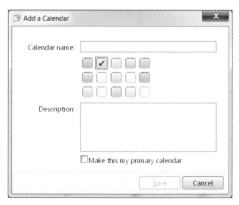

FIGURE 7.6 Creating a new calendar

As you can see, the information necessary for creating a new calendar is nearly the same as what you saw in Figure 7.5 when setting properties. You can enter a title, select a color, and enter a description. You also can determine whether this is your primary calendar. The primary calendar is the calendar that will be used by default when you add events. Once you've set the information, you can click the Save button to create the calendar.

The new calendar will then be listed in the left pane with your other calendars. If you check the box to the left of the calendar, then its events will be displayed. If you uncheck the box, then that calendar's events will be hidden.

You can also choose to hide the calendar from the list of calendars by clicking on its name and selecting Hide this calendar from list. When you hide a calendar, you also hide it events. You can redisplay hidden calendars by clicking on the name of one of the other calendars and selecting Add hidden calendars to list. You can also add hidden calendars back by selecting Add hidden calendars to list from the Windows Live Mail's View menu.

Working with Events

A calendar is nice if you want to know what day it is, but an electronic calendar becomes more valuable when you start adding events. Events can be meetings, people's birthdays, holidays, vacations, or anything else that you want to remember or keep track of on a calendar. You can add events to any of your calendars.

Adding Events

You can add an event in a number of ways. The following are all ways you can add a new event:

- ▶ Right-click on a date within the calendar. Select New event from the menu that is displayed.
- ▶ Select New → Event from the toolbar.
- ▶ Select the File menu and then go to New → Event.
- ▶ Click Ctrl+Shift+E.
- ▶ Click on one of your calendars in left pane. Display New event from the menu that is displayed.

Regardless of the manner in which you choose to create a new event, you will be prompted to enter information for your event, as shown in Figure 7.7. Depending on how you selected to add the event, some values might already be selected. For example, if you used the first option of right-clicking on a date to add an event, then that date will be entered into the dialog shown.

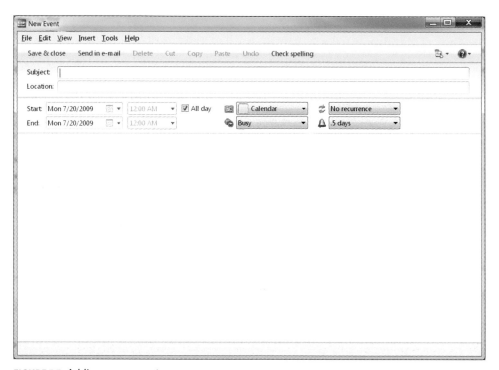

FIGURE 7.7 Adding a new event

There is a lot of information that can be entered for an event. The Subject is the information that will be displayed on the calendar. This should identify the event. The more descriptive, the better; however, you'll want to keep this relatively short since it will be displayed on the calendar. Location is free-form text for where the event will be located. You don't have to enter a location.

If an event is going to last all day, you can check the All day box. If it is not all day, then you'll want to make sure the All day box is unchecked. Once you uncheck the All day box, you'll be able to select a start and stop date and time for your event. You can schedule events that last no length of time at all to events that go across days.

In addition to setting the time, there are several other options for your event. You can set which calendar to add your new event. Unless you selected to add an event to a specific calendar, then the defaulted calendar will be listed.

> **NOTE** *The default calendar can be changed by right-clicking on a calendar in the left pane when in the calendar view. On calendars you control, you'll be able to select an option from the pop-up menu, called Set as default calendar. This will make the calendar the default when adding events.*

Not all events require that the time covered be blocked. For example, a birthday happens, but it does not preclude you from doing other things as well. To account for this, you can set a status for how an event will use your time. You can set the status to Busy, Free, Tentative, or Away. The status will determine how your availability will appear to others who you allow to view your calendar. Busy will let others know that you are unlikely to be available for other tasks or events. Free indicates that, although something is scheduled, you are likely to be available for something else. Tentative indicates that you are busy but might have time for something else as well. Away indicates that you are not likely to be at your computer at that time and, thus, are unlikely to be available.

If you want a reminder that you have an event about to happen, then you can set a reminder time. You can set a reminder from the actual time the event starts (0 minutes) or up to two weeks before the event. You can also choose to set no reminder.

If you do set a reminder, you'll need to be signed into Windows Live Mail in order to get the reminder. Additionally, you'll need to have set up Windows Live Mail Alerts. Setting up the alerts is covered later in this chapter. When you get an alert, it can be as an instant message, a message sent to your phone, or simply as an email, as shown in Figure 7.8.

The remaining item that you can set is recurrence. If a meeting can happen more than once, then rather than entering it into your calendar multiple times, you can set it to reoccur. For example, a birthday reoccurs every year on the same day, you might have a meeting that occurs every week on the same day at the same time, or you might have a vacation that happens for several days in a row.

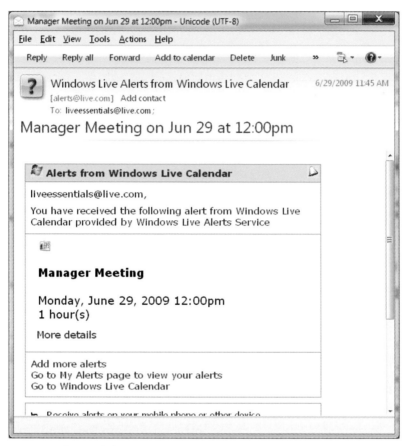

FIGURE 7.8 An email alert

Rather than entering each item separately, you can set values for recurrence. If you look at the list, you'll see a number of options, including:

- ▶ No recurrence
- ▶ Daily
- ▶ Every weekday
- ▶ Every Mon, Wed, Fri
- ▶ Every Tue, Thu
- ▶ Weekly
- ▶ Every 2 weeks
- ▶ Monthly

▶ Yearly

▶ Custom

If none of the regular options works for what you want to set, you can choose Custom. This will present a dialog where you can be more specific on when you want the events to occur and how many times.

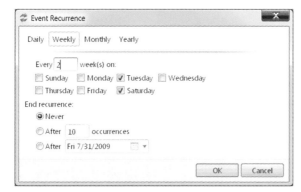

FIGURE 7.9 Event recurrence options

Below all the setting areas within the Event dialog shown in Figure 7.9 is a free-form area where you can enter any notes or comments about the event. Alternatively, you can leave the area blank. Either way, once all your values are entered, you can click Save and close on the toolbar to save the event and add it to your calendar.

Changing an Event

If you find you need to change something about an event, then you can simply open it and make changes. To open an event, double-click on it within the calendar. Alternatively, you can right-click on an event and select Open. Either way, the event will open, and you'll be able to change any of its values.

If the event is part of a series, then before it opens, you will be prompted with a dialog similar to Figure 7.10 asking if you want to edit the specific meeting you are opening, or if you want to edit the entire series.

Once you've opened an event to edit, you can make changes to any of the values in the same way you originally added them. Once done, simply choose to Save and close.

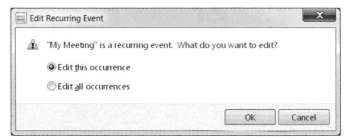

FIGURE 7.10 Editing a series

Deleting an Event

There may come a time when you want to delete an event from your calendar. To delete an event, click on it to select it. You can then press the delete key on your keyboard, or you can right-click on the event and select Delete from the pop-up menu.

> **WARNING** *Once you delete an event, it is gone. If you want it back, you'll need to create a new event, then recreate the values.*

Setting Up Reminders

In order to get reminders, you need to set up how you want to get them. This can be set up by selecting Tools → Deliver my reminders to… on the Calendar menus. This will launch Windows Live Alerts online.

You'll be prompted to set delivery on a web page to set where you want your reminders sent. As you can see in Figure 7.11, I have the option to have reminders sent to Messenger, via email, or to my mobile device. You can choose any or all of these options.

You can also select the Advanced delivery options link to get additional options for sending alert messages when you are, or are not, logged in to Windows Live. Once you've made your selections, click Save to continue. You'll be taken to a page to set calendar options, as shown in Figure 7.12. You can chose to change ay options on this page, or you can simply click Save to get back to your calendar. The options will be applied to all of your calendars both online and off.

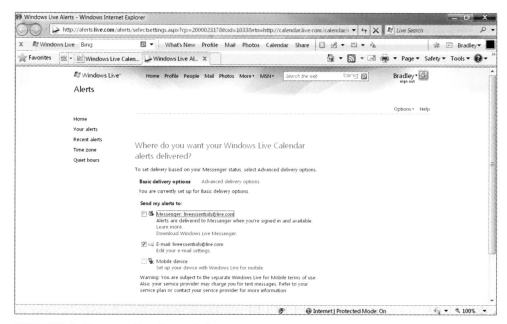

FIGURE 7.11 Setting up options for reminders

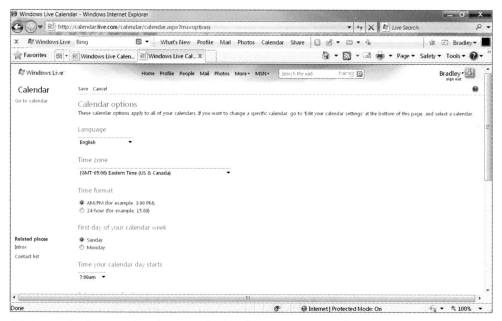

FIGURE 7.12 Setting up options for your calendar after setting up reminders

Once you've selected to Save the options, your calendars will then be set up to receive alerts.

Printing Your Calendar

Windows Live Mail gives you the ability to print out your Windows Live Calendars. You can choose to print a day, week, or month view. You can click on the Print option in the toolbar or you can choose Print… from the File menu. Either way, you will be prompted to print your calendar, as shown in Figure 7.13.

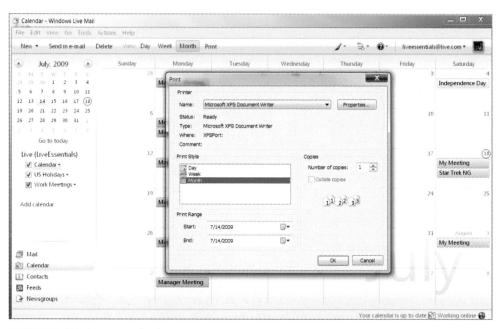

FIGURE 7.13 Printing your calendars

As you can see in Figure 7.13, in addition to setting whether you want to print Day, Week, or Month views, you can also set the date range that is printed on your calendar. Once you've selected the options to print, click OK to start printing. Figure 7.14 shows a printout of the Month view. As you can see, the printout is very similar to what is displayed in the calendar program.

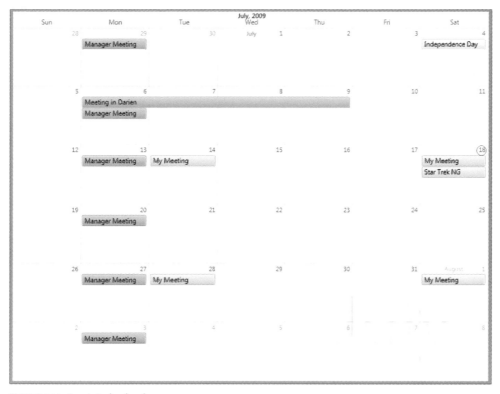

FIGURE 7.14 A printed calendar

Windows Live Calendar Online

At this point, you've learned most of the features of the Windows Calendar that are available on your local machine as a part of Windows Live Mail. There is also the Windows Live Calendar that is available online. The online calendar is similar to the offline calendar in many ways, but it contains a number of additional features as well.

It is worth noting again that if you sign in to the Windows Live Mail calendar with your Windows Live ID, then if you sign in to the online calendar with the same ID, your two calendars will be automatically synchronized together. In Figure 7.15, you can see the Windows Live Calendar that has been synchronized from the local calendar. To get to the online calendar, go to `calendar.live.com`, or go to `home.live.com` and select Calendar from the Windows Live menu.

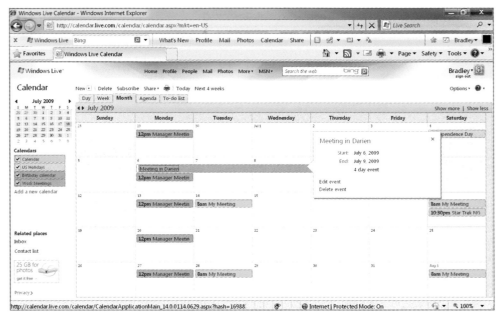

FIGURE 7.15 The Windows Live Calendar online

Adding calendars and events to the online calendar is very similar to using the local calendar. There are a few additional options for events such as the ability to add charms to events. Otherwise, the information is pretty much the same.

> **NOTE** *Charms are little graphics you can add to an event that will be displayed in the calendar. You can see the default list of charms in Figure 7.16. You can use these charms to make it easier to identify different types of events. If you use a charm on an event, only the charm will be displayed on the calendar instead of the event name. You can see that a charm was used for an event happening in the calendar shown in Figure 7.15.*

FIGURE 7.16 The default charm options

Another option you have with the online calendar is the ability to share your calendar. To share your calendar with others, from the online calendar, click on the Share option located right above the calendar. This will list your calendars. Click the one you want to share to select it.

This will then take you to the sharing options. When you click on the Share this calendar option, you'll see options as shown in Figure 7.17.

FIGURE 7.17 Sharing your online calendar

You'll be able to select the share options you want form this page. Depending on which option you select, additional details might be requested. For example, if you choose to share with friends and family, you can then choose to add the specific people that are allowed to share your calendar.

Once you've made your selections for sharing, click the Save button. If you decide you want to change the settings, simply go back to the Share options again and make your changes.

In Conclusion

In this chapter, you learned about the calendar features that are available to you in the Windows Live Mail application. You learned that this calendar automatically synchronizes with the online Windows Live Calendar as well. Using the calendar, you can schedule your meetings, events, birthdays, and other appointments. You learned not only how to schedule appointments but also how to organize them by using multiple calendars. Of course, you also will find reminders a valuable feature of the calendar program, as it allows you to know that you have an event about to happen. Finally, you learned how to print your calendars so that you can take your appointments with you.

Socializing with Windows Live Spaces

IN THIS CHAPTER, YOU WILL:

▶ Learn how to create and customize a Windows Live Space

▶ Add a blog

▶ Use email to publish to your Space

▶ Determine who can view your Space

▶ Set up communications preferences

▶ View statistics

▶ Develop an understanding of how to delete your Space

EVEN THOUGH the Internet is a huge place, you can carve out your own personal part of it with Windows Live Spaces. Spaces lets you build a personal web page that includes a variety of social features such as blogging, a guest book (similar to the wall in Facebook), photo sharing, and more. By integrating it with other Windows Live Essentials products and services, your new Space can become a key part of how you keep in touch with family and friends.

A Windows Live Space has two modes of operation. As the creator and owner of a Space, you can enable an edit mode where you can change the look-and-feel of your Space and add new content modules. How you decide to design your Space is completely a matter of your own personal style and interests. Visitors to your Space will see the published version of your site, and you can control if the site is open to the general public or to just people you decide can view it.

Creating and Customizing Your Space

Creating a Windows Live Space is a fairly straightforward process. To begin, locate the More menu (shown in Figure 8.1) on the top of any Windows Live web page. Click the menu and select Spaces from the list.

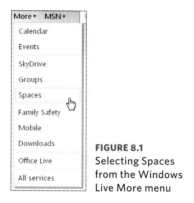

FIGURE 8.1
Selecting Spaces from the Windows Live More menu

Assuming that you haven't yet attempted to create a Space for your Windows Live ID, you will see an initial getting started page like the page depicted in Figure 8.2. Click on the Create your space link, and you're off and running.

FIGURE 8.2 Initial getting started web page for Spaces

The initial version of a Space created by Windows Live is fairly spartan. You can see an example of the start of a Space about this book in Figure 8.3. Windows Live starts your Space with a simple title and includes modules for your profile and your network, as well as a handy Welcome to your space module and some other links to get you going.

FIGURE 8.3 An example of a brand new Space

You'll notice that the web address for your newly created Space is an internally generated ID followed by .spaces.live.com. Since you'll most likely be sharing this site
with others, a friendlier name is probably in order. To create a web address, click the
Choose web address icon, and type in a name you prefer in the web page field shown
in Figure 8.4. Click the Check availability button to see if your name is unclaimed,
then click Save.

Choose web
address

FIGURE 8.4 Choosing a web address

WARNING *It's worth taking a few moments to decide what web address name you'd like to use here. Once you enter and save your web address, you can't change it later.*

Now the real fun begins. It's time to turn the pedestrian site that Windows Live initially created into something that matches your own style. Windows Live is prompting you to get started with some tips in the middle of the page. Click on the Customize your space link, and you'll see the options shown in Figure 8.5.

Customize (Use keyboard accessible version)
Choose from the options below. Drag modules to rearrange them.
Save Cancel

Modules   Themes   Layout   Advanced

FIGURE 8.5 Options for customizing your Space

 TIP *You can also access these customization options using the Customize menu (see Figure 8.8) near the top of your Windows Live Space.*

Adding Modules

You can work left-to-right across these customization options, starting with modules. Clicking on the Modules link will open up a tab and a list of available modules to add. Windows Live provides a wide variety of modules to use to get started, some of which you can see in Figure 8.6.

Try adding two of them by changing the view option from Hide to Show next to Guest Book (under Featured modules) and Weather (under Gadgets). Click the Close tab button, and you'll notice the new modules on your page with a reminder to also click the Save button (near the top of the page) to exit the edit mode of Spaces and save those new modules to your site. After saving, the Space you see is the same as what your visitors will see and should look similar to Figure 8.7.

 TIP *Check out the Windows Live Gallery (gallery.live.com) for other Spaces gadgets created by Microsoft and other developers.*

FIGURE 8.6 Adding modules

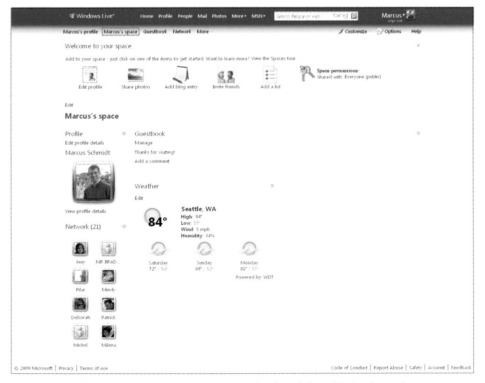

FIGURE 8.7 Updated Space with Weather and Guestbook modules added and saved

The Space is starting to take shape, but it might be nice to change things to make it a little more visually appealing. Windows Live includes some themes you can select, plus you can do more advanced look-and-feel changes (more on this later in the chapter). To return to edit mode, click the Customize menu (shown in Figure 8.8), and then click Change the theme.

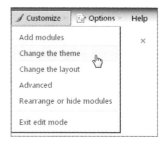

FIGURE 8.8 Customize menu

Since this Space is all about a book, the pencil-and-paper theme seems like a good choice and is reflected in Figure 8.9. What you pick is completely up to you, and you can change the theme at any time—for example, changing to a new theme for a new season like winter or summer. When you have the theme that you prefer selected, click the Close tab button and then click Save to exit edit mode.

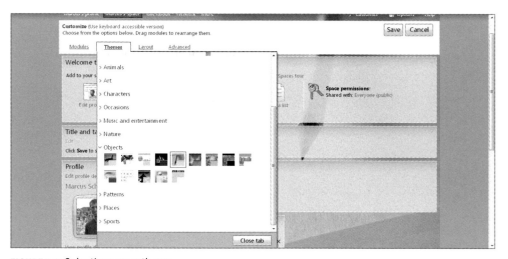

FIGURE 8.9 Selecting a new theme

Layout Customizations

The next customization option to explore is the overall layout for your Space. Click on the Customize menu, and then click Change the layout. Here you can select from a variety of layouts, much like you'd find in a magazine, newspaper, or another web site. In the example shown in Figure 8.10, the layout with two smaller columns and one larger column is used. Pick the layout that best matches the content you'll have on your site. If you plan to write a lot of text in a blog, you might want a layout with at least one wider column to make reading your blog posts easier.

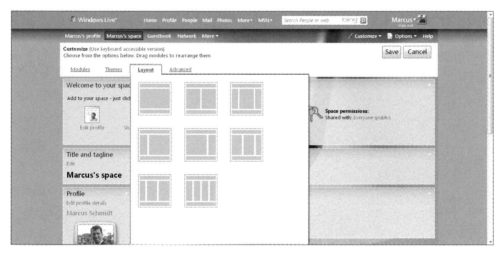

FIGURE 8.10 Selecting a layout

When you've finished picking a layout, click the Close tab button. Before you click Save, however, notice that you can drag and drop the modules around the page to get the right content in the right parts of your new layout. Simply left-click on a module, hold down the mouse button, and drag it to another part of the page. In Figure 8.11, the weather module has been moved to the right column, the profile and network in the right column, and the guestbook in the middle.

As you start to experiment with new layouts and modules, you'll find that some modules are better suited to some parts of different layouts.

> TIP *You can also quickly jump into rearranging and hiding modules by choosing the Rearrange or hide modules option under the Customize menu (see Figure 8.8).*

FIGURE 8.11 New layout after rearranging by dragging and dropping modules

There is a lot more that you can do to modify and customize your Space. Since you now know how to use the Customize menu, you can now hide the Welcome to your space module at the top of your page. Click on the down arrow in the upper-right corner of that module to reveal the module's menu, and then select Hide (see Figure 8.12).

FIGURE 8.12 Accessing the menu for a module, with options for configuring settings or hiding the module

Click Save to exit edit mode with all your new layout changes applied to the Space.

The finishing touch to any Space is the Title. As you may recall from earlier in this chapter, Windows Live provides you a starter title that includes your first name (e.g., Marcus's Space). Click on the Edit link in the upper-left corner of the title module, immediately above the current title, to make some changes in the dialog box that pops up, as shown in Figure 8.13.

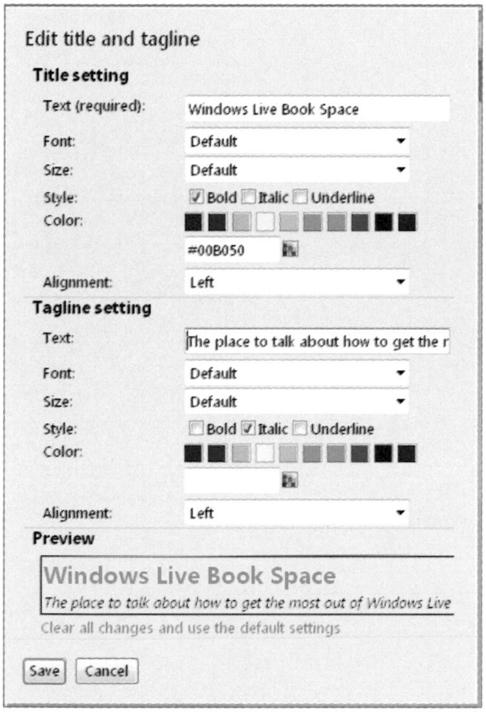

FIGURE 8.13 Editing the title of the Space

Not only can you edit the title itself, but you can also provide a tagline and customize the fonts and colors of the text. Everything is previewed at the bottom of your screen. When you like the changes you've made, click Save. You can also click the Clear all changes and use the default settings link in the preview area to revert back to the original titles, fonts, and colors. Figure 8.14 shows the updated version of the Space with the new title and tagline.

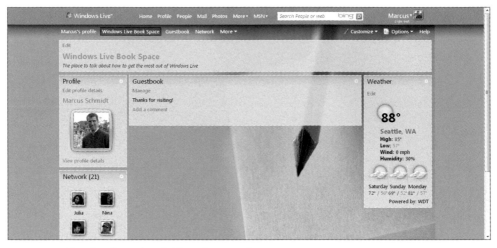

FIGURE 8.14 Showing the updated title and new tagline

Advanced Options

If you're ready to move beyond the confines of the colors, images, and fonts available in the built-in Spaces themes, it might be time to check out the Advanced options available under the Customize menu (see Figure 8.8). These options are under the fourth major link (or "tab") in Customize area you see when you're in edit mode (see Figure 8.5). The advanced options you can set include

▶ Text colors and fonts for standard text and hyperlinks (shown in Figure 8.15)

▶ Background colors for the page, body, selected, and hover

▶ Background images

▶ Colors and fonts for modules on the page

 You aren't limited to the standard color selections shown. Click on the Color picker icon to view a larger palette of options.

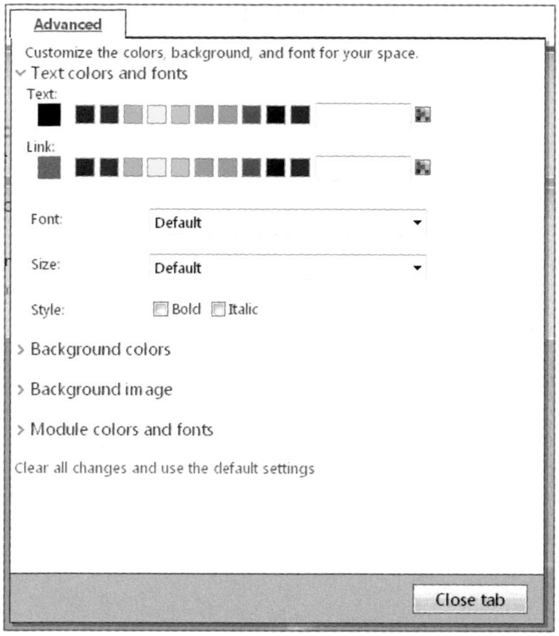

FIGURE 8.15 Setting up advanced options

Adding a Blog

Everyone can be an author when they become a blogger. Writing a blog (short for web log) is more commonly referred to as blogging, and the person doing the writing is the blogger. What do people blog about? Anything and everything. There are blogs about travel, food, pets, hobbies, politics, technology, and on and on.

When you're ready to start blogging, Windows Live Spaces provides an easy place to get started. A blog is simply another module within your Space. To enable it, click the Customize menu (see Figure 8.8), click Add modules, scroll to the Blog section of the module list, and click the show link next to the Blog module as depicted in Figure 8.16.

Then click the Close tab button followed by the Save button to exit edit mode with your new blog module added. Your Space should look similar to Figure 8.17.

FIGURE 8.16 Showing the blog module

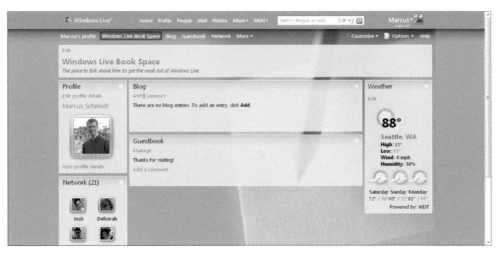

FIGURE 8.17 Updated Space with blog module showing

You can start blogging within Windows Live Spaces or you can use a specialized blogging application that is included with Windows Live Essentials, called Windows Live Writer. To learn more about Writer as a blogging tool, refer to Chapter 4.

Blog Entries

Click on the Add link in the Blog module to start a new blog entry. Figure 8.18 shows a new blog entry being created inside Spaces.

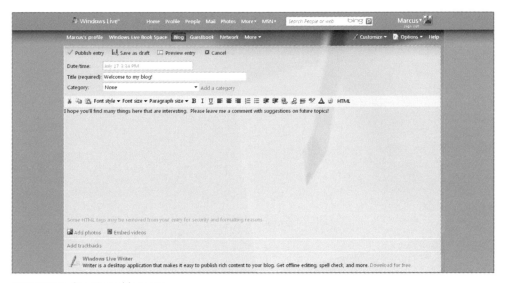

FIGURE 8.18 Creating a blog entry

Each blog entry requires a title and can be optionally assigned to a category, either one of the default categories supplied by Windows Live or one of your own (just click the Add a category link). The text of the blog entry has all the same editing tools found throughout Windows Live, including those for changing fonts, adding links, adding emoticons, and even doing HTML editing.

A picture or video can sometimes literally be worth a thousand words of blogging. Windows Live Spaces provides links at the bottom of the entry page to add Photos from your PC or online albums, or to embed video codes from popular video-sharing sites like YouTube.

When you're satisfied with your first blog post, click the Publish entry link at the top of the edit page. Alternatively, you can save the entry as a draft for later editing or preview the entry to see how it will look before publishing. Click Cancel if you want to abort this particular blog entry. The updated Space with a new blog entry is shown in Figure 8.19.

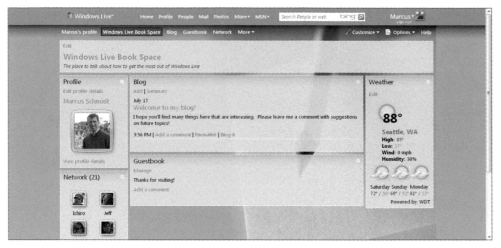

FIGURE 8.19 Updated Space with new blog entry

Use Email to Publish Entries to Your Space

If you want to keep your Space (and your friends and family) up to date while you're on the go, Windows Live provides a handy, but rather oddly named, feature known as email publishing. This capability allows you to publish blog entries and photos to your Space by sending them in email. This is especially useful when sending email from mobile devices like cellular phones. As you see something happening, you can quickly text a message that becomes a blog post or snap a photo to post to your Space.

Turn on email publishing by selecting the Options menu near the top of your Space (next to the Customize menu). Select E-mail publishing from the list of options, as shown in Figure 8.20.

FIGURE 8.20 Options menu

Begin by checking the Turn on e-mail publishing check box at the top of the page illustrated in Figure 8.21.

FIGURE 8.21 Setting up email publishing

After you have enabled publishing, you have five steps left:

1. Add the email addresses that you will be using to send in blog entries or photos. These can be email addresses associated with your mobile device (e.g., `4255554321@txt.att.net`) or any other email address.

2. Enter a secret word that will create an email address to publish to (e.g., `windowslivebook.secretword@spaces.live.com`). This is the where you'll send your blog posts or photos.

3. If you want photos to go into specific albums, you can create short secret words for those as well. These secret words are added to the secret word you selected in step 2 to create an address such as `windowslivebook.album1.secretword@spaces.live.com`.

4. Determine if you want to publish entries immediately or as drafts. It's recommended that you publish them as drafts, so you can later review, possibly edit, and then post them.

5. Jot down your new email addresses generated from the secret words you created in steps 2 and 3. Remember to keep these private.

 NOTE *Your mobile carrier may charge you fees for sending and receiving information. Contact your carrier for details.*

Determining Who Can View Your Space

The entire world might be a stage but you don't necessarily have to put your newly created Windows Live Space out into that world for all to see. It's up to you to decide if your Space is wide open to the public or restricted to being seen by only those people you select.

To configure the permissions for your Space, click on the Options menu (see Figure 8.20) and then select Permissions. By default, as shown in Figure 8.22, all new Spaces are shared with everyone. This means that these Spaces are publicly viewable by anyone, even if that visitor doesn't have a Windows Live ID or isn't signed in to Windows Live. To restrict permissions, uncheck the Everyone (public) box and select from the following:

▶ My Network (with the option to also include My extended network or the network of your friends and family)

▶ Categories of people (such as Favorites in Figure 8.22)

▶ Or individuals specified by email address, name, or selected from your contact list. Click the Select from your contact list link to show contacts to choose from, or start typing, and Windows Live will try to auto-complete a matching contact.

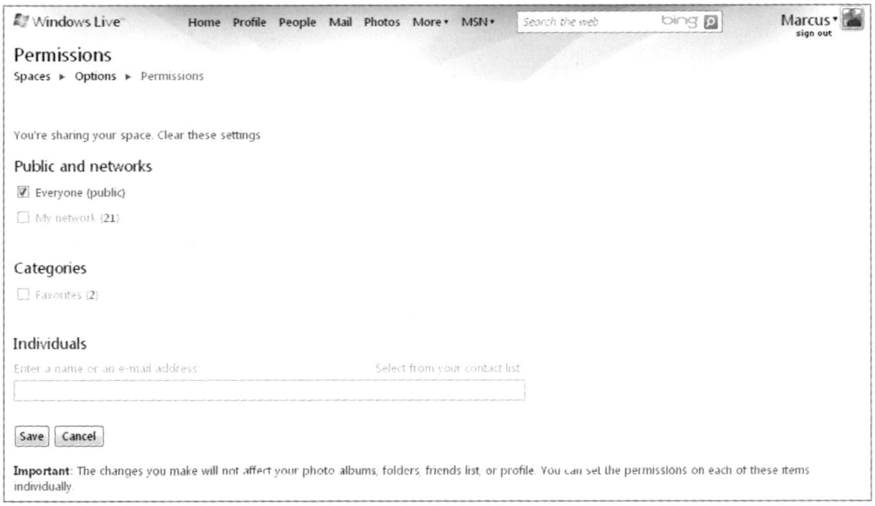

FIGURE 8.22 Setting up permissions

Setting Communications Preferences

After you optionally restrict access to your Space, you can control who (if anyone) can request access to view your Space. This communication setting is found along with the other Windows Live communication settings. Click on the Options menu (see Figure 8.20), then click More options, and finally click the Communication preferences link under Related options, shown in Figure 8.23.

The Spaces option is the second communication option listed on the Communication preferences page (see Figure 8.24), located between Network and Groups and events. Click on the drop-down list, and choose from the following for who can ask to view your secured Space:

▶ Anyone

▶ People in your network

▶ People in your extended network (the Windows Live network of your friends or family members)

▶ No one

Leave the check box enabled for email notification when you get these requests, or turn it off and manage the requests by returning to your Space and reviewing the requests there.

FIGURE 8.23 Main Spaces options page

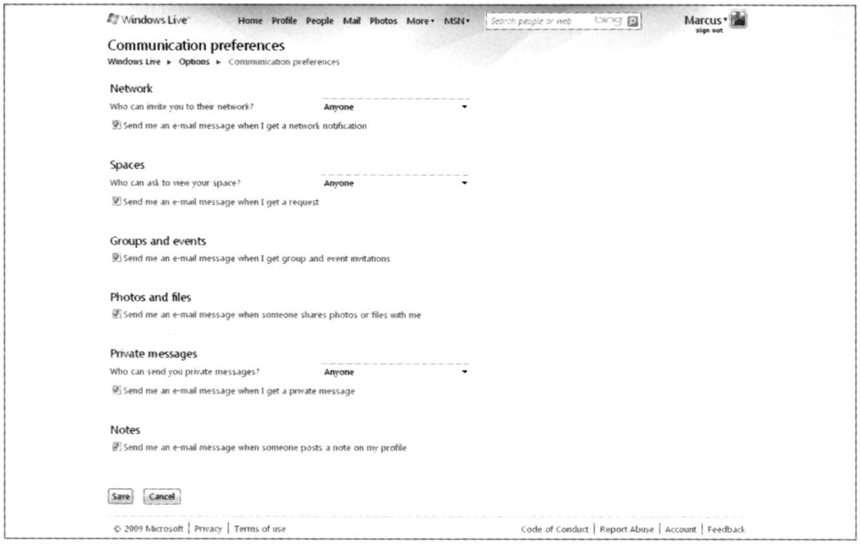

FIGURE 8.24 The communication preferences options for Windows Live

Viewing Statistics for Your Space

You've got a Space. You're blogging up a storm. But is anyone coming to visit your new corner of the Internet? Spaces has a relatively minimalist statistics feature that you can use to see how many page views your Space has received in total, plus how many views happened in the past hour, day, or week. You can see which pages were viewed along with any referring addresses. The referring addresses can be insightful to know if your Spaces content, especially blog posts, are getting picked up by search engines. Figure 8.25 shows a portion of a statistics page from a Space that has been around a little while.

To view the statistics for your Space, click on the Options menu (see Figure 8.20), and select Statistics.

FIGURE 8.25 Example of statistics

Deleting Your Space

Windows Live Spaces even has a "do over" feature that can delete your entire Space and get you started back on square one. If you ever find that you've overcustomized or tweaked your Space into a place where it would be easier to start over than trace back through all your steps, this is the button for you.

Click on the Options menu (see Figure 8.20) and select General to reveal the page shown in Figure 8.26. You'll see a few familiar items here, including those that give you the ability to edit your title and tagline, adjust the date and time format, and others. At the bottom of the page is the Delete your space button.

FIGURE 8.26 General options include the choice for deleting your Space.

WARNING *If you delete your Space, all your modules, customizations, guestbook entries, blog entries, lists, and web address will be deleted. Your core Windows Live profile, photos, files, and network will not be deleted.*

In Conclusion

In this chapter, you found out more about how Windows Live Spaces can be your own personal web site. You walked through the steps for creating and customizing your Space, as well as creating a blog within your Space. In digging into the options for Spaces, you explored how to use email to publish entries to Spaces and set permissions for viewing your space and communication preferences for requests to view your space. You also found out how to get statistics for the page views of your Space and, if needed, how to delete your Space and start anew.

CHAPTER 9

Interacting with Windows Live Groups

IN THIS CHAPTER, YOU WILL:

- ▶ Learn how to create a Windows Live group
- ▶ Manage membership
- ▶ Discuss topics of interest
- ▶ Configure group options
- ▶ Use email to contact the group
- ▶ Maintain a group calendar
- ▶ Add group photos and files
- ▶ Instant message with your group

WHEN YOU think about groups of people, what comes to mind? Perhaps it's your extended family. Or maybe it's your bowling league. How about your book club? It seems that everyone is a member of at least one group. Keeping those groups organized and the members in touch with one another can sometimes be a challenge. That's where Windows Live Groups can help.

Windows Live Groups provides an online place for your group to interact. Members can discuss topics, share a group calendar, and even store and share important files and photos. As part of the Windows Live product family, Windows Live Groups works together with other Windows Live Essentials applications and Windows Live Services.

Creating a Windows Live Group

Starting a new group in Windows Live is easy. Just sign-in with your Windows Live ID and then select the Groups option from the More menu at the top of any Windows Live web page, as shown in Figure 9.1.

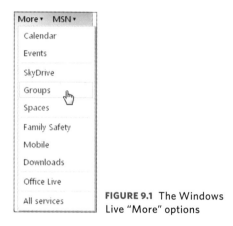

FIGURE 9.1 The Windows Live "More" options

Assuming that you aren't already a member of any groups, you will be taken to the initial page shown in Figure 9.2, which explains Windows Live Groups and includes the option for creating a new group of your own.

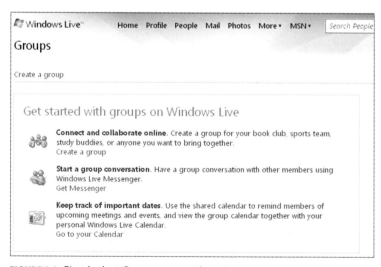

FIGURE 9.2 First look at Groups page with option to create a group

Click on the Create a group link, and you're ready to get started. As you think about the group you're creating you'll need to decide on:

▶ A name for your group

▶ A web address for your group

▶ Whether you want your group to be open for membership requests or by invitation only

▶ What sort of graphic theme you want for your group's web page

▶ Whether your group will have more than 20 members

You can enter all this information in the Create a group page. In the example shown in Figure 9.3, a group for book club members who love to read mystery novels is being created.

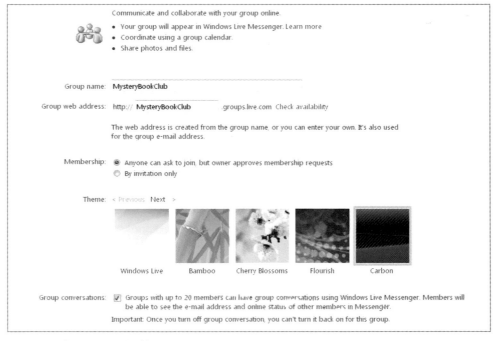

FIGURE 9.3 Options required for setting up a new group

Windows Live Groups will create a group web address based on your group's name. You'll be able to use this web address to directly access the group. Clicking on the Check availability link will tell you if that address is available. If it's not, or if you don't like what Windows Live has created, just type in a new name and check its availability as well before proceeding.

WARNING *If you want to use Windows Live Messenger to keep in touch with your group, it must have no more than 20 members and you must leave the group conversations check box turned on. If you turn this off, you can't turn it back on. Look later in this chapter for more on instant messaging and groups.*

Click the Create button and you'll be taken to the brand new web page for your group, shown in Figure 9.4. The example used here is for a book club for people who enjoy mystery novels.

FIGURE 9.4 New Group web page

NOTE *The web address you select will be used both for your group's web site as well as for the group's email address, as shown above.*

You'll notice the group has a membership of only one (you) and doesn't have a whole lot going on right now. In order to get things going, people will need to be invited to join.

Managing Membership

Groups aren't really groups without members. To invite people into your new group, just click on the Invite people link near the top of the page. You'll see an invitation form like the one shown in Figure 9.5.

FIGURE 9.5 Invitation form for a group

If you want to invite people who are already contacts in Windows Live, just click the To button and your contacts will be displayed. Pick the ones you'd like to invite. If your invitees aren't in your contact list, you can just type in their email addresses. You'll also want to include a brief (less than 300 characters) invitation message. Click Send and your group is well on its way.

The people you send invitations to don't have to have a Windows Live ID initially. They will be asked to sign in to accept the invitation, at which time they will be asked for a Windows Live ID. If they don't have one, they can sign up to get one. Anyone you invite will have to get a Windows Live ID to continue to participate in the group.

To continue to manage the membership of the group, click on the Membership link on the left side of the web page shown in Figure 9.4. This will display the Group membership page where you can invite more members, remove members, and change the role of members to make anyone a co-owner of the group.

TIP *It's often advantageous to have co-owners of a group to help maintain membership, moderate discussions, and manage other group requests.*

Discussions

One of the top features of Windows Live Groups is discussions. This is where you and the rest of your group can talk about anything you want. Everyone can stay up to date with the discussions as they appear in the What's new with your network section of your Windows Live Profile's home page. You and your members can also just stop by the group's web page and see what's being discussed without having to join the discussion.

To begin a new discussion, click on Start a discussion on the main web page of your group. You'll be shown a page similar to Figure 9.6, where you can title your discussion topic and provide the first entry for others to view.

FIGURE 9.6 Begin a discussion in your group

You have a lot of formatting control over your message. Use the fonts, layout, color, and emoticons, and even edit HTML to dress up your message as much as you'd like. You can also include links to other web sites using the Hyperlink icon.

Click Preview to look at your entry as others will see it, or click Publish to start the discussion going with this first entry. The discussion will be added to the discussion list, as you can see in Figure 9.7.

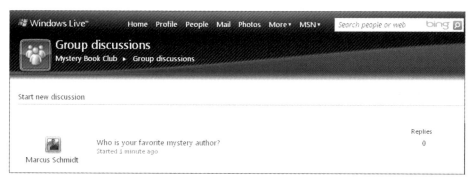

FIGURE 9.7 List of discussions in your group

Now any member of the group can click on the discussion title and add his or her own thoughts. They will be greeted by your initial entry (shown in Figure 9.8), with the options to Reply or Quote your original message in a reply. If the message is your own, you'll also see links to Edit the message or Delete it.

FIGURE 9.8 First message in the new discussion

Members of your group can start other discussions, and you can have several under-way at any one time. You'll see them all listed on the main web page of your group, shown in Figure 9.9.

FIGURE 9.9 Updated main web page for the group

Configuring Options

Now that your group is underway, you might want to adjust a few of the options Windows Live provides to make your group even better. To explore the options you have for your group, click on the Options menu link on the right side of the page, as shown in Figure 9.10, and then select Group options.

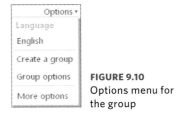

FIGURE 9.10
Options menu for
the group

Under Group options, you have six main categories to choose from:

> ▶ General
> ▶ E-mail

▶ Group Conversations

▶ Personal

▶ Leave group

▶ Delete group

Starting with General options (shown in Figure 9.11), you'll see many of the choices displayed here that you made when you first configured your group. However, there are a few more things you can set that customize the group a little more.

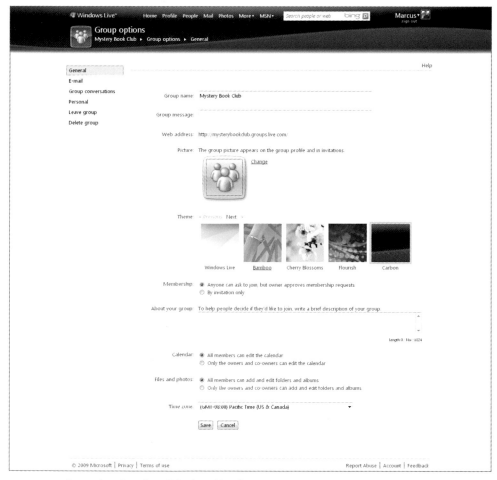

FIGURE 9.11 General options for a Windows Live Group

The new options you can set include adding a group message that will be displayed below your group name on your main web page, changing the group picture, describing more about your group, and setting permissions for both the group calendar and files/photos (more on each of these later in this chapter). The Mystery Book Club's options can be updated with a better group picture, a message, and a new theme. The updated web page for the group is shown in Figure 9.12.

FIGURE 9.12 Updated web page for the group

The General options contain the most choices for changing your group. But there are other options to consider as well. Here is a brief discussion of the other options you can set:

▶ **E-mail:** Turn group email on or off, as well as manage members who are either banned from sending group email or who are not receiving it because of delivery problems or if they have opted out of receiving it.

▶ **Group Conversations:** Enables you to turn off group conversations in Windows Live Messenger for groups of up to 20 members.

▶ **Personal:** Where you or any member can opt out of receiving email messages from the group.

▶ **Leave group:** Where you or any member can decide to leave the group,

▶ **Delete group:** Where you as a group owner can decide to delete the whole group.

WARNING *If you delete a group, all discussions, photos, files, and other information is permanently deleted. Your group is also removed from messenger and your group web address won't be available to be used again for 60 days.*

Email and Groups

As groups get larger and larger, it can be difficult to remember everyone's email addresses. With Windows Live Groups, however, you have one single email address to remember to contact everyone in the whole group. It's easy to remember the address. It's the same as your web address, followed by @groups.live.com. So, for the Mystery Book Club, the address would be MysteryBookClub@groups.live.com.

If you recall the group options discussed previously, any member of the group can decide to no longer receive group email. This option is set by clicking on the Personal link on the left side of the web page shown in Figure 9.11. The owner or owners of the group can see who has opted out of receiving group email by clicking on the E-mail link on the options page shown in Figure 9.11.

Group Calendars

Most groups not only like to gather online, but they also want to meet face to face. The calendar that is built into Windows Live Groups makes coordinating everyone's schedule much easier. The calendar used by Windows Live Groups has most of the same features as the personal calendar discussed in greater detail in Chapter 7.

To start using the calendar for your group, just click on the Calendar link on the left side of the main group web page (shown in Figure 9.12). Before you can begin using your calendar, however, Windows Live may ask you to set your time zone if you haven't already specified it as part of your previous use of Windows Live.

After selecting the correct time zone, click Go to the group's calendar, and you'll see an empty calendar with today's date highlighted, as shown in Figure 9.13.

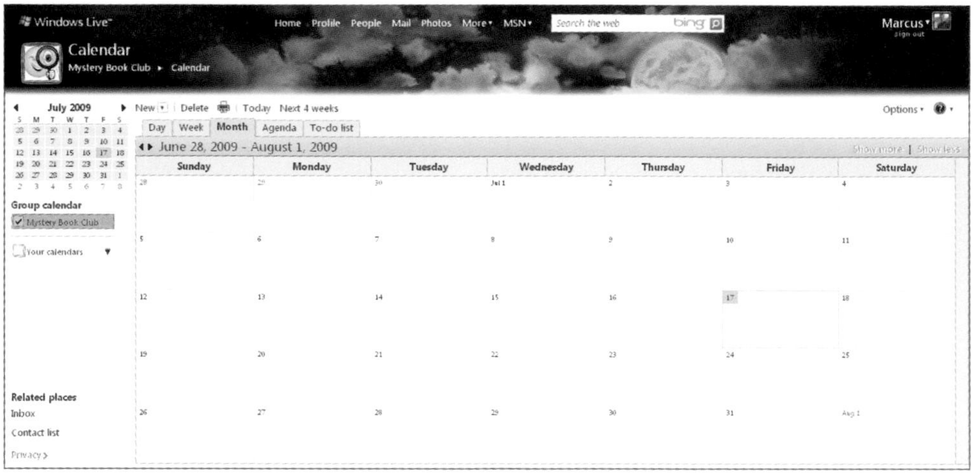

FIGURE 9.13 The Windows Live Group calendar page

The calendar web page for your group has a lot of very useful capabilities. To get started adding an event to the calendar, click the New menu. If you click New, you will be shown a form for adding a new event. But if you click the down arrow, you'll be prompted as to whether you want to create a new event or a new to-do item, as shown in Figure 9.14.

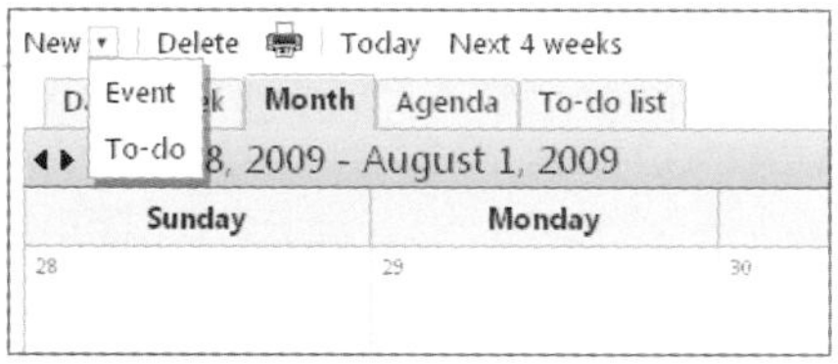

FIGURE 9.14 Options for New items in the calendar

The book club meets once a month, usually early in the month. The event being created for the July meeting is shown in Figure 9.15. Windows Live provides helpful pop-up calendars and times to choose from as you create your event. If you want to add additional details, such as adding an event charm (a small icon shown for the event), making the event recurring, or adding an extended description for the event, just click on the Add more details link.

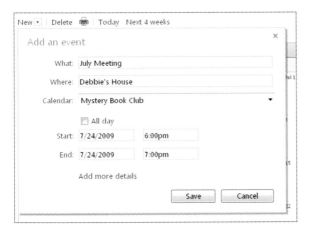

FIGURE 9.15 Meeting details area

One of the handiest features of the calendar is the ability to show multiple calendars in one view. To do this, click on the Your calendars link on the left side of the calendar web pages (shown in Figure 9.14) and then check each calendar you want to view or check all calendars. You'll see the entries from each, color-coded on one calendar, much like Figure 9.16.

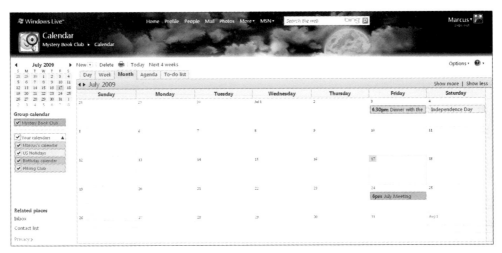

FIGURE 9.16 Viewing multiple calendars together

Windows Live makes it easy to avoid scheduling conflicts between your personal plans and your group plans.

For more information on other calendar features, please turn to Chapter 7. The way your personal calendar and group calendar works in Windows Live is similar.

Group Photos and Files

So far, you've learned how to get your group started, discuss topics, email, and schedule events. But what about sharing? That's something groups (especially family groups) really like to do.

The same sharing features that you use as an individual in Windows Live—namely Windows Live SkyDrive and Photos—are available for your Windows Live Groups as well. Each group has its own storage space for sharing photos in group albums or sharing files.

 NOTE *Each group is allocated 5GB of SkyDrive storage space, versus the 25GB allocated for personal SkyDrive use.*

To access your group's Photos or SkyDrive storage, simply click on the Photos or SkyDrive link on the left side of the main group web page (see Figure 9.12). For more information on Photos, see Chapter 5; and for more information on SkyDrive, see Chapter 10.

Instant Messaging and Groups

Email, discussions, and meetings are great, but sometimes you and your group just want to chat about things right away. You could use Windows Live Messenger to talk back and forth with everyone individually. Even better, however, is being able to talk to your whole group at once.

To get started with instant messaging among your group, just launch Windows Live Messenger as you normally would. You'll see all your contacts listed, but now you'll also see a new entry for the group you've just created, as shown in Figure 9.17.

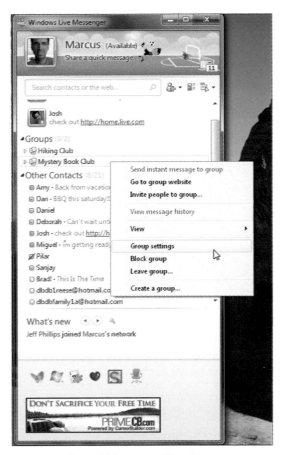

FIGURE 9.17 Instant Message options for groups

NOTE *This feature is only available for groups of up to 20 people. It can also be disabled for any size group using the options discussed previously in this chapter.*

If any of the group members are online, you can start an instant messaging session with all of them at the same time just by double-clicking on the group's name. You can also right-click on the group name and choose from any of the following options:

▶ Send an instant message to group (same as double-clicking)

▶ Go to the group's website

▶ Invite people to group (opens an invitation window to select and invite new members)

▶ View message history

▶ View Photos, SkyDrive, or Discussions

▶ Examine the group's settings

▶ Block the group from instant messaging you

▶ Leave the group

▶ Or create a whole new group

For a complete discussion of Windows Live Messenger, please refer to Chapter 2.

In Conclusion

In this chapter, you learned about Windows Live Groups. You discovered how to create a group and manage members. You also explored how to create group discussions, group calendars, and share photos and files among the members of a group. Additionally, you investigated the communication options for Windows Live Groups, ranging from group email to instant messaging.

Storing Things Online with SkyDrive

IN THIS CHAPTER, YOU WILL:

▶ Learn what SkyDrive is

▶ Learn how to set up SkyDrive

▶ Learn how to create and use folders for organizing your files

▶ Learn how to store things on your SkyDrive

▶ Learn how to post photos onto your SkyDrive

▶ Learn how to share access to areas of your SkyDrive

▶ Learn how to share links to items on your SkyDrive

▶ Discover how to share links or files in your blogs

THE PRIMARY storage space for most computers is the hard drive. This is where you can store files, photos, videos, documents and more on your computer. You can also load applications onto your hard drive. For example, if you downloaded the Windows Live Applications, then you copied the programs onto your hard drive.

Of course, if you don't have your computer with you, then your files and applications are not likely to be accessible to you. Additionally, if your computer were to crash or if your hard drive were to break, then unless you had created a backup of your files, they could be lost.

It is a good idea to copy your files to a place where you can always get to them whether you are on your computer or someone else's. The Internet makes this much more possible. In fact, one of the Essentials you can tap into is Windows Live SkyDrive.

SkyDrive is like having a hard drive out on the Internet. Not only can you access it from your computer, but you can also access it from any computer that is connected to the Internet.

At the time this chapter was written, you could use SkyDrive freely. In fact, Microsoft provides 25GB of storage for you to use to store your files. All you need to do to start using SkyDrive is to have a Windows Live ID or Hotmail account!

Getting to Your SkyDrive

To start using SkyDrive, you simply need to access it online. To access SkyDrive, open your browser and go to home.live.com to access your Windows Live Home page. You can then select SkyDrive from the More menu, as shown in Figure 10.1.

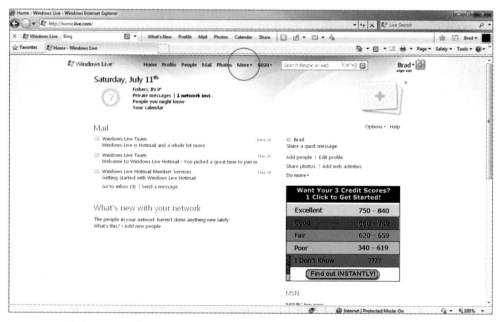

FIGURE 10.1 Navigating to SkyDrive from your Windows Live Home page

Once you select SkyDrive, it will be loaded as shown in Figure 10.2. Your page might show a few slightly different items, but the overall look should be similar.

FIGURE 10.2 SkyDrive main home page

You'll notice that there are several folders already on your SkyDrive. By default, you should see folders for Documents, Favorites, Shared favorites, and Public. If you look closely at these folders, you will notice a few small icons that give you clues about the folders. For example, on the Documents and Favorites folders, you'll see that there is a small lock. This lock indicates that the folder is restricted so that others can't see the contents of the folder. Alternatively, the Public folder has a small globe on it to help indicate that it is shared with the world. You'll learn more about how to change the permissions later in this chapter.

To get a better view of your SkyDrive, click on the All folders option under the Folders area on the left side of the page. This will display your SkyDrive and all of its folders. As you can see in Figure 10.3, these are organized a little better than the SkyDrive home page.

Now that you can access your SkyDrive and get to your default folders, it is time to learn how to take advantage of it. Before showing you how to add files and how to create folders, there is one additional tidbit of information worth noting.

FIGURE 10.3 SkyDrive All folders page

In Figures 10.2 and 10.3, you should have noticed a small status bar on the right side of the page. This status bar will tell you how much space you have on your SkyDrive and how much space is left. When you initially set up your SkyDrive, no space will have been used, so your status will look like Figure 10.4. After you start using space, the status bar will be updated to show you the amount of space you have remaining.

FIGURE 10.4 SkyDrive usage status

 NOTE *You can use SkyDrive for storing backups of files on your computer. You can also use it to share photos, videos, and other files.*

 TIP *You can go straight to your SkyDrive by going to* `skydrive.live.com.`

Working with Folders

If you are going to start placing files on the SkyDrive page, you'll want to consider organizing them within folders and within subfolders. You have the ability to create new folders in the base of your SkyDrive or within any of the existing folders.

Creating New Folders

Any folder you create will exist in the area where you start the creation process. For example, if you were in the home directory of SkyDrive, then your folder will be created there. If you want to create a subfolder within another, you should select that folder first by clicking on it. Clicking on the Documents folder will open it and display its contents. The first time you open the Documents folder, it will be empty, as shown in Figure 10.5.

When you are ready to create a folder—whether on the home area or within a folder such as Documents—you simply click on the Create folder link. You can see this link in Figure 10.3 above the Documents folder area as well as in Figure 10.5 in the options listed in the middle of the page.

FIGURE 10.5 The empty Documents folder on SkyDrive

What you will see when you click the Create folder link will depend upon whether you are in the base SkyDrive area or within a folder. If you are in the base area, you will be given more options than if you are already within a folder.

If you are within a folder, then when you click on the Create folder option, the dialog shown in Figure 10.6 will be displayed. For example, if you've never created anything in the Documents folder before and you click on the Documents folder, and then click Create Folder, then you'll see exactly what is in Figure 10.6.

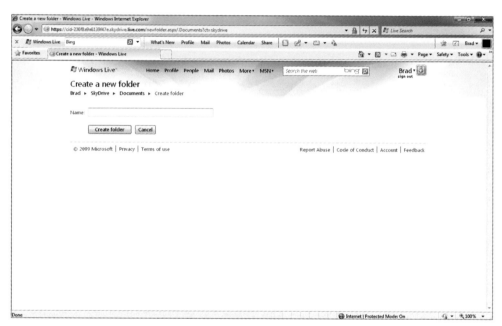

FIGURE 10.6 Creating a new folder on SkyDrive

To add your new folder, you'll fill in the information on this dialog, specifically the name you want to give your new folder. You then click the Create folder button. The new folder will be created as shown in Figure 10.7. At this point, you'll be able to add files to the folder.

If you had created the folder in the base SkyDrive area, then the dialog you were prompted with would also include a prompt asking who you want to share the folder with. You'd be able to select Just me, Everyone (public), My network, or Select people. Later in this chapter you'll learn more about these different permissions, including how to change them. You can give your new file a name, select the permission you want, and this time click Next instead of Create folder. This will create the new folder as well as open the folder so that you can start adding files. If you don't want to enter files at this time, you can click the Cancel button on the Add files page, and you'll be returned to the Folder view.

> **NOTE** It is important to point out that if you create a folder in the base SkyDrive area, you have to set permissions. If you create a folder within an existing folder, the permission will be the same as the folder in which you are creating the new folder. Later in this chapter, you'll learn how to change the permission on the parent folder.

Removing an Existing Folder

If you create a folder and realize that you don't actually want it, you can remove it. Additionally, you can remove folders you no longer want to use. You remove a folder by deleting it.

To delete a folder, navigate through SkyDrive until that folder is selected and its contents are displayed. In Figure 10.7, you can see the folder called Essentials is open and that it contains one file. Additionally, you can see that the More menu has been selected to show its options.

FIGURE 10.7 Getting ready to delete a folder

Within the More menu, you can select Delete. This will cause a dialog similar to Figure 10.8 to be displayed asking if you are sure you want to remove the current folder and all of its content.

Message from webpage

You're about to permanently delete Essentials and all of its contents from Windows Live SkyDrive.

OK | Cancel

FIGURE 10.8 Deleting a folder and its content

If you don't want to delete the folder and its content, then click Cancel in the dialog. If you do want it deleted, click OK. The folder and all of its contents will be removed from your SkyDrive. Once you click OK, you can't change your mind—the files and folder will be gone.

WARNING *Once you delete a folder, it and all of its contents will no longer be on your SkyDrive. There isn't an "undo" to get your files back.*

Modifying an Existing Folder

If you want to give a folder a different name, you can always delete it and create a new folder. Of course, it is easier to simply rename the folder. You can rename a folder in much the same way that you delete a file. If you look at Figure 10.7, in addition to the Delete option, there is also a Rename option on the More menu. To rename a folder, navigate to that folder, then select Rename on the More menu. As you can see in Figure 10.9, you will be prompted with a dialog similar to what you saw when you created the folder.

You can select Cancel on this page, and your folder will retain its original name. If you want to change the name, though, then enter the new name in the New name box and then select Save by clicking on it. Your folder will be renamed.

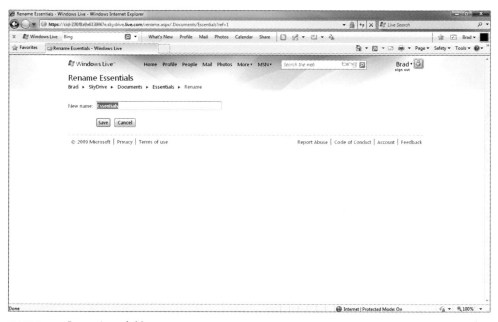

FIGURE 10.9 Renaming a folder

Adding Files (Uploading)

Of course, folders are good for organizing things, but you obviously need things to add to your folders. You can upload pretty much any type of file to the folders on your SkyDrive. At the time this book was written, the main limitation is that the maximum file size you can upload is 50MB. The other limitation is that you are limited in total storage space as indicated earlier.

There are two ways to upload a file or photo. There is a standard upload page and there is a Windows Live Upload tool that can be used. Either method will let you upload your items. The Windows Live Upload tool gives you the ability to do it by dragging files from your local system and dropping them within an area on a page within your browser. In the following sections, you'll learn how to use both ways to upload an item.

> **NOTE** *While you can upload and share files on your SkyDrive, you should remember to honor copyright and other laws when doing so. For example, it is possible to upload MP3 music files, but you should make sure that you don't violate any licensing.*

Uploading Using the Standard Upload Page

When you first create a new folder, you are prompted to start adding files. At that time, you can click the link to begin the process. Alternatively, to start adding files to your SkyDrive, you can first go to the folder where you would like to upload them. Once there, you can click on the Add files option. In either case, the result should be nearly the same, which is a dialog similar to Figure 10.10.

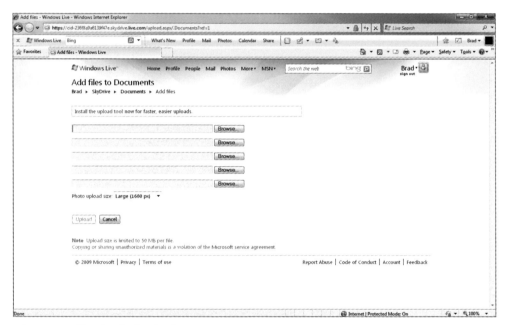

FIGURE 10.10 The standard upload page

As you can see, you have the option to upload five files at a time. To upload a file, click on the Browse button. This will open a standard Windows dialog as shown in Figure 10.11. Note that Figure 10.11 shows the dialog from Windows 7. If you are using a different version of Windows, the dialog will be slightly different; however, it should be familiar.

You can navigate to the document, photo, or other file that you want to upload to your SkyDrive. Once you've found it, select it and click Open. This will place the filename in the dialog. Once you've selected a file, the Upload button will be enabled so that you can begin the upload processes. You can choose to select additional files or upload them at any time.

FIGURE 10.11 Selecting a file to upload

If you are uploading an image, you have an additional option on the page. This option allows you to set the size of the photos you are uploading. Many digital cameras can take pictures with very large resolutions. This results in very large file sizes. You can use the Photo upload size option to reduce the size of the files being uploaded. In general, you can choose to upload the file in the original size, in a large size with a width of no more than 1600 pixels, or in a medium size with a width of no more than 600 pixels. In general, it is up to you to decide which size to set. You can see these three options in Figure 10.12. Additionally, you can see that there is one file ready to upload.

If you choose a Photo upload size and you are not uploading any pictures, then it will have no impact on what you are doing. Regardless of whether you are uploading pictures or other files, once you've entered up to five files, you can click the Upload button. This will start the uploading process, as shown in Figure 10.13.

You should note that very few details are given during the uploading processes. Additionally, if you are uploading large files, the process can take several minutes, depending on your Internet connection. You can look at the browser status bar to see part of the status of the upload. Otherwise, you have to sit and wait.

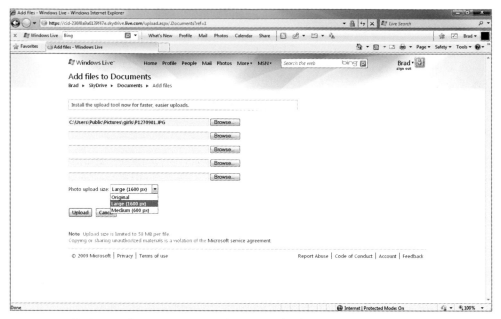

FIGURE 10.12 Options to change picture sizes during an upload

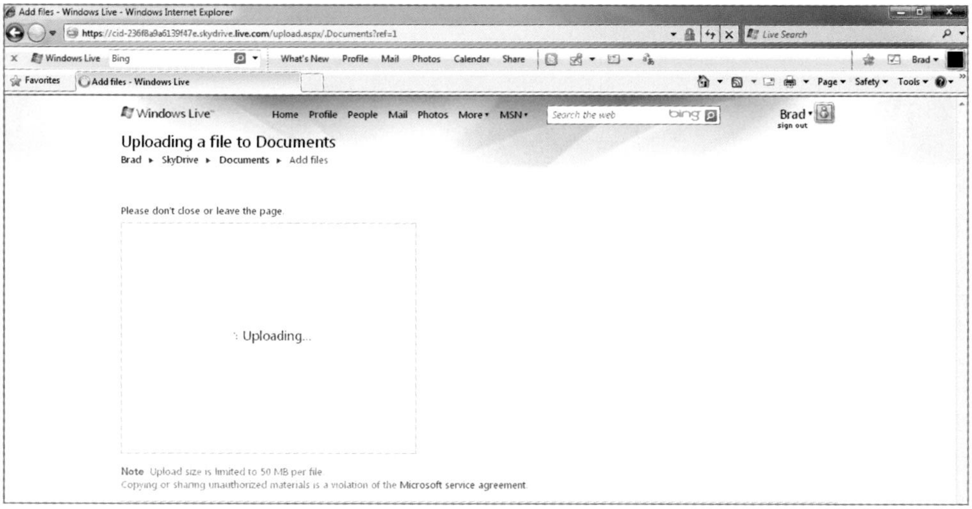

FIGURE 10.13 Uploading the files

Once the files have been uploaded, the folder where you started the process will be redisplayed with the new items in it. You should note that these items have been copied from your computer. Thus, they now reside in both places. This means that you can manipulate them on your SkyDrive, and this will have no impact on the files on your local computer.

Uploading by Dragging and Dropping Files

Microsoft Live SkyDrive has an easier way to select and upload files. You can drag files from your local computer and drop them onto a location within a browser window. This drag and drop option can be used as an alternative to the standard upload dialog in the previous section. To enable dragging and dropping in SkyDrive, you need to install the Windows Live Uploading Tool.

In Figure 10.10, you saw a box on the standard upload dialog showing that you can install the uploading tool. Go to any folder on your SkyDrive and click Add files. You'll get a dialog similar to Figure 10.10. Click on the Install the upload tool option. This will start the process for installing the tool by displaying a prompt asking if you want to run or save a file, as shown in Figure 10.14.

FIGURE 10.14 Starting the install process for the uploading tool

Click the Run button to get the installation started. You should then follow any instructions presented. You might see several status boxes as Windows installs the tool.

Once the tool has been installed, the dialog you see for uploading files will no longer look like the standard dialog you saw in Figure 10.10. Rather, it will look more like Figure 10.15.

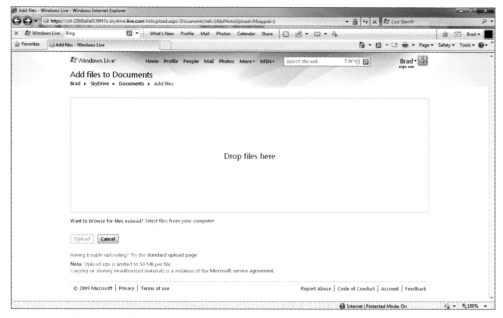

FIGURE 10.15 The installed uploading tool

You can now drag files from other Windows applications such as the Windows Explorer, or from your Desktop onto this browser page and drop them into the area marked as Drop files here. Because you are using Windows dialogs or your desktop, you can use standard Windows selection techniques to select more than one file at a time. As you can see in Figure 10.16, I've selected a set of thirty pictures from my Windows Picture folder and am dragging them to the upload tool.

You can see in Figure 10.16 that as I drag the files over to the browser, Windows 7 shows the number of files being copied; in this case thirty files are being copied. Once they are above the dialog and dropped, their icons will be added as shown in Figure 10.17. Be aware that at this point, the files have not yet been copied. Rather, they are simply ready to be copied.

You should also notice in Figure 10.17 how the browser window has changed. The top portion of the dialog now shows the icons for the files that are to be uploaded. The area to drop new files is now smaller and is below the icons. You can continue to drag and drop additional files into the drop area. If you find that you dragged and dropped a file you didn't want to upload, you can click the little X in its upper-right corner. This will remove the item from the file uploading tool, and thus it won't be uploaded.

FIGURE 10.16 Dragging files to the uploading tool

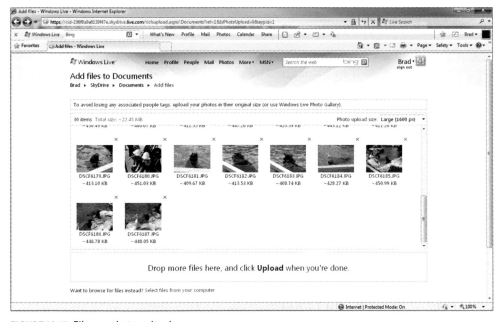

FIGURE 10.17 Files ready to upload

Once you've selected all you want, you can begin the upload process by clicking the Upload button. Unlike the standard tool, the uploading tool shows you the progress of the upload (see Figure 10.18) as well as provides a button that you can use to stop the uploading processes. Once the uploading is completed, you will be shown the SkyDrive folder with the new items added.

Sent: 1.08 MB of 18.96 MB

Stop

FIGURE 10.18 The progress of an upload

> **NOTE** *Once you've installed the file uploading tool, it will be the default dialog you see when uploading folders. If you want to go back to using the standard uploading tool, there is a link on the uploading tool page to go to the standard dialog. If you want to permanently remove the uploading tool, then you should use the Windows Control Panel to remove the uploading tool from the list of programs on your computer. Consult your Windows documentation on removing programs to accomplish this.*

Viewing and Sorting Files

Once you've added many files to a folder on your SkyDrive, it can begin to get a bit cluttered. You are offered a few options to make finding files a little easier. This includes options for viewing what is in a folder as well as for sorting what is in a folder.

Setting a View Option

You generally have three options for viewing the items in a folder on your SkyDrive. The view options are for Icons, Details, or Thumbnails. You can change the view by selecting the View drop-down menu above the file icons within a folder. The default view is Icons, as shown in Figure 10.19

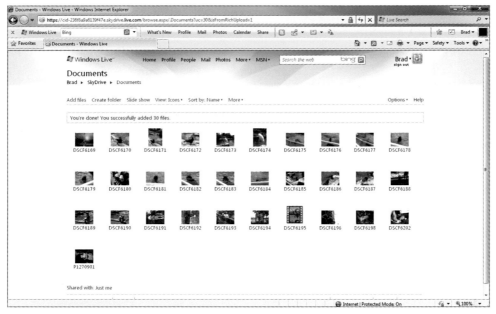

FIGURE 10.19 Icons view

The Details view provides a more textual list of information about the items in your folder. This information includes the name of the item, the last date it was modified, the item's type, and the item's size. The Thumbnails view is nicer for pictures and photos as well as other files because it gives a more "picture like" view of items. Figure 10.20 shows the Details and Thumbnails views of the same folder shown in Figure 10.19.

Sorting Your Files

Similar to changing the view, you can also sort the items in a folder. To sort items, you can use the Sort by drop-down list provided in the folder navigation. This will let you sort your files in a variety of ways. To do a simple sort, you can select Name, Date, Size, or Type, and the items will be sorted accordingly.

If you have images in your folder, you can also get a sort option of Arrange Photos. This option will give you a thumbnail view of your photos. You can then drag these into the order you want them displayed, as shown in Figure 10.21.

FIGURE 10.20 The Details and Thumbnails views

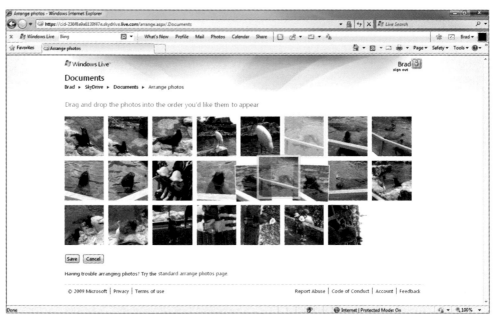

FIGURE 10.21 Sorting pictures manually

Once you are satisfied with the order, you can click the Save button to be returned to the folder. If you decide you don't want to do this custom sort, then you can click the Cancel button to ignore any changes you might have made.

Manipulating Your Files and Photos

Of course, there are bound to be times when you place a file into the wrong spot on your SkyDrive, when you decide you want to give it a new name, or when you simply want to remove it. You have the ability to do all of this directly on your SkyDrive.

To do any of these actions, you should first select the item you want to delete, move, copy, or rename. When you click on an individual item, it will be displayed on a page with a menu to perform each of these actions. If the item is a picture, you'll see that a larger version of it will be displayed. Figure 10.22 shows the page with a spreadsheet selected. As you can see, an icon is displayed for this file.

There might actually be additional items displayed beyond what is shown in Figure 10.22. For example, if a photo is selected, then there will also be menu options for doing a slide show, for tagging, and more. These options for photos are covered later. If there are more options, they will be placed under a More drop-down list.

FIGURE 10.22 Viewing an individual item on SkyDrive

Before showing you how to manipulate an item, it is worth exploring some of the other items shown in the item page. For example, in Figure 10.22, you can see the text "Add a description" below the icon. If the item were a photo, then you'd see the text "Add a caption" instead. In both cases, clicking on this text will allow you to add a descriptive piece of information to the file.

If you look on the lower-right side of the page, you will see that there is also information about the file presented. For the item in Figure 10.22, you can see the file type, the size, dates, and more.

Deleting an Item

To delete an item, simply click the Delete link. You will be asked if you are sure you want to permanently remove the file from your SkyDrive. If you are, then click OK, and the file will be removed. Otherwise, you can click Cancel, and the file will be retained.

Renaming an Item

Earlier you learned how to rename a folder. You can also rename an item within a folder. You won't be able to change the item's extension, but you can change its name.

After selecting an item, you can rename it by clicking on the Rename option. This will provide you with a dialog to change the filename. The original name will be displayed, as shown in Figure 10.23. You'll be able to enter a new name. Click the Save button to save the change.

Copying an Item

The process of copying an item is a bit more complex than deleting or renaming one. When you click to copy an item, a dialog is presented to you that will allow you to select the folder where you want to place the copy of the file. The specific folder or subfolders you chose is the path where you'd like the file to be placed. In Figure 10.24, you can see this dialog for selecting the path. Simply click on the folder and subfolders until you get to the location on your SkyDrive where you want the file placed.

FIGURE 10.23 Renaming an item

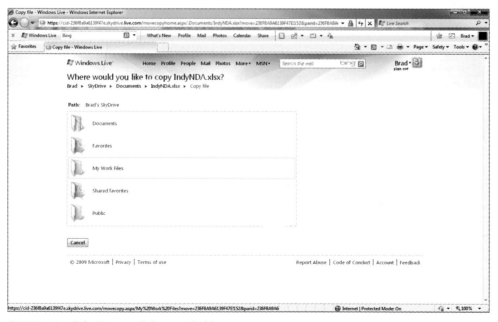

FIGURE 10.24 Selecting a path for a copied item

Once you select a folder, you can choose a subfolder if one is available. You can also choose to create a New folder in which to place the item. Selecting New folder within the Path box will allow you to create a new folder in which to place the copy.

Once you have selected the folder where you want to place the file, you can select the option to copy the file into the folder. The folder you selected will be displayed with the copy presented. The copy will have the same name as the original file, so you might want to rename it.

NOTE *You won't be allowed to copy a file into the same folder where it originated.*

Moving an Item

Moving an item works exactly like copying an item. The only difference is that the item will be shifted from the original folder to the new folder you select. You will be presented with a folder selection dialog similar to the one in Figure 10.24. As when copying a file, you cannot move an item to the same folder from which it originated. You must select a new folder.

Adding Additional Information about Your Items

In addition to being able to take one of the preceding actions, you'll also see that you can add additional information about your item.

To move an item, you should first select it. This will take you to a page that gives you a number of options, including deleting, downloading, renaming, copying, and moving it.

NOTE *You might also see additional options. If so you can learn about those features in Chapter 5.*

Downloading an Item

When viewing general items, there is an additional option beyond those already covered. That is the Download option. When you add items, you are uploading them to your SkyDrive. You can also download individual items by selecting the Download option.

When you select the option to download an item, you will be prompted with the standard download dialog that you see whenever you use your browser to download. This will be a dialog similar to the one in Figure 10.25.

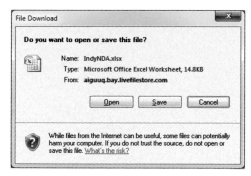

FIGURE 10.25 Downloading an item

From this dialog you can choose Save to download and save the item to the local machine, or you can select Open to open the file. Opening a file requires you to have the proper software on your local machine to actually open the file.

Downloading from Your SkyDrive

While you've seen how to download an individual file, you also have other options for downloading files. When available, these will be presented in the options on the page you are viewing. On folder pages with multiple items, you will be given the option to download all the files as a compressed zip file. On folder pages with photos, you'll also be given an option to download with Windows Live Photo Gallery.

Downloading Items in a Zip File

To download a zip file, you select Download as zip file from the options. This might be under a More drop-down or under a Download option on the More drop-down. Once you select this option, you will be given a standard File Download dialog similar to the dialog you saw earlier in Figure 10.25, except the file will be a zip file. The compressed file will contain all of the files from the current folder.

Downloading to Windows Live Photo Gallery

If you have photos in a folder, you will also have the option Download to Photo Gallery. Selecting this option will pull the photos into Windows Live Photo Gallery. You'll be able to select this just as you are able to select the other options on a page.

When you select Download to Photo Gallery, you will be prompted to open a program on your computer with a dialog similar to Figure 10.26. You'll have to select Allow to be able to continue. Depending on your security settings in your browser, you might have to respond to a few additional prompts as well.

FIGURE 10.26 Giving permission for a program to run on your machine

Once you've addressed the security dialogs and given permission for Photo Gallery to run, the process of retrieving the photos will begin. You'll be given a dialog to show the status of the information retrieval as shown in Figure 10.27.

FIGURE 10.27 Status of retrieving information for Windows Live Photo Gallery

If all goes well, you will be prompted to select the pictures or videos that you want to download into Windows Live Photo Gallery. Figure 10.28 shows an example of the dialog that will be presented. You can uncheck any items you don't want to download.

FIGURE 10.28 Selecting the items to download to Windows Live Photo Gallery

Once you've selected the item you want, you can click the Download button to begin the download. Each of the items will be downloaded. Once the downloads are completed, Windows Live Photo Gallery will be opened with the items displayed. You can see Chapter 5 for more on working with photos in Windows Live Photo Gallery.

> **NOTE** *You must be logged into a Live account that has permissions to Windows Live Photo Gallery in order to download the images to Photo Gallery. If you are not, you will be prompted to Enter another Windows Live ID before the download will occur.*

Setting Access Permissions for Sharing Folders

You've seen how to add folders and files to your SkyDrive. You also have seen that different levels of permission can be used on folders and files. The permissions that are set in a folder at the base level of your SkyDrive carry through to subfolders. Therefore, if you create a folder in the existing Public folder, its permissions will be the same as the Public folders, which is public (everyone) by default. Similarly, if you create a new folder in the Documents folder, then it will have the same permissions as the Documents file.

In a subfolder, you can view its permissions by selecting the View Permissions option. For a subfolder, you will see a dialog similar to Figure 10.29.

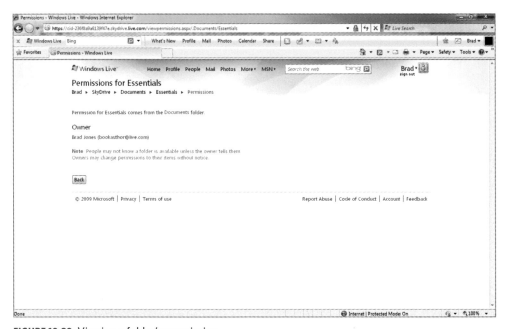

FIGURE 10.29 Viewing a folder's permission

As you can see in Figure 10.29, you can determine who owns a folder and where the permissions originate. In the case of the Essentials Files folder in Figure 10.29, its permissions come from the Documents folder. In this case only the owner has access.

Of course, if you want to change the permissions to a folder, you need to change the base folder's permission. You do this by first selecting the folder. Once you've selected it, choose the Edit Permissions from the options that are presented. This option might be located under the More drop-down. You will be presented with a page similar to Figure 10.30 that will allow you to set the page's permissions.

FIGURE 10.30 Setting permissions

From this page, you can change permission for groups or for individuals. Additionally, you can click on the Clear these settings to clear the customized permissions. Regardless of what changes you make, you need to click the Save button to finalize the changes.

Granting Group Permissions

From the Edit permissions page shown in Figure 10.30, you can set permissions for a group of people. There are three primary types of groups you can set; everyone, a network, or a category of people.

You can check the Everyone option to provide access to the most people. In this case, you make the folder, any subfolders, and all contained items publicly available to everyone. That means the world can view your files. Note that everyone can view your files, but they don't have access to change them.

You can also choose to give permission to your network of people by checking the box next to My network. This allows people in your Windows Live network to access your files. These are people in your Windows Live Messenger contacts and Windows Live profile contacts. If you select to give this group access, you can then choose, as shown in Figure 10.31, to give this group access to either view files or to actually change and delete your files.

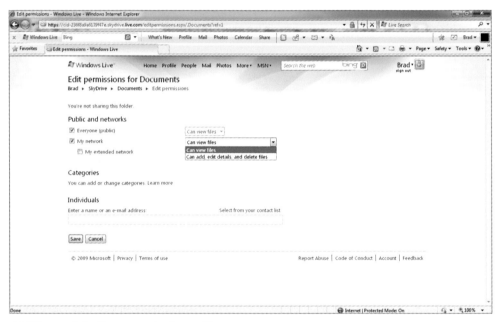

FIGURE 10.31 Selecting groups to share with

Additionally, if you choose to give your network access, then you can also choose to give your extended network access to view your files. Your extended network includes your network and the friends (contacts) of those in your network.

The third group type that you can give access to is Categories. If you've set up categories, you will have the ability select them and assign rights to them. You learn about categories in Chapter 2.

Granting Individual Permissions

If you want more control over who gets access to the files in a folder on your Sky-Drive, then you can assign access to individuals. To add individuals, you can either select them from your contacts one-by-one, or you can enter their name or email address into the box shown in Figure 10.31 for Individuals.

If you want to select them one at a time, then you should click on the text, Select from your contact list. This will present a list of your contacts to select from similar to what is shown in Figure 10.32. As you can see, each name is listed and can be selected by clicking the check box to the left. That will place the name below the People box and then allow you to select whether the individual can view or edit and delete files in the given folder and its subfolders.

FIGURE 10.32 Giving permissions to individuals

You can also give permission to individuals who are not contacts in your profile. You do this by specifically entering their email addresses into the box specified on the page, and then pressing Tab or Enter. This will add the individual and again allow you to determine if they can only view files, or if they can edit and delete them as well.

Once you've set up the individuals and their permissions, you can click Save to save the changes. If you added permissions only to individuals, you will be prompted to send a notification to the people you added. As you can see in Figure 10.33, you can add your own message or you can simply send a notification as is. If you don't want to send a notification, you can click the Skip this button to continue back to the folder with the new permissions in place.

FIGURE 10.33 Notifying individuals of the permission change

Storing Your Browser Favorites on Your SkyDrive

In addition to storing files and photos on your SkyDrive, you can also store your favorites. Favorites are links to web pages and web sites that you like or want to keep track of. You can add favorite links by using the Windows Live toolbar you learned about in Chapter 1 or by adding them to one of the Favorites folders on your SkyDrive.

Adding favorites is like adding files. In folders set up for holding favorites, you will be given the option to add or create a favorite just as you are given options to add folders in the regular folders. When you click the link to add or create a favorite, you will be prompted to enter the corresponding information, as shown in Figure 10.34.

Once you save this information, it will be stored in your Favorites folder for you to access later. You can add as many favorites as you want. When you add a favorite, it will be listed in the Favorites folder as shown in Figure 10.35.

FIGURE 10.34 Adding a favorite

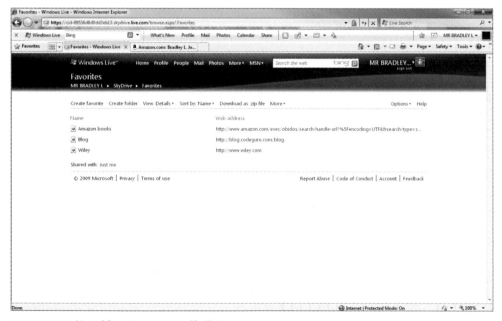

FIGURE 10.35 Listed favorites on your SkyDrive

NOTE *Favorites are treated like folders. You can share them, comment on them, and otherwise treat them like files. The biggest difference is that favorites include a link that you can click to take you to a web site.*

In addition to adding favorites to your Public favorites within the SkyDrive folders, you can also add new favorites from the Windows Live toolbar within your browser. To add the current page from your browser into your favorites, you click on the Share button on the Windows Live toolbar. This will display a box, as shown in Figure 10.36, where you can enter a description to associate with the current link. The saved favorite will be placed on your SkyDrive.

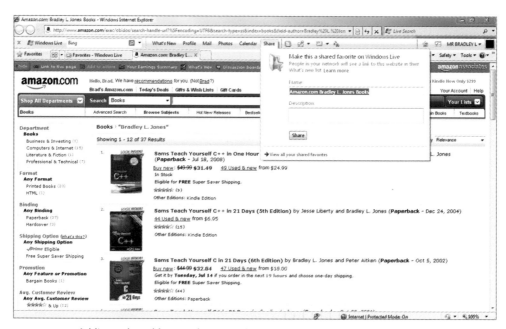

FIGURE 10.36 Adding a shared favorite from your browser

In Conclusion

In this chapter you learned how to use Windows Live SkyDrive to store your files, photos, and favorites. You learned how to create folders, how to add files, and how to organize all of them. You also learned how to set permissions to allow others to access items on your SkyDrive.

Index